Research Skills for Journalists

D0165209

Research Skills for Journalists is a comprehensive, engaging and highly practical guide to developing the varied skillset needed for producing well researched, quality journalism across a range of platforms.

Illustrated with original interviews and case studies, the book guides readers through a clear understanding of the sources of news, as well as illustrating the skills needed to undertake successful digital and non-digital research and to conduct interviews for a variety of media. It examines the skills needed for basic data journalism and presents an in-depth exploration of the different research skills specific to producing print and online text as well as those for broadcast and multimedia journalism.

Key research skills explored in the book include:

- developing digital research skills including researching through search engines, message boards, discussion groups and web forums, social media, apps and using user generated content;
- working with data, including sourcing, auditing and analysing data, data visualisation and understanding the importance of accuracy and context;
- essential non-digital research skills including telephone techniques, using libraries and working with librarians, understanding copyright, working with picture libraries and research services and producing Freedom of Information requests;
- working directly with people to research stories including the power of persuasion, tracking down great contributors, managing and protecting sources, planning and managing interviews and interviewing vulnerable people; and
- researching for multimedia production of stories including researching a radio story, podcast or video story and planning for outside broadcasts.

Research Skills for Journalists also explores specialist research skills needed for working overseas and investigates new areas, which could be used for journalism research in the future.

The book is illustrated with original contributions by journalists from a variety of backgrounds including veteran investigative journalist John Pilger, pioneering data journalist Simon Rogers and The Bureau of Investigative Journalism's award-winning reporter Abigail Fielding-Smith. It is an invaluable guide for students and practitioners of journalism to the skills needed for finding and developing original news stories today.

Vanessa Edwards is a journalist, broadcaster and educator with nearly thirty years' experience. She began her career in local independent radio and in regional television before spending more than a decade as a broadcast journalist at the BBC in London. She spent several years teaching journalism at Bournemouth University and she now works as a freelance journalist and consultant.

Research Skills for Journalists

Vanessa Edwards

Routledge
Taylor & Francis Group

LONDON AND NEW YORK

First published 2016
by Routledge
2 Park Square, Milton Park, Abingdon, Oxon OX14 4RN

and by Routledge
711 Third Avenue, New York, NY 10017

Routledge is an imprint of the Taylor & Francis Group, an informa business

British Library Cataloguing in Publication Data
A catalogue record for this book is available from the British Library

Library of Congress Cataloging in Publication Data
Names: Edwards, Vanessa, 1965– author.
Title: Research skills for journalists / Vanessa Edwards.
Description: Milton Park, Abingdon, Oxon : New York, NY : Routledge, 2015.
Identifiers: LCCN 2015032848| ISBN 9780415734271 (hardback) | ISBN 9781408282977 (pbk.) | ISBN 9781315646275 (ebook)
Subjects: LCSH: Journalism – Research. | Online journalism – Research.
Classification: LCC PN4784.R38 E39 2015 | DDC 070.4/3072 – dc23
LC record available at http://lccn.loc.gov/2015032848

ISBN: 978-0-415-73427-1 (hbk)
ISBN: 978-1-408-28297-7 (pbk)
ISBN: 978-1-315-64627-5 (ebk)

Typeset in Sabon
by Florence Production Ltd, Stoodleigh, Devon, UK

For Patricia Edwards, who is always an inspiration.

With special thanks for their support to:
Dr Julia Round, who made this book possible, Sharon Mason,
Julia Briginshaw, Helen Creeke, Miriam Darby, Janice Jeffrey,
Miranda Watson, Suzanne Widdup and Georgina Wilson.

Contents

Figures

(All other images are © Vanessa Edwards)

Acknowledgements

Thank you to all the researchers, journalists, broadcasters and other professionals who contributed their time and expertise to this book. Especially:

Katherine Baldwin, Myriam Balezou, Martin Belam, Robin Britton, Mathew Charles, Chris Coneybeer, Harry Crawford, Claire Edwards, Matthew Eltringham, Abigail Fielding-Smith, Nicholas Gibbon, Tom Gillmor, Lottie Gross, Ben Kreimer, Ross McFarlane, Louise Matthews, Claire Miller, Leigh Montgomery, Nigel Nelson, Amber Phillips, Nigel Phillips, John Pilger, Venetia Rainey, Matt Rhodes, Simon Rogers, Matthew Schroyer, Robert Sharp, Jennie Slevin, Katy Stoddard, Esther Vargas, Samantha Watt, Mark Watts, Suzy Wheeler and Tania Willia.

1   Introduction

Over the past three decades, the working conditions of journalists have changed beyond imagination. It's almost inconceivable now, but before the 1980s, reporters typed their stories on electric typewriters, making copies with carbon paper. They travelled with coins for public telephones, and broadcasters recorded their reports on magnetic tape, even in some cases film. Many journalists who started in those dim and distant days (the author included!) are still working, having adapted and developed their practice, during a time of unprecedented technological revolution.

Despite these dramatic changes, the basic skills required by a good journalist remain the same: the 'nose' for something new, compassion for our fellow humans, the creativity to tell compelling, original stories and the desire to hold those in power to account. As US journalist Glenn Greenwald, wrote in 2013, 'A key purpose of journalism is to provide an adversarial check on those who wield the greatest power by shining a light on what they do in the dark, and informing the public about those acts'.

Over the early part of the twenty-first century, our profession has come under intense scrutiny and rightly so. Journalists starting out in the profession today face the difficult challenge of building a new future for journalistic practice.

This book aims to bring together many of the research skills needed by the modern journalist. It examines the traditional skills, which would have been familiar to reporters of generations past, alongside some of the newest journalistic and technological innovations. Its aim is to provide a detailed and practical grounding, alongside discussion of the ethical dilemmas modern journalism can present. Perhaps most importantly, this book is illustrated with the words, ideas and experiences of many working journalists (Figure 1.1).

The journalist as researcher

In its simplest terms, research is the collection, organisation and analysis of information. It covers a wide range of activities, from carrying out light-hearted surveys to the scrutiny of public administration and cutting edge scientific research.

In a journalistic context, the concept of research is equally as complex. Great journalism is built on a foundation of credibility. While most journalists would be happy to admit their profession rarely deals with a totally undisputable fact, the pursuit of 'the truth' remains the central goal of most journalistic work. Whether you're working for a regulated broadcaster with an absolute requirement for impartiality or a website with a strong political agenda, few professional journalists want to deliberately mislead.

Journalistic research always has the same starting point, the collection of new and relevant information. At this point, the process broadly remains the same wherever you're working,

John Pilger is one of the most influential journalists of his generation. In a career of more than 50 years, he has produced iconic reports from Cambodia and fought for the victims of Thalidomide. His documentaries have won numerous awards including a BAFTA and an Emmy.

'Remember that all journalism ought to be investigative. That means accepting no assumption, no official truth, and the word of no vested interest without scrutiny. Reject all jargon and clichés. Claud Cockburn said, "Never believe anything until it's officially denied". That should be scratched on the bathroom mirror of every budding investigative journalist.

Almost all lies, all undemocratic manipulation, all big crime comes from the top, rarely from the bottom. Remember you are or you ought to be, an agent of people, not power, and that established authority uses the media to deceive routinely and that much of "mainstream" journalism colludes with this.

Of all the journalism awards you can win, the most important comes with no ceremony, no trophy; it's your independence.'

Figure 1.1 John Pilger

but how this information is subsequently processed is determined by a complex web of factors. Each day journalists consider the opportunities and restrictions of their chosen media; the preferences and expectations of their audience; any legal, regulatory or ethical restrictions; the style and agenda of their publisher and the practical limitations of time and location. It's a complicated process, and it's no wonder that the production and distribution of journalistic work can be a topic for heated debate.

How important is research?

Good research is a vital skill to develop, both for the journalistic profession as a whole and by each individual journalist. Despite the many crises of confidence in journalism, research by YouGov (2014) suggests that some areas of journalism retain considerable public respect. Nearly two thirds of people in the UK still trust journalists from the BBC, and more than 40 per cent retain their faith in the more upmarket newspapers. Just over 10 per cent of the public trust the red top tabloids. Interestingly though, Wikipedia was seen as being more trustworthy than any traditional news outlet. If the public's remaining faith in the journalistic profession is to be maintained and hopefully rebuilt, the ability to source accurate content and present this in an accessible and credible way is clearly vital.

On a more personal level, every professional journalist has tales of crazy investigative missions, impossible deadlines and insatiable editors, all needing great research skills. All journalism is fed by information and every stage of the journalistic process relies on research to prime the production line with fuel.

Novelty is at the heart of the highly competitive daily news environment. Finding a shocking revelation, uncovering a new angle, or hunting down the most revealing interviewee can make

Figure 1.2 Journalists at work in the *Daily* and *Sunday Mirror* newsroom © Mirrorpix

the vital difference between a publication staying afloat and going bust. Researchers working in the broadcast media not only chase stories, but they may also be required to track down suitable locations for recordings and organise the practical and technical requirements needed to transport a journalist, crew and interviewees to that spot. Even outside the tough world of daily news, the shelves are packed with women's magazines whose main content is the 'real life story'. These interviewees must be found and persuaded to share their most private experiences.

So the journalist as researcher must not only establish and verify information but also decide which content is most recent, most pertinent and interesting to their particular audience. They will be required to provide interviewees or contributors to illustrate their research. They can also be asked to research and gather video and audio content, along with still images. With the growth of data journalism, many researchers are now expected to research and marshal vast quantities of data and even learn the skills of computer programming. It is a highly complex and demanding process.

So, wherever a journalist works, research skills are the core of his or her role and a great researcher can be worth their weight in gold. Yet new journalists often underestimate how important research skills will be to their future careers.

What makes a great researcher?

Curiosity is often cited as a vital skill for a great journalist and that's clearly just as true, if not even more so, when it comes to research. If you're not interested in the world around you and fascinated by human beings and their experiences, it will be hard to maintain the focus and attention needed to be a successful researcher. It's that curious streak that will lead a great journalist to be observant, spotting unusual and fascinating information around them and to dig deep to uncover injustice or law breaking.

While the requirement for curiosity is crucial, a great journalist needs another important skill: the ability to be creative and generate ideas. It's pretty clear that some people have a natural talent for creativity, but it is possible to learn to be more creative. That talent can be honed, and ideas come more easily when they are built into a framework of habit and hard work.

Journalists at work

Robin Britton is Head of News at ITV Meridian. He's an experienced journalist and multi award-winning programme maker. He explains why excellent research skills form the basis of great journalism.

'Having the right skills to find out what we don't know – or to confirm what we believe to be true – is the hallmark of a great researcher. In today's information environment there is so much information out there it's easy to be swamped in opinion. The key challenge for anyone carrying out research is to find the facts. What we write to be read or heard relies on the quality of the research we have done.

The reputation of individual journalists and the organisations they represent depends on a bedrock of excellent research that validates the stories they share. That builds the trust with the audience and makes the difference between a news service that thrives and one that fails to survive'.

Knowing your audience

Having outlined the central research skills common to all journalistic work, it's clear this work is done in a wide variety of environments and outlets. Traditional print journalists work in publications which vary from trade papers serving highly knowledgeable niche audiences, through newspapers, to mass-market magazines and high-end political journals. These publications can be daily, weekly and monthly. Online journalists might work alone on a personal blog, in a small website team or a large news organisation website. Their work can be published from minute to minute on a live blog, or be the culmination of a long-term investigation. Along with text and images, digital journalists may well be producing audio, still and moving images, along with data visualisations and even programmes. Television and radio journalists work in a regulated environment, often as part of a large media organisation and multimedia newsroom. Each of these different working environments has its own requirements and expectations and the skills needed for research are constantly evolving.

Wherever they work, a great researcher must understand their audience. Not only will the reader, listener or viewer determine the kind of stories that are chased; the audience will also be at the heart of the material included; and knowing what an audience wants, will drive the journalist's choice of interviewees and case studies.

For most journalists the first chance to consider how an audience influences their work comes during their training. Newspaper and magazine circulation is measured by the Audit Bureau of Circulations (known as ABC), and the organisation also provides digital audit data for websites. The bureau measures not only print versions of publications but, from 2013 also included some digital versions. Radio audiences are recorded and analysed by Radio Joint Audio Research (called RAJAR). It's owned by the BBC and the Radio Centre on behalf of the commercial radio sector. Television audiences are recorded by the Broadcasters' Audience Research Board (BARB), which is owned by the main television companies and the Institute of Practitioners in Advertising. BARB measures live viewing figures and then combines them with streamed and time-shifted viewing. There are a variety of free and paid-for analytical tools available to measure and analyse website and social media audiences. They measure different things and provide different forms of audience data. The most commonly used is Google Analytics.

An 'angle', scope and depth

Journalists working in book publishing, in-depth investigation, features and long-form programme making will have the time and the relative luxury to research freely, exploring the depth, breadth and context of a subject. It's the kind of investigation that researchers relish and can lead to innovative new work and truly inspirational journalism. Interestingly, researchers in these areas may well find themselves using some of the most traditional resources, such as libraries and archives, alongside the newest and most innovative forms of journalism, like data mining and visualisation, but it's an unfortunate truth that most in-depth and groundbreaking forms of research require money and time.

For news journalists, research is likely to be driven far more by the need for fresh content and an 'angle'. Spotting a new angle is not easy. It's one of the most difficult aspects of journalism to learn and can take time and practice to get right. Academics often speak of 'news values' or the rules governing the way journalists pick the most relevant news stories for their audience. These values are relatively easy to identify and explain, but the way they work together is incredibly complex and they each form an interrelated factor for the journalist to consider when researching a story.

With limited time and resources, the need to find a news angle will limit and direct the research process. News journalists will usually identify one or two likely angles and then work to prove or disprove those main ideas. As a result of these limitations, news reporters often find themselves following a research 'template' that helps them to construct a story swiftly, to meet their publication's requirements and the interests of their audience. Once the main thrust of a story is identified, the journalist will seek a 'case study' to illustrate the impact of the story, relevant interviewees and evidence to support two sides of any debate. If there's room they'll seek expert opinion to add authenticity and background information.

The daily news research formula is a highly effective system, which delivers a solid and accessible news story in a relatively short amount of time, but the process can limit the breadth of research and the means. There may not be time or resources to challenge assumptions, dig deeper or provide truly innovative storytelling. Many of the criticisms of daily news reporting centre on its perceived 'shallowness' and 'formulaic' structure. In many respects, these criticisms are fair and much could be done to make daily news more challenging and original, but time and money will always place limitations on what can be achieved.

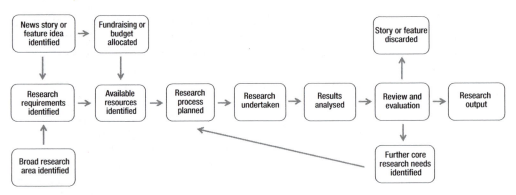

Figure 1.3 Journalism research workflow

The process of research

While journalistic research may be carried out in widely differing environments and for very varied purposes, in its simplest term the process remains broadly the same.

Research starts from two basic points. The journalist will either have identified an area, which they want to explore with the hope of identifying a story or feature idea, or alternatively, they will already have a story or idea, which they want to research.

As you can see from Figure 1.3, the amount of time and money available will play a key part in deciding how to carry out that research. Reviewing the resources available may be nothing more than a quick decision made by a news reporter with just a few moments to research and write a short piece of copy or a significant part of the budgeting process when planning a major long-form documentary. When the budget and timeframe have been established, a plan for the research can be put together. Once again, for journalists working in daily news, this plan might be nothing more than a few moments of thought before making some phone calls. But, for an in-depth piece of investigative journalism, much time and planning will go into the research process. After the basic research is complete, the information will need analysis. This is the point where the researcher considers how ideas and themes can be drawn from the data and what their research material might mean. There should always be an opportunity to review the success of the research and analysis. Has the research identified the information needed? Does the story still 'stand up'? Is more work needed or has a better angle become apparent? At this point, sometimes a story may have to be abandoned. Alternatively, if the research process is complete and comprehensive, then the job of editing the information and writing the story can begin.

Ethics

The ethical framework of British journalism has rarely been under more scrutiny than in the early 2000s. With the phone hacking revelations, allegations of illegal payments made to public officials and complex debate about the activities of Wikileaks, every journalist should be prepared to examine the ethical grounding of their research and newsgathering techniques.

We each draw the line between what is ethical and unethical in a different place, but it is important that we pause regularly to reflect on where that line has been drawn and whether unwittingly or deliberately we have crossed it. This is not a book about ethics, but wherever relevant, ethical issues surrounding journalistic practice are raised and discussed. Any guidance has been written with reference to the relevant law, regulatory guidelines and ethical codes.

Places to learn more

Books and journals

Davies, N. 2009. *Flat Earth News*. London: Vintage.
Kovach, B. and Rosenthiel, R. 2014. *The Elements of Journalism*. 3rd Revised, Updated Edition. New York, NY: Three Rivers Press.
Marr, A. 2005. *My Trade: A Short History of British Journalism*. Reprints Edition. London: Pan.
Pilger, J. 1998. *Hidden Agendas*. London: Vintage.
Randall, D. 2011. *The Universal Journalist*. 4th Edition. London: Pluto Press.

Online resources

Audit Bureau of Circulations Website	www.abc.org.uk
BARB Website	www.barb.co.uk
Glenn Greenwald at Salon	www.salon.com/writer/glenn_greenwald/
John Pilger's Website	www.johnpilger.com
Knight Foundation	www.knightfoundation.org
Pew Research Center	www.journalism.org/resources/j_tools
The Poynter Institute	www.poynter.org/
RAJAR Website	www.rajar.co.uk
Trust and Journalism in a Digital Environment (Blöbaum, B. Reuters Institute)	https://reutersinstitute.politics.ox.ac.uk/sites/default/files/Trust%20and%20Journalism%20in%20a%20Digital%20Environment.pdf

References

Greenwald, G. 2013. *Edward Snowden's worst fear has not been realised – thankfully* [online]. London: The Guardian. Available from: www.theguardian.com/commentisfree/2013/jun/14/edward-snowden-worst-fear-not-realised [accessed 8 July 2015].

Jordan, W. 2014. *British people trust Wikipedia more than the news* [online]. London: YouGov. Available from: https://yougov.co.uk/news/2014/08/09/more-british-people-trust-wikipedia-trust-news/ [accessed 6 July 2015].

Where not referenced, quotations are from interviews, emails or social media conversations with the author.

2   Sources of news

Introduction

One of the central requirements of great journalism is the ability to find and tell stories. A professional journalist is nothing without first-rate contacts and fresh ideas. Indeed, one of the most common criticisms of modern journalism is its tendency to be derivative, replicating facts without detailed research or verification. The copying and re-using of news stories has been dubbed 'churnalism' and there has been considerable debate about the effect this has had on the quality and credibility of modern journalistic practice.

Despite the growing trend for re-using or 'aggregating' news, most reputable media organisations still set great store by original journalism, and a reporter who is able to generate new ideas and angles is still seen as an irreplaceable member of the production team. As columnist Caitlin Moran observes, coming up with ideas is a constant challenge for working journalists (2012).

> If I were driving an ambulance with a child dying in the back, it would still not stop me writing a column idea down. There's nothing like the horror of knowing that in four hours you have to have filled the page and having nothing.

This chapter concentrates on the basic and most common sources of news. It looks at building networks, developing a patch and the differences between primary and secondary sources. If you're interested in more complex investigative journalism, dealing with confidential information, leaked material and whistleblowers, you'll find more in Chapter 6.

This chapter covers:

- Developing contacts and sources
- Networking and cultivating a patch
- Primary sources
- Secondary sources
- The life cycle of a news story

Developing contacts and sources

People are at the heart of every news story, and a good journalist is unable to function without great contacts. Most professional journalists would say the ability to get on with people is one of their most valuable skills. Luckily, being able to network effectively and maintain contacts is a skill that can be learned and developed.

Most successful journalists carry a small notebook or keep careful notes on their smartphone. You should get into the habit of making notes both at work and while out and about. It's always worthwhile keeping your eyes and ears open in everyday life. Learn the names of local shopkeepers, pub managers, and postmen or women, as they may provide useful contacts or become cooperative case studies. You never know when you may need an interviewee for an important feature on the future of small businesses. Make a note of shops and businesses that are closing or opening, as you may be the first to spot a trend. Watch out for people doing interesting or unusual things. Posters in shop windows and cards in newsagents provide a rich hunting ground for local news reporters. Keep an eye out for things that might seem wrong or unfair. Is there an injustice to be investigated? Casual conversation with contacts may often reveal a mine of useful information. Where does the person live? What does their partner do? What are their hobbies? Whether you're reporting on your neighbourhood for a hyper-local website or covering an international conflict, the process remains much the same. Talk to people, listen to them and keep in contact.

Any information you keep about your contacts should include helpful hints and reminders about where you met them and a note of any particular areas of interest they might have revealed. A public relations professional (PR) for a local company may also be a keen jet-skier or have raised a million pounds for charity. A managing director who is off on maternity leave in a few weeks might provide a great case study for a feature on executive mums. A little personal information also provides you with a great opening gambit when it comes to contacting that person many months into the future. It's much easier to send an email asking for a favour when you can also enquire about someone's children or their recent holiday. If you show a genuine interest in people, they're much more likely to talk to you.

In a professional environment, networking should be carefully structured. There are a variety of excellent books on business networking available, but the general advice is to get out and meet people and always take a note of their contact details. Business cards are still a vital networking tool. Many larger companies provide staff with cards, but they can also be ordered cheaply from the Internet or high-street printers or even printed at home. Exchange business cards with other journalists, PR and marketing professionals and anyone you interview. Information can be transferred to your contacts book at a later date and there are now apps to allow you to take a photo with your smartphone and store the details digitally.

General reading and off-duty Internet browsing can also provide story ideas. When you're scanning a newspaper or clicking through the Internet, make a note of the names and job description of interesting interviewees. If you have a spare few moments, you can research their details further and transfer the information into your contacts book.

Contemporaneous notes

When you start your journalistic career, keeping careful, dated notes may seem a little over zealous, but it's a really important part of journalistic research. If you get into the habit of keeping a dated notebook or digital file with records of all your work conversations, you will find it much easier to keep notes when you're researching controversial or difficult investigations.

It's up to you how you choose to keep notes, but you may well find that in this digital world, an old-fashioned reporter's notebook still does the job best, and being able to write shorthand will allow you to make the most accurate record of your conversations. If you can't write shorthand, jot down as much as you can clearly or consider making audio recordings of your discussions.

Accurate contemporaneous notes may be required as evidence in a court of law. For example accurate notes may be used when trying to pass the 'responsible journalism' test for the Reynolds Defence in a defamation case. In 2000, the *Leeds Weekly News* successfully defended itself against a defamation claim, following the publication of a story about a salesman trying to sell karate lessons. One of the key pieces of evidence was the reporters' notebook, because it showed her good practice and the steps she had taken to verify her story.

Accurate notes are also a professional requirement. In 2014 the Press Complaints Commission reviewed a complaint against the *Kentish Gazette* after a woman complained about comments attributed to her and printed in the newspaper following the conviction of the publicist Max Clifford. The woman claimed she had not given an interview and the quotes published were not only incorrect but taken from comments made while advising the journalist she was not prepared to speak about the court case.

The complaint was upheld, and in its ruling the PCC wrote (2014):

> The newspaper has a positive obligation to provide evidence substantiating its position, such as a contemporaneous note or audio recording. In this instance, there was no such record. The newspaper was not able to demonstrate that it had taken care over the accuracy of the reported comments.

The PCC found the Gazette had been in breach of Clause 1(i) of its Code of Practice. Although the PCC no longer exists, its replacement IPSO has retained the same clause in its code.

Remember:

- People are at the heart of every news story.
- Keep your eyes open in your own community.
- Network in a structured way.
- Regularly record ideas and thoughts.
- Keep accurate contemporaneous notes – it's good journalistic practice.

The contacts book

You don't have to spend long browsing journalism job advertisements, before you come across the requirement for a 'bulging contacts book'. For many years, ownership of an ancient address book filled with business cards and tatty bits of paper was a matter of professional pride. Serious researchers kept their contact details in card filing systems. Now of course contacts are generally stored in a mobile phone or on email or database software. However it's done, an organised up-to-date system of contacts remains a vital journalistic tool. Any journalist can phone a press officer, but only a well-organised one will have a note of the managing director's mobile number and details of her holiday home in the south of France. For the purposes of this book, the term 'contacts book' refers to any systematic cross-referenced record of professional contacts (Figure 2.1).

Figure 2.1 Whether it's paper or digital, all journalists must record notes and contact details

Every journalist has their own personal preference for organising their contact information. With a paper-based system, alphabetising surnames is the most obvious method, but this relies on you remembering the correct names of many dozens of contacts and this can be tough when you have several hundred. Another option is to use an alphabetical system arranged around subject headings such as 'space' or 'agriculture', but occasionally, this can cause problems when you're trying to track down a specific contact and can't recall under which category they are filed. One solution is to use a mixture of both systems, keeping most contacts under subject areas, but replicating the names of the most useful sources under their surnames also. If you're using a paper-based system, it's also a good idea to get into the habit of photocopying the entire book once a year. This may seem dreary and time-consuming, but it's worth every minute the first time you tip coffee over the pages and watch many of the names and numbers dissolve. Deputy Editor of the *Waitrose Chronicle* Caroline Cook writes about her early mistakes in her blog (2011) 'When I first started out as a proper real life journalist. I didn't write everyone I came across into my book. I know, shudder, horrible, terrible thought . . . Now pretty much everyone goes in'.

With modern digital storage such as mobile phones, tablets and smartphones, the filing system is less important, as most software allows you to search for keywords. It still remains important though to 'tag' all your contacts with suitable search categories and regularly back-up all the information. There are a variety of ways to do this, including software that synchs your phone with your PC or Mac, cloud storage or even external memory sticks or devices. Whatever method you choose, the importance of making back-up copies of all your contacts can't be emphasised enough.

Whenever you conduct an interview, you should ask the contact whether they are happy to do further interviews for you. You should clarify when and how they are prepared to be contacted. Are they happy to be phoned in the evening or at weekends? Can they give you their personal mobile number? Many daily news journalists have their own valuable group of contacts, who will happily answer the phone at three in the morning and provide a quote or interview. You'll be surprised how many professional commentators make a reasonable living by ensuring they're available at short notice and charging a small fee for regular television and radio appearances. Others are simply passionate about their area of expertise and enjoy providing advice and help. If a contributor is reluctant to give you their contact details, it's always worthwhile reminding them of the valuable publicity this might mean for their organisation. Take a note of their mobile or home numbers on the back of their business card or tap the information directly into your phone.

Data protection

Once you start storing people's contact and personal details, you must comply with the requirements of the Data Protection Act 1998. If you're working for a large media organisation, your managers will have a data protection policy, and a member of staff will be responsible for looking after data and monitoring its usage. If you are a freelancer or part of a small company, then you should assume that you might be held personally responsible. The basic requirement of the Act is that you treat people's information fairly, are open about the way you will be using it and keep the information secure. You may only break this basic guidance if it is in the public interest (Figure 2.2).

Many of these requirements can be easily followed by ensuring you take a few basic practical measures:

1   When taking someone's telephone number, email or card, ask whether they're happy for you to keep the contact for future use. Also check when they are happy to be contacted (i.e. within or outside office hours).

The Information Commissioner's Office provides a very useful guide for journalists about keeping contact data: Data protection and journalism: a quick guide (2014). It identifies eight key points, which must be followed:

1   Collect and use information about people fairly and lawfully, without **unwarranted** harm or intrusion into their private life.
2   Don't use the information for any other incompatible (i.e. non-journalistic) purposes.
3   Ensure the information is adequate, relevant and not excessive for your purpose.
4   Ensure the information is accurate and (where necessary) kept up to date.
5   Don't keep it for longer than necessary.
6   Comply with individuals' rights (e.g. to access their information, or to object).
7   Keep the information secure.
8   Don't send it to anyone outside the European Economic Area without adequate protection.

Figure 2.2 ICO Guidelines: The ICO provides clear guidelines on complying with the Data Protection Law

2   Check through your contacts book regularly. Make sure any material is still relevant and delete anything that's out of date.
3   Protect any digital contacts or research notes with a secure password and encryption if possible. If you use a paper contacts book, you should find a place to lock it away when you're not using it. And obviously don't leave it lying around.
4   Don't pass on your contacts to colleagues unless you have asked the contact's permission first.

Most organisations, which keep public data, need to register with the Information Commissioner. If you're working for a media organisation, they will have done this on your behalf. Freelancers keeping their own records may need to register and should check on the Information Commissioner's website for further guidance on when and how to do this.

Networking and cultivating a patch

When newspaper journalism was in its heyday, the heart of every reporter's job was his or her 'patch' or 'beat'. The word patch is generally used to refer to a geographical area that a journalist is responsible for covering. The word beat can also mean a geographical area, but can also be used to describe a subject area such as local government, environment or business stories. In many cases now, the two terms are used interchangeably.

With the dramatic change in the newspaper industry over the past decade, many such specialisms have been lost. General reporters spend less time in their communities and are expected to carry out a good deal of their work from the office. However, patches and beats haven't completely disappeared. With the growth of digital journalism and online communities, a patch might well now be virtual, covering a particular social network or online interest area such as tech blogging or political campaigning. In whatever way a patch is formed, developing a close personal connection with real people leads to the best original journalism.

So how do you start building your patch? If you're assigned a new geographical patch, you should begin by researching the area. What kinds of people live there? Where are the emergency services and hospitals? Who are the major employers? Some of this work can be done online, but it's vital to take time to drive or walk around and follow the advice in the early parts of this chapter; speak to local campaigners, shopkeepers and business people. Hand out your business cards and most of all show an interest in the area and its residents. Explain why you're working the patch and why you're keen to report local news and represent local residents.

The process for building a subject-area patch is much the same. Read the work of other journalists covering the same area. Check out trade journals and online publications. Make a list of key players and jot down their contact details in your contacts book. Subscribe to their blogs and social network feeds. Introduce yourself to press officers and campaign groups with a brief phone conversation. Once again, it's vital to appear enthusiastic and interested in the area concerned. Many young print journalists start their careers on trade journals with niche areas of interest. An ability to develop a sincere interest and expertise in obscure subject matters will transfer well as your career develops.

While many local papers have been forced to cut their coverage of so-called 'hyperlocal' news and to reduce the reporting time they can devote to local councils and court hearings, in some areas that gap has been filled by a new breed of local bloggers and community websites. Although many of these websites are run by volunteers and few cover their costs, they provide a valuable service and a great opportunity for new journalists to gain experience. Jason Cobb runs the hyperlocal sites the 'Colchester Chronicle' and the 'Wivenhoe Forum'. He not only has a geographical area for his patch, but also specialises in a local government beat:

> I don't have enough time, but the resources are there. I mainly cover local council issues. Most of my time is spent reading council reports and agendas. The information is always available. Finding the time to plough through it is another matter. I have learnt quickly to only write about what I know about. I often get leads to cover a local story that is of no interest to me and also probably the core readers of my site. They come to me to learn about local council developments. Sadly I haven't the time to research these leads in full, and so I stick with writing about issues that I understand.

As we've already discussed, beats are becoming increasingly virtual in nature, with much of the news, conversation and information happening online. There are some beats, however, which are entirely digital. Most larger news organisations now have a social media team whose beat is based around online social networks. They monitor online communities, share information and use their knowledge to research stories. There will be more on using social networks for research in Chapter 3, but it should be remembered that whether a patch is real or virtual, the best journalists find stories by developing sincere and ethical relationships with their sources. Etiquette and ethics should not be overlooked in the online environment. An ill-advised post on a message board or status update can quickly be passed around and can alienate large numbers of potential contacts.

There is one other area of concern when developing a patch. As with any job, there is a danger of becoming too involved with professional contacts, and this can be particularly problematic when focusing closely on one subject or geographical area. It's natural to form personal friendships with people you see and report on regularly. There is nothing wrong with this, and it is central to being a good patch journalist; but a successful reporter should also monitor such relationships constantly to ensure they remain ethical and professional in nature. It can be difficult to balance the importance of representing your local community and reporting their views and concerns while at the same time maintaining the level of balance and impartiality required to remain credible.

For journalists who are employed, the ethical boundaries of working with their contacts will generally be defined by the rules and guidelines laid out by their employer. In smaller newsrooms and for freelance journalists, monitoring professional relationships can be more difficult as there may not be the time or money to produce such guidelines. This is when many young journalists may revisit their training and review their working methods within the ethical framework taught at college or university. For practical everyday advice, the IPSO and Ofcom Codes are good starting places. The National Union of Journalists also has its own Code of Conduct, which can provide a valuable resource, and the BBC has published its editorial guidelines online for public use.

Primary sources

A primary source is the person or information right at the heart of the story. Getting a story from a primary source usually means getting it 'from the horse's mouth'. When you speak to a primary source, you may still need to check or corroborate their information, but that's because they may have a limited viewpoint or a vested interest, not because they've received their information second-hand.

Interview

Abigail Fielding-Smith is a reporter for the Bureau of Investigative Journalism and a former Beirut correspondent for the *Financial Times*. Here's her advice on networking and building contacts.

New journalists are always told about the importance of developing a network of contacts, but that can be really hard when you first start out. What practical advice can you offer?

There are two types of contacts you need to develop when you're starting out: the editors who are likely to commission work from you and the people who are likely to deliver you stories. The best way to get the first is shameless persistence: go to talks and events, introduce yourself, force yourself to ask for their card. It can seem like a closed door, but in some ways journalism is quite meritocratic. A good story idea is a good story idea whoever proposes it, and editors know that. I think editors also respect pushiness because you need it to deliver your stories.

In terms of potential sources, once you have established the kind of stories you want to write about, the techniques are similar. Go to talks and public events and conferences where people who are involved in the area you want to report on are likely to be. Introduce yourself, try to get a follow-up meeting for coffee, tell them what you're interested in, ask them if they know anyone else who knows anything about it. After a while you get a cascade effect where people introduce you to more people. I think the key is to stake out a beat and focus on that.

How does a successful journalist investigate beyond the 'obvious' and bypass those with vested interests to get to the heart of a story?

I think most journalists want to get beyond the obvious and bypass those with vested interests, and the biggest obstacle to them doing this is not being given enough time to report. Someone once told me to be good at the job you have to be an obsessive, and I think that's right. Most journalism jobs these days require you to turn out a high volume of content, and won't give you the time to develop those unusual contacts, and so if you want to do stories that stand out, you have to invest a lot of your spare time in thinking about them. So I guess the best advice I can think of is to find something that you care enough about to want to report on and find out more about in your evenings and weekends.

Check calls/web checks

In many local and regional daily news organisations, the working day is punctuated by regular checks with the emergency services. This can sometimes be known as doing 'the calls'. This may be a regular ring-around of some of the major emergency services to get details of accidents, criminal activity and police investigations, or it can now be checks to see what the organisations have posted on their websites. It is vital that the calls are done regularly, particularly in news agencies and broadcast and online newsrooms where news stories are being updated continually. Many dozens of fruitless checks may be made each day, but a missed call can also mean being beaten to a great scoop by a rival. For many reporters, the telephone numbers called five or six times in one shift become etched into their memories.

The editor or news editor usually puts the regular calls list together. It will generally include phone calls to or URLs of the local police force/forces, ambulance service, and fire services and in coastal areas the Royal National Lifeboat Institution and the Coastguard. Which individual contacts are included in the calls list will depend very much on the type of news organisation and its relationship with the local police, fire and ambulance services. Some emergency services have very strict rules that all press calls must go through the press office, while others may be happy for reporters to contact senior officers or the control centres directly.

Many of the emergency services post updates about on-going stories on their websites or recorded telephone message services known as 'voicebanks'. Such standardised messages make distributing information far more efficient for the organisation concerned and free up press officers and senior managers to do other work, but from the journalist's point of view, the system is extremely limiting. It means every news organisation has exactly the same information and this can make it very difficult indeed to dig out new leads. It can also be virtually impossible to bypass the press office and speak to staff working on the ground. When covering a big breaking story, this is where it clearly becomes vital to make personal contacts with police officers and other emergency service staff, who may well be able to supply 'off the record' information.

It's also well worth crosschecking details in these statements between the different emergency services. The fire service may well release information ahead of the police or vice-versa, which can then be corroborated, and if you're lucky enough to have a friendly press officer or police contact, you might even be able to glean a little more information from another source.

Some editors view information supplied by the emergency services as primary source material, which can be presented as undisputed fact. Many editors, however, will require this information (and that from the police in particular) to be clearly attributed and presented alongside other accounts of a story. This increasingly questioning attitude has been fuelled by a number of high-profile cases in which the police accounts of major news events were subsequently found to be inaccurate for a variety of reasons. Such cases included the Metropolitan Police information released about the shooting of Jean Charles de Menezes at Stockwell Underground Station in 2005 and the death of newspaper seller Ian Tomlinson during the G20 protests in 2009, which have since been the subject of intense scrutiny. The advice, as in many of these editorial issues, is to check the policy of your newsroom or publication before you start work.

Tip-offs

A tip-off is a news story or piece of information given to a journalist by a contact or member of the public, often in a discrete or anonymous way. A tip-off can come in the form of a social media message, text, email or phone call. Or a story or piece of gossip may be mentioned in conversation with a familiar source.

When receiving a tip-off, the first stage should be to try to identify the source (if not known) and ask whether they will keep in contact and if they want to remain anonymous. Most will not wish to give their names, but occasionally people will call or email information and are quite happy to be contacted again or even be interviewed. If a source is adamant they wish to remain anonymous and the information they are offering may put them in danger, then the journalist should take action to protect their identity. Basic measures to do this are outlined in Chapter 6.

The next (and absolutely essential) stage is to check the information. Tip-offs may be primary sources, but they are not considered to be reliable. Make a list of all the possible people or organisations involved in the story and contact them directly. You will be held personally liable for not checking out such stories, and there is also the danger of defamation if you publish a critical story, which you have not properly verified.

There is only one exception to this process and that is when giving an organisation or person prior warning about a significant news story may allow them to evade an investigation or even hide evidence. It's important to discuss stories like this with your editor and consider other ways to research the story without giving prior warning to the central player. It may be that you complete the investigation and then contact the organisation or person implicated shortly before publication for a comment.

The Internet

There will be much more on sourcing and researching stories on the Internet in Chapter 3, but it should certainly be mentioned here briefly as an invaluable source of news stories. These can reach a journalist in a whole variety of ways, from a tip-off via an anonymous email, to an update spotted on a social network, to a press release posted on a company's website.

Information on the Internet can be found in such a huge variety of locations that each piece of information must be treated on its own merit and can be seen either as a primary or secondary source. Instantaneous commentary from a reliable source on Twitter might be seen as a primary source. Whereas content or advice posted on a sponsored blog might well require a great deal of checking, probing and verification before it can be used. The problem with Internet content is that it is completely unregulated, and discerning between genuine first-hand accounts, useful information and complete fabrication is incredibly difficult.

News conferences and briefings

News conferences or press conferences are organised in a whole variety of ways for a wide range of reasons. They can be of virtually any size from an impromptu group of people gathered outside a courtroom to a large choreographed event held in an auditorium (think about some of the massive consumer technology launches). On the surface, most news conferences would seem to have the same purpose: to allow a person or organisation to disseminate information to as many journalists as possible in the shortest period of time. Looking a little deeper though, news conferences are organised to serve a whole variety of functions. They might be (Figure 2.3):

- *A promotional event to raise publicity*
  A typical example might be a press conference held for a big film or music album launch. In many cases, the journalists who attend such events are vetted by the organisers, and the questions highly controlled. There are sometimes suspicions that when an actor or musician behaves badly during such a conference, the actions may well be a pre-planned 'publicity stunt'.

- *An update to keep journalists informed about a breaking story*
  This might be a news conference organised by an ambulance or fire service after an emergency call. It may well start with a prepared statement followed by some supplementary

Figure 2.3 Journalists attend a news conference given by the science writer Simon Singh © Robert
    Sharp, English Pen

questions, which in this case are likely to be mostly factual. Reporters will often try to
glean exciting new details from these events, but it can be very hard to do.

- *An attempt to 'spin' or distract from the real story*
  Companies involved in controversial news stories will often call news conferences to attempt
  to manage media coverage. This is known in the public relations industry as 'crisis
  management' and can involve considerable planning and preparation. Often a participant
  will read out a prepared statement and then may take a couple of questions from
  journalists. The journalists themselves may be totally independent, but the PR team can
  sometimes decide in advance which journalists will ask more sympathetic questions and
  those will be chosen from the audience. The plan is often to divert attention away from
  less flattering elements of a news story by offering detail on other less critical aspects or
  to concentrate headlines on positive news coverage rather than more negative features.
  Sometimes, companies or politicians will even deliberately release one unflattering news
  story to detract the media from an even more controversial one.

- *A highly managed 'media opportunity'*
  Political parties will allow journalists to attend public meetings or campaign events
  with local people in schools, factories or universities. The media are allowed to record
  and report the event, but it should be remembered that most, if not all, of those attending
  are party supporters and those asking the questions can often be party officials briefed
  in advance. This technique was repeatedly used during the General Election campaign of
  2015.

- *A police 'fishing exercise'*
  Occasionally, police forces will organise news conferences in order to establish what reporters know about an on-going investigation. This can allow them to prepare for any adverse or unexpected press coverage. They may also deliberately release particular pieces of information, which may enable them to question a suspect more effectively in future.

- *Putting police suspects under pressure*
  This is a controversial topic, but it's claimed that some police forces have organised news conferences involving criminal suspects to place them under pressure and monitor their reaction. It's suggested that the pressure of appearing in a public place and answering multiple questions might encourage them to slip up or reveal information they had not previously mentioned during a police interview.

Whichever type of news conference you are attending, the key to making the most of the opportunity is good preparation and having realistic expectations. Consider in advance how valuable your news organisations' coverage might be to the organisers of the news conference. Who do they want to speak to? Who makes their audience? Are you likely to help them reach those people? For example, a police news conference organised to appeal for witnesses to a road crash may well favour local news outlets, while a conference planned for the release of a large company's annual results will naturally be aimed at national and international business media. If the organisers aren't keen to get coverage from your publication or broadcaster, it may be harder to ask questions and get access to the speakers. Journalists who attend such conferences are often in a hurry and may well be expected to 'file' within minutes. It's important that you research the story thoroughly and prepare questions in advance to ensure you get the right soundbite or quote. You should also seize any opportunity to ask more difficult or challenging questions.

Interview

The anonymous police officer below is a sergeant working in a police force in the south of England. The officer has asked for his/her identity to be protected in order to speak more frankly, but they have worked closely with the media. The interview offers valuable insight into reporting on crime stories and also how detectives use journalists to help their investigations.

How important are journalists in helping the police with their work?

They are vital, in terms of engaging public support for specific investigations and also in changing public attitudes towards the police, in terms of police being seen in a positive light.

Most police forces now have professional press office teams. How has that changed the way you deal with journalists?

Professional media relations departments have deliberately placed a buffer between individual officers and the media. This has controlled the flow of information, but has made it more difficult for individuals to form professional relationships based on mutual trust because they require regular contact. I would normally now default to directing a journalist to the media department, which may be seen as obstructive or bureaucratic.

What advice would you give a new journalist, working on their first crime story?

Concentrate on the personalities involved to understand why a particular story is emotive or interesting. Build up a trusting relationship with the force media relations dept. If police methods seem unduly odd or slow, check why before going to print. There may be a genuinely good reason and giving balance by explaining that will be noted by the force. If appropriate don't be afraid to criticise the police, but do so from a non-partisan viewpoint. Even for the most horrific crimes, remember fear of crime has a massively negative effect on people's lifestyles. Often this is unnecessary in terms of how likely a person is to become a victim. Taking a non-sensationalist stance will also be noted and appreciated by forces, if not editors.

Many journalists believe the police deliberately release or withhold information on an investigation to help with their enquiries. Is that your experience? And if so why is this done?

Absolutely we do, for many reasons. We might tactically withhold or release information to avoid compromising the integrity of an investigation. For example releasing suspect details is a big step as it can 'potentially' jeopardise a conviction dependent upon corroborating evidence. Often, crucial information which would only be known to the offender is withheld. This allows the investigating officers to establish the innocence of a suspect. Some information is also withheld if it could lead to the identification of a victim who might otherwise wish to remain anonymous.

Similarly, information released in the wrong way or at the wrong time could jeopardise the safety of a source (informant). For example, if the information could only have come from them. The police have a statutory duty to protect that source. There could also be legal reasons for withholding information. For example, a suspect's name is normally kept private (or at least not confirmed) until they're charged and in front of the court.

News conferences in practice

When you arrive at a news conference, think about where to sit. Many television and radio stations now broadcast news conferences live. Their own reporters will be keen to ask questions and mention their channel live on a rival's news programme, so they'll often sit near the front. Shouting out an employer's name and warning a contributor they're live on TV or radio has become a bit of a competitive sport for broadcast journalists who want to ensure they appear on as much news coverage as possible. It's also a coded warning to speakers that they should avoid swearing.

You might sit near or in front of the TV's star names in order to catch the organiser's eye. Alternatively sitting at the very back can be a good move. Press officers will often be keen to spread questions fairly around the room and will be looking for journalists at the back. If you are given the opportunity to ask a question, ensure what you ask will get you the answer your editor needs. It doesn't matter if it's something obvious or something that has already been asked, as it's your job to get material tailored for your organisation. You may consider reframing a question that has been used earlier in the hope of eliciting additional information, getting a better sound bite or even catching a more relaxed participant off guard.

Keeping notes of the press conference is obviously crucial. If you have time to transcribe proceedings, you can use your phone or a digital recorder; however, the quickest way to make accurate notes during a press conference is to use shorthand. Print journalists in particular are under pressure to get news conference quotes absolutely accurate when they may have already appeared in the broadcast media a few hours before or can be accessed for checking online.

However great your preparation, it should always be remembered that the modern PR industry is extremely sophisticated and it's unlikely you'll catch out any participant or get any unexpected information at a news conference. Perhaps the biggest achievement for a new journalist might be to appear well prepared, professional and confident in an important public arena.

Reports, surveys and other research data

Journalists are bombarded with hundreds of pages of reports, surveys and statistics from a wide range of sources. Stories can come from academic journals, quirky online surveys or the release of important government data. Journalists may also acquire such material by submitting their own Freedom of Information requests. Dealing with such sources can be extremely complex and challenging, and much more information can be found in Chapter 4.

The criminal justice system

Along with politics, crime reporting forms the very backbone of most British journalism, and subsequently, court cases are also invaluable sources of news. No professional journalist can work in daily news without a good understanding of English or Scottish law and the rules surrounding court reporting. There are a number of excellent books on the subject, which is beyond the remit of this book. There is a basic guide to planning and preparing to cover a court case in Chapter 7.

Many cash-strapped local newspapers have given up having dedicated court reporters to monitor cases on a regular basis. Instead, like broadcasters, they only send journalists to high-profile cases or to the last few days of a longer case. This has dramatically reduced court coverage, and many would argue reduced the level of journalistic scrutiny required to ensure the criminal justice system operates fairly. This cost cutting does offer opportunities though for new journalists to source and sell stories that might not otherwise be covered. Sitting through a few days' regular court proceedings can uncover hidden gems that might make great copy for a new freelancer or secure a valuable 'foot in the door' at a local newspaper. In addition making contact with the court staff and gaining their trust will prove very useful when returning to cover more high-profile cases.

Politics and public administration

When was the last time you heard or saw a news bulletin that didn't include at least one political story? Letting the public know about the activities of those who govern them is a vital role for journalists. When you start out it's easy to be a little in awe of politicians, particularly those seen regularly in the media or those who are personal heroes. It's important to put that admiration aside and remember that it's your job to represent voters and ask difficult questions. There's much more about political reporting in Chapter 8.

Weather

The prominence given to weather reporting in both the British press and broadcast media is a growing trend. It reflects the increasing 'personalisation' of news and the desire of media organisations to connect more intimately with their audience. Clearly it's virtually impossible for most people in the UK not to have a connection with the weather. Picturing snowdrifts, heat waves or torrential rain on a television news bulletin or newspaper front page is almost always guaranteed to get an audience.

Much of the weather data and forecasting in the UK comes from the Met Office, which is a commercial body currently overseen by the government's Department for Business Innovation and Skills. It employs more than 1800 people around the world, taking a staggering ten million weather readings each day. Along with providing a public weather forecasting service, it offers weather information to a huge variety of public and governmental bodies and private clients including many of the major news organisations. Another large provider of weather forecasting services is the private company MeteoGroup, which is owned by the Press Association. Recent clients include Sky News and Channel Four. Reports on flood risks come from the Environment Agency in England and Wales and from the Scottish Environment Protection Agency in Scotland. There is currently no flood warning system in Northern Ireland, but the Met Office does issue weather warnings.

Deciding when weather becomes news is not an easy judgement. Make too much of an adverse forecast and you can cause widespread panic. Ignore a weather warning and your organisation can be accused of failing its audience. The key advice for most new journalists is to get reputable professional advice wherever possible, use common sense and attribute your information. When weather warnings are issued, explain clearly what they mean and make sure you update them so that people know when the danger has passed.

Sport

Sports news forms a hugely important part of daily news reporting. There is regular sports news on almost every mainstream television and radio station, but fresh and insightful sports reporting remains one of the reasons why many people still buy daily newspapers. Sport reporters set great store by the accuracy of their reports, and this is clearly important when publishing the results of sporting events. It's always a good idea to go back to the primary source of sports results (such as the clubs or leagues) before adding them to your copy or broadcast. Most of this material is now available directly online, and it only takes a few seconds to ensure your report is correct.

Remember:

- Primary sources are the best places to find and check news stories.
- Some primary sources are very reliable. Others may need checking.
- News conferences serve a variety of purposes.
- Crime, politics and sport form the backbone of British news reporting.
- Weather reporting is growing in importance.

Secondary sources

Secondary sources are generally those which provide 'second-hand' information. They should always be treated with caution since, by their very nature, the information you receive has in some way been processed or 'mediated'. Most news organisations have their own policy on verifying secondary sources, and you should check this with your editor when you start work.

The wires

'The wires' is a collective term for the news services being supplied by news agencies whether local, national or international. Many years ago such agency stories were distributed to subscribers by telegraph wires, and such organisations were known as 'wire services'. There are still many hundreds of journalists across the world whose early newsroom careers were accompanied by the insistent 'tap, tap, tap' of teleprinter machines in the background. The machines received stories via the telephone wires and printed them out on reels of paper, which were often known in broadcast newsrooms as 'rip and read'. Later on, the stories were sent by satellite link and eventually directly into computers as a 'wire feed'. With the development of technology, video and audio footage is played out via satellite links for broadcasters to record and re-use. Increasingly now though, the material is available online for reporters to immediately download.

Most news organisations will use at least one wire or agency service, whether it's paying for individual items from a local news agency or subscribing for regular updates from national or international news agencies. The four largest and most-used international news agencies in the UK are the Press Association, Reuters, Associated Press and Agence France-Presse. All four provide news stories in text along with still images and video. The profile of these news agencies has increased as they have been able to publish their reporting directly onto the Internet. They also provide news to some of the major online aggregation organisations such as Yahoo News. Most news organisations will treat stories from reputable news agencies as 'primary sources' and assume the information they provide does not require checking, although it is vital that you confirm the policy of the newsroom where you are working.

Most countries have their own national news agencies and those which are genuinely independent, such as Germany's Deutsche Presse, often have excellent reputations. There are also a whole host of government-owned news agencies in countries which do not have a fully democratic press, such as Xinhua in China and Itar-Tass in Russia. Information from these agencies should be treated with great scepticism but can certainly give an interesting insight into the 'official government line' on news stories in these countries.

Many cities and regions in the UK have their own news agencies. Some agencies have their own large newsrooms, such as Caters News in the West Midlands and Mercury Press and Media in the North West of England, while others are local journalists working from home and selling their stories individually. Such freelance journalists are known as 'stringers', and they rely on a personal reputation built up through their body of work. They often have a close working relationship with local newspapers, radio and television stations or can sometimes be paid a retainer.

There are critics who argue that the proliferation and wide spread use of national and international news agencies by publishers and broadcasters is seriously compromising the variety and quality of the news agenda. They claim that re-using the same stories from a limited number of sources leads to the homogenisation of news, narrows down world views to a particularly westernised agenda and increases the likelihood of misinformation being repeated and rebroadcast.

Press releases, public relations and Electronic Press Kits

Whether they like it or not, professional journalists spend a considerable amount of time dealing with PRs, whether they're working in press offices, trying to promote press releases or providing background research to promote their employers' interests. It would be a rare day in a newsroom if a reporter didn't speak to at least one PR or press officer.

In the public eye, the line between journalism and PR is becoming increasingly blurred. Even in reputable publications, press releases can be published verbatim without corroboration, and few people would be able to spot the difference between a well-written press release and a genuine news story. In the digital world, it can be almost impossible to distinguish material produced by independent journalists from the terabytes of sponsored content created for promotion and marketing purposes. If the editorial policies of a website are not transparent, and sources are not clearly given, then the content should always be questioned.

For the purposes of this book, I would like to draw an absolute distinction between professional journalism and PR. A professional journalist should always start with the goal of independently establishing the facts, challenging decision makers and providing a fair analysis of those facts and their implications, whether that's done impartially in the regulated media or tailored to a newspaper or online audience. A PR in contrast, starts with the sole aim of presenting their client or employer in the best possible light. In most situations, these goals are polar opposites and will leave the work of journalists and PRs in conflict. Whenever one does their job well, they are by their very nature hindering the job of the other. Some professional journalists speak of their PR counterparts with barely hidden contempt, while PRs like many members of the public (and with considerable justification in recent years) have very little respect for working journalists. Perhaps the most pragmatic approach is to suggest that it is quite possible for both professions to work alongside each other and, in some cases, to work together, as long as both retain a very healthy sense of scepticism.

So what does this relationship mean in practice? In the first instance, it should mean that a working journalist should assume that a press or public relations office is very rarely the source of a news story and is unlikely to provide much useful background research. A PR might reasonably be expected to provide some very basic factual information about their employer or client and will often (sadly) be the first and only source of comments or quotes, but that should always be seen as the starting point (Figure 2.4).

Other publications and broadcasters

While our primary aim as journalists is always to seek out and tell untold stories, the practical truth is that much of our time is spent following up scoops from other newspapers, websites and broadcasters. In fact, it's generally one of the first jobs of the day to checkout the opposition, whether it's reading through the local paper, checking the nationals or watching the most recent TV news bulletin.

One way to make sure you monitor your main competitors is to set up a routine. If you have enough time during your shift, it's worthwhile starting with a read-through of all the newspapers, a check of the main news websites and a listen to any broadcast news outlets that share your audience. If you don't have time in the newsroom, you can still listen to the radio in the car or on your phone on the way to work and catch up with at least one newspaper, even if it's a free one. Getting into the habit of monitoring a variety of media regularly and when you're off shift will make it much easier to work effectively in the newsroom. When a rival has a story that you don't, there is a big decision to make. Do you chase it? Or do you leave the story to them? In every instance, the decision will be a different one, but if it's a

Figure 2.4 The team at Reuters in London monitor broadcasters and rival agencies © Esther Vargas

major development in a story you're already covering, it's likely your editor will ask you to check out the new angle.

It is unwise (and unethical) to reproduce a story from a media rival without checking it first. For those of us working in print and broadcast, it's one of the few advantages we still have over the many news aggregation websites on the Internet. If your reader or viewer trusts you, they also expect you to verify a story for them and put it into some context. The most straightforward way to check a story is to go back to a primary source. This may be as simple as ringing the person quoted in a newspaper article and asking them to confirm whether the piece is accurate. Alternatively, it may involve carefully sifting through some complicated statistics and checking the calculations. It's not uncommon to find simple mathematical errors in data that can completely invalidate a story.

In the case of a major news scoop, many editors will willingly credit their rival. For example, it may be impossible to check the veracity of leaked documents or an anonymous source, but if the report is in a reputable publication, it may be republished or broadcast and attributed to the original newspaper or programme.

Remember:

- News agencies are a major news source.
- Journalism and public relations are very different jobs.
- Treat your PR colleagues with both respect and scepticism.
- Get into a routine to monitor other news organisations.
- Never use news stories from other news organisations without verification.

The life cycle of a news story

One invaluable skill for a news journalist is the ability to think creatively around a news story, looking for alternative approaches, angles and interviewees. Finding those new ideas and treatments will often come from a real understanding of a publication's audience. If you know your reader, you will also know instinctively what they care about and what will interest them. Each news story has its own life cycle, which can help a reporter to identify ways to widen their research or identify a potential new angle. There are broadly two different types of news story, which fill the bulk of daily news reporting.

Diary stories

These are stories, which can be anticipated, such as elections, anniversaries and product launches. They will often be prompted by a news release or note in the newsroom diary. Most newsrooms keep some form of news diary. This can be a filing cabinet with labelled files for each day or week or a digital diary with attached notes and planning documents. Much of the news diary content will be genuine news stories, which will require planning and the production of pre-prepared content, such as the many events throughout 2015 to mark the centenary of World War I.

The research and preparation for diary stories tend to be in advance. In large news organisations, stories like this will often involve journalists working in dedicated planning teams. It is much easier in these conditions to tailor the style and content of the material to suit the news organisation's audience. Researchers will be working to a strong brief, with a plan and an idea of the finished product.

Press Officers also understand the opportunities offered by the News Diary. Journalists have seen a proliferation of special days and weeks organised by PR specialists. A brief experiment with Google quickly turned up 'National Chip Week', 'Befriending Week' and even 'Colon Health Wellness Week'. These PR creations may sound ludicrous, but on a quiet news day, they can provide a valuable peg for a feature piece or interview. Remember too, that there will be specialist trade publications and websites, which focus on fast food or public health, and these campaign weeks may well be big events in their calendars. Well-prepared press officers will often ring newsrooms to suggest interviewees connected to a big upcoming story. If the interviews are relevant and timely, it's very easy for a busy journalist to say 'yes' (Figure 2.5).

Breaking news

Breaking news stories (by their nature) can't be planned in advance. The bulk of the research effort is required as stories are developing or 'moving'. Researchers can be working under pressure, and those on the ground are often dealing with the very difficult conditions, which

Figure 2.5 Life cycle of a diary story

may have caused or exacerbated the news story in the first place. For example reporters working in an earthquake zone will have problems travelling, keeping safe and avoiding infection and even finding enough food. It's often in these circumstances that aspects of a story can be missed, misunderstood or glossed over. It's later in the life cycle of a breaking story that there may be time for reflection and analysis (Figure 2.6).

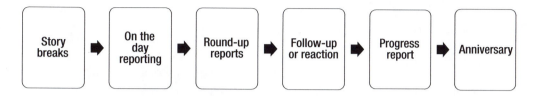

Figure 2.6 Life cycle of a breaking story

Interview

Jennie Slevin is an advanced content writer for Trinity Mirror's local news website Get Reading. Based in the Thames Valley, it's her job to cover events and use her digital expertise to build an online audience. Here's how she and her team planned the world famous Royal Ascot race meeting in 2015:

How did you go about planning the coverage for Royal Ascot, getting ideas and making contacts in advance?

We put together a 30-day plan, which helps us with Google rankings. Every day for the 30 days leading up to the event we ran a piece of content about Royal Ascot. This worked as the day before Royal Ascot our site was ranked second on Google just below the race-course website. I created a content schedule with details about what we would be doing each day and shared with the office who all pitched in.

What sort of research did you do in advance, and how did you get ideas of preview pieces?

We used Google Trends to find out what sort of things people search for and when they search for them in the run up to the event. We also brainstormed ideas of everything you could ever need to know and put together information pieces. Rather than doing one main information piece, we did individual pieces for food, drink, what you need to take, how to bet on horses etc, to spread out our coverage.

How did things change on the day? Did you go to Ascot, or did you process material from the newsroom?

On the day, myself and a photographer went to the event, while another colleague ran a live blog from the newsroom. I used social media tools like Twitter, Vine and Periscope to send different pieces into the office which were then embedded in the live blog and used the racecourse media centre to put together galleries from our photographer. I also wrote several pieces each morning based around weather, races, the Queen's procession and any other specific events happening each day. The live blog was used for breaking news including police updates on arrests and pushing all the content we had produced in the 30 day plan.

How long did you use follow-up material from the story?

Only around the week but the great thing is we'll be able to use a lot of the pre-pieces again next year. The follow-up material consisted mainly of photo galleries, but we also did a round-up piece the following Monday with links out to each day's coverage.

Things to do

Start a contacts book

If you don't have one already, start your contacts book. Consider whether you'd prefer to use paper or digital storage, how you'll update the information when you're out on a story and how you'll keep back-ups.

Practise your research

Find out the biggest employer in your hometown or local patch. Find out what it does or produces. How many people work for the organisation? Has the workforce grown or shrunk in the past 10 years? Use the Internet to start your research, but follow-up with phone calls to the organisation itself. Try to get past the press office to speak to some of the key staff or union leaders. Dig out archive online news reports on the organisation.

Research in action

Following on from the research above, imagine you have secured an interview with the most senior manager at this large local employer. Using your research, plan what you might ask your interviewee.

Now prepare a brief pitch to sell your profile of the company and its manager to an editor. First, consider how you might pitch the interview to your local newspaper and then how you might approach a monthly business publication. How would your angle, questions and writing style change?

Issues to discuss

The public relations industry is growing in size and sophistication. Many organisations are taking advantage of new technology to place publicity and marketing materials directly on the Internet. What does this mean for the work of professional journalists?

Newspapers and broadcasters are making increasing use of material from news agencies. How does this affect the variety of news stories available on mainstream news organisations? Do you think the use of such material improves or reduces the quality of their news coverage?

Places to learn more

Books and journals

Barry, A. 2002. *PR Power: Inside Secrets from the World of Spin*. London: Virgin.

Davies, N. 2009. Flat Earth News: An Award-Winning Reporter Exposes Falsehood. *Distortion and Propaganda in the Global Media*. London: Vintage.

Dodd, M. and Hanna, M. 2012. *McNae's Essential Law for Journalists*. Oxford: Oxford University Press.

Fenton, N. 2009. New Media. *Old News: Journalism and Democracy in the Digital Age*. London: Sage.

Pilger, J. 2005. *Tell Me No Lies: Investigative Journalism and its Triumphs*. London: Vintage.

Simpson, J. 2011. *Unreliable Sources. How the Twentieth Century Was Reported*. London: Pan.

Townsend, H. 2011. *The FT Guide to Business Networking*. London: Pearson.

Online resources

About.com – Journalism	http://journalism.about.com/
BBC College of Journalism	www.bbc.co.uk/academy/collegeofjournalism
Bureau of Investigative Journalism	www.thebureauinvestigates.com/
Centre for Investigative Journalism	www.tcij.org/
Data protection and journalism: a guide for the media	https://ico.org.uk/media/for-organisations/documents/1552/data-protection-and-journalism-media-guidance.pdf
IPSO	www.ipso.co.uk/IPSO/index.html
Journalism.co.uk	www.journalism.co.uk
National Union of Journalists – Code of Conduct	www.nuj.org.uk/about/nuj-code/
Press Gazette	www.pressgazette.co.uk/
Response Source	www.responsesource.com/
The blog of David Wilcox – 'Social Reporter'	http://socialreporter.com/
US Society of Professional Journalists	http://blogs.spjnetwork.org/

References

Cook, C. 2011. *The contacts book: A journo's most prized possession?* [online]. Reading, UK: Broadsheet Boutique. Available from: http://broadsheetboutique.com/2011/02/09/the-contacts-book-a-journalists-most-prized-posession/ [accessed 5 July 2015].

GKR Karate Ltd vs Yorkshire Post Newspapers Ltd. 200. WLR 2571, 361, 362

Information Commissioner's Office. 2014. *Data protection and journalism: a quick guide* [online]. London: Data Commissioner's Office. Available from: https://ico.org.uk/media/for-organisations/documents/1547/data-protection-and-journalism-quick-guide.pdf [accessed 6 May 2015].

Press Complaints Commission. 2014. *A woman. The Kentish Gazette* [online]. London: Press Complaints Commission. Available from: www.pcc.org.uk/cases/adjudicated.html?article=OTAyMg== [accessed 20 May 2015].

Scirrotto, J. 2014. *Q&A: Caitlin Moran tells it like it is* [online]. New York: Colombia Journalism Review. Available from: www.cjr.org/critical_eye/moranthology.php [accessed 5 July 2015].

Where not referenced, quotations are from interviews, emails or social media conversations with the author.

3 Digital research

Introduction

It seems strange that in a world where almost unlimited information is at our fingertips, getting close to the truth can be harder than it's ever been. For journalists, the speed and research opportunities offered by the information age may be both enabling and obstructive at the same time.

Digital technology changes daily and keeping up to date with the knowledge and skills to do our job can be a full-time occupation in itself. This chapter doesn't promise to be comprehensive and within a few months some of the ideas and advice offered will be out of date. I hope, though, that the key themes will endure. The need for researchers to be meticulous, take considered decisions, and be well informed will never change, as also the requirement to provide information that is tailored to their audience's needs and preferences. Matthew Eltringham is the Editor of the BBC College of Journalism website:

> Understanding how the online and social media world works is crucial for any journalist of today. It doesn't replace 'traditional' journalism techniques but builds on and complements them. It's where so many stories now play out.
>
> For that reason developing research skills in these areas has been a major focus for BBC journalists, those who hire them and those who train them. BBC journalists are expected to be able find stories and research them through social media and the digital world as naturally and effectively as their predecessors used shoe leather and notebooks.

To understand the digital world, you still need to understand people. A good journalist knows how to use technology, but just as importantly they recognise how people relate to that technology and where in the digital world they work and play. As researchers, we need to remember that human fallibilities are as common online as they are in the physical world. By being thorough and cautious in our research and taking the trouble to fact-check and verify our sources, we will hopefully retain and even build public trust. That trust is a valuable commodity in a confusing digital world.

This chapter covers:

- Search engines
- Searching smart
- The deep, invisible and Dark Web
- Message boards, discussion groups and web forums
- Social media
- User generated content
- Approaching sources online
- Crowdsourcing stories
- Apps for research
- Useful web resources
- Organising information

Search engines

Everyone knows the easiest way to find any basic information online is to 'Google' it, but this offers just a tiny glimpse into a universe of digital information. There are many alternative search engines and each has its own way of finding information and different ways of organising it. Understanding how to use search engines effectively can dramatically improve your ability to source information that is relevant, accurate and new.

Search engines only scan and index a tiny section of the Internet. Almost all look at the most visible part, called the World Wide Web. You'll find the terms 'Internet' and 'web' used interchangeably, but the web is actually only a small part of the entire Internet. Search engines use programmes called 'spiders' to look through web pages. This process is rather creatively known as 'web crawling'. The spiders for different search engines use different methods to scan the contents of a page. Their instructions are programmed using a list of rules known as an 'algorithm'. Once the spider has found the information required it's compiled into an 'index'. This is the information that is accessed when you type in your search request and it's automatically collated into the 'search results'. The search engine programmers are constantly changing their algorithms, to make the engines work better, so it's very hard indeed to know in detail how they scan each web page. However, gaining some understanding of the basics will help you to choose the right search engine for the job. Reading an engine's Webmaster Guide can give some insight into the way the algorithm has been designed.

At the time of writing, Google is by far the most popular search engine in the UK, used three times as often as its most popular rivals Bing and Yahoo combined, but its popularity has dropped a little recently (Statista, 2015). Search engine popularity does change. Older readers might remember AltaVista, which was one of the most used search engines of the late 1990s, but was closed down in 2013. There are a number of websites, which keep reliable league tables of the most popular search engines. It's worthwhile checking these occasionally to keep track of the most popular sites and spot any up-and-coming engines that might use innovative search technology.

Bing, Yahoo and Google each look different, but Bing actually powers Yahoo, so their searches work similarly. Broadly, Google looks for websites with a high number of links and prefers material that is regularly updated. So it's particularly good for finding news, recent blog posts and social media content. Bing prefers more established material and it's thought to be far better at finding multimedia content. Straight away, we can see how used together Google and Bing could offer a researcher more varied search results.

When your search results appear, each of the search engines presents them differently. One key point to remember is the prominence given to paid content. Before clicking on the first link offered, just pause for a moment to check whether it is actually the best response to your query or an advertisement. In Google, the first couple of options generally have the word 'Ad' next to them and are used to generate revenue for Google. Another very simple way to access more unusual or interesting material, is to look at the third or fourth page of the results. It's thought that fewer than 10 per cent of people who make a Google search look any further down the list than page 3.

One way to quickly access several search engines at once is to use a meta search engine. These engines retrieve and index the results provided by a number of other search engines. They have some advantages in that they allow you to make swift combined searches, but there are disadvantages in the ways that they filter and index the information. If you're looking in a hurry, or for a fresh perspective on material, then meta search engines can be useful tools. Two popular meta search engines are WebCrawler, which searches using both Google and Bing, and Dogpile, which uses Google, Bing and the Russian search engine Yandex.

While Google may dominate much of the western world, it's not the most popular search engine everywhere. Yahoo is the most popular engine in Japan (Statista, 2014). If you're looking for content in Russia, then Yandex is a valuable tool (Robertson, 2013). In China the most popular search engine is Baidu (Robertson, 2013). Some have English versions or you can use an online translation service.

There are a variety of other niche search engines that can help you track down valuable images, video or contact details. Again, the best way to keep up with the rise and fall of these is to subscribe to relevant blogs and online publications. Some that are useful at the moment include Duck Duck Go, an engine that offers some anonymity when web searching; Giphy, which allows you to search for short clips of online video; Blinkx, an engine that helps you to search video by content rather than just title; Slidefinder searches the remarkable number of presentations posted online (it's a great source of expert comment and information) and FindSounds searches for audio files (valuable for audio producers).

One search engine that merits its own special mention is Way Back Machine. It's an archive and search engine that allows you to visit websites as they appeared in the past. The site was set up in 1996 by the non-profit organisation the Internet Archive and keeps regular snapshots of websites over time.

Wolfram Alpha is another search engine that has attracted a huge amount of interest. It uses a completely new way to answer a search request. Rather than simply trawl the web for data and present a number of answers for you to review, it accesses a huge database and analyses the results to try to offer a single relevant answer. It's also programmed to interpret natural language, so it will do its best to figure out what you want to know.

Aside from answering someone's maths homework, it is particularly good with facts and figures. If you ask Google what the biggest company in the world is, you get more than three hundred million hits, each giving an answer. Wolfram Alpha picks one answer and explains why it has chosen that response. You are able to change the criteria for choosing the biggest company, if you believe the search engine has misunderstood you or made an incorrect assumption. Wolfram Alpha is in its earliest stages and it can be hard to use, but it's fascinating to get a glimpse of a new way of searching the web.

Interview

Katy Stoddard is a Senior Researcher for The Guardian News and Media and writes for *The Guardian*'s revolutionary Datablog. She's worked for the organisation for around fifteen years and has seen a dramatic change in her role and the resources available to researchers.

How has the work you do as a professional researcher changed over the past few years?

It's changed dramatically. There are fewer of us, but the workload has increased as we work with different departments, and with developments in digital technology. We're working in a very different way. When I started, there were fifteen of us, including five trainees and seven researchers; now, we have six in all.

When I was a trainee, the department still maintained the cuttings files, clipping articles from every national paper every day, and filing them away. We stopped in 2001. When I started as a researcher in 2002, most of our time was taken up with research for journalists, finding background for stories, statistics, contacts, writing sidebars etc. Basic research takes far less time now, for a number of reasons. We've rolled out some subscription services, so journalists can search themselves for agent details, for example; journalists can find some information easily using Google and other web services; and advances in web searching, and the creation of the digital archive, means it takes far less time to search.

We can collaborate on projects as a team, using Google spreadsheets, and also collaborate with other departments. For example, we work with the website to update timelines directly on the web, such as Phone Hacking Interactive and our General Election Database. The site was powered by a massive spreadsheet – we found the information on each candidate, entered it and uploaded it to the site, a huge amount of work.

I work on *The Guardian's* home for data journalism, finding statistics, formatting them in Google spreadsheets, uploading them to the web and writing the accompanying article. I've written on everything from Glastonbury and the film awards season to birth rates, plastic surgery and US healthcare.

Do you think trainee journalists overlook the importance of developing their research skills?

I think there's a risk of assuming research is easy, with the ready availability of web resources like Google and Wikipedia. I've come across journalists who assume that everything can be found in two minutes with one click of a mouse! A lot of information requires complex search techniques, and can take hours to compile or access to databases and subscription services that aren't freely available on the web.

Then there's the issue of reliability on the web. Just because the information is out there does not mean it is true! It is incredibly important to get your facts right before you publish, particularly on legally sensitive issues, and journalists have been caught out by relying on suspect Internet sources. Even Wikipedia, which can be reliable and is certainly one of the most comprehensive free online reference sources, needs corroborating, which is fairly easy, as everything should be cited and therefore can be checked quickly.

How do you collaborate with journalists and what do both professions gain from working together?

The level of collaboration varies depending on the job and the journalist! Some journalists come to me for background info. If someone is planning an interview, for example, they'll email, call or pop over and ask for articles on the person, and I'll email the results; or a journalist will call for a phone number and I'll do an electoral roll search and ring them back. If the newsdesk wants a sidebar to accompany an article, they tend to call with details and I get on with it. Sometimes they send the copy first. Some stories require much more collaboration. Longer term projects, where the research is on-going, web interactives for example, can mean working more closely, keeping in contact as the project progresses. The best case scenario would be that the library is consulted and listened to at the beginning of a project, so that we can explain what can realistically be done in the time given, with the resources we have, but this doesn't always happen! Likewise with a basic search, my job is much easier if I'm given all the information and context.

What's your top research tip for a journalist starting out on their career?

Take time to consider what you're searching for. What is the best resource to use, be it calling someone or choosing a database? What are the best keywords to use? If you choose the right tools before you begin you can save a lot of time.

Searching smart

One of the simplest ways to improve the success of your web search is to use the search engines' advanced search feature. Both Google and Bing offer advanced searches.

These sites change their designs regularly, but in most cases the advanced search option can be found easily from the main search page and the principles remain broadly the same. An advanced search allows you to narrow down your criteria and look for particular forms of content (such as videos or blogs). One of the most important facilities is the ability to search for material by date. Most journalists don't want older posts or information and so it can really help to focus a search. You can also select material by country of origin or its language, and if you look for material in another language, the translate function will give you a rough idea of the content. Scholar is a great tool for finding experts and peer-reviewed data, which can add authority to your work.

Google in particular uses a wide variety of 'operators', or terms that you can include in a search to improve your success. Most people are familiar with basic Boolean searching using the words AND, NOT and OR. Google will also allow you to search for specific web content using more complex terms. Using the word 'site' with a colon allows you to search a single website, while using the word 'cache' with a colon allows you to search for the site as it appeared the last time Google's spiders crawled it. For example, the search *sparrow site:bbc.co.uk* will only find mentions of sparrows on the BBC website. A search for *cache:guardian.co.uk* will reveal what the newspaper's website looked like when it was last crawled. It's a useful way to find controversial material that may have been deleted by the Webmaster.

> **Remember:**
>
> - Search engines work in different ways and provide different results.
> - Search engines only crawl a small section of the Internet.
> - Meta search engines index material from several search engines.
> - Overseas search engines and those in other languages can be useful.
> - Keep up to date with specialist search engines.
> - Using the 'advanced search' makes searches more accurate and productive.

The deep, invisible and Dark Web

As we've already mentioned, search engines only scan a small section of the Internet. Even in the areas they do scan, careful design and coding can ensure web content stays invisible. Some research tasks may require you to dig a little deeper or reach further out into the area known as the 'deep' or 'invisible' web. The vast majority of this material is accessible, innocuous and can be extremely useful to journalists.

The deep or invisible web

There is a huge quantity of perfectly legitimate material available online that is either invisible to search engines, or ignored by the crawlers for a variety of reasons. It's often valuable for journalists, as it can contain facts and figures few others have seen. Many hundreds of 'draft' web pages also exist in this space. They may be awaiting publication or archiving but not clearly visible when you visit websites. Professionals who have a particular area of expertise or interest also curate some of this information, which can make it reliable and useful for more detailed analysis. Finding this material requires persistence, some skill and may be made much faster with the assistance of a professional researcher. Some content that can't easily be found with a search engine is:

- *Unusual file formats*
  Search engines are becoming better at finding material stored as more unusual file formats. Word and Excel documents and .pdf files now regularly appear in search engine results, but there are a whole variety of more unusual file formats that can be stored online and don't regularly pop-up on search engine crawls. In particular, many data journalists are interested in information stored in databases. (More on this in Chapter 4).

- *Password protected or paid-for material*
  The vast majority of academic writing is stored on password-protected sites, run by academic publishers. If you want to access original research for your work you may need to purchase access to these sites, or visit a library which offers access and can provide a specialist search tool.

- *Dynamically assembled pages*
  These pages are compiled in response to an online research request. Think about the pages that appear online when you search for train times or book a hotel. There are many millions

of these pages produced each day and search engines generally ignore them (mostly for practicality, but also because they are of little interest to anyone except the person using them).

- *Deliberately excluded web pages*
  Search engines only include a sample of pages from sites. To make searches more manageable they deliberately only present a snapshot of relevant pages. What is excluded will depend on the search engine. Website designers can also exclude pages from searches by including specific lines of code.

Finding hidden material online

The most straightforward way to find material that is invisible to one search engine is to use an alternative. That's why researchers will often start a search by using two or three different search engines. The ubiquity of Google means that using another search engine can immediately reveal information the vast majority of journalists have missed.

Using the advanced search tools on Google and other engines is the next step for searching more deeply. If you know a particular website has relevant material for your research, then try using Google to access only that website. If you're looking for a particular type of material, then make this part of the search criteria. For example, if you're looking for data on road accidents, then add the term 'database' to your search. Keep up to date with new and relevant search engines that might provide material relevant to your patch or beat. If these tools aren't available to you, then try what some journalists have done – begun writing their own 'web mining' code, to allow them to find relevant data. More information on coding for journalists can be found in Chapter 4.

If you're focusing on a particular website, but finding it hard to navigate to the pages you require, the sitemap can be a useful tool. A good sitemap is an instant indication of what's on a website and how the site is organised. The link to the sitemap is often hidden in material at the bottom of the site's homepage. Links that may be broken on the pages of a website, or disabled to hide material may still be available on the sitemap. Most sitemaps are clickable and are particularly useful on very large websites, or on those that are poorly designed.

The Dark Web

There is an entirely different part of the Internet, known as 'the Dark Web' which is completely ignored by the main search engines and where the vast majority of users remain anonymous. There are many estimates of the size of the Dark Web, but it's probably reasonable to assume it's hundreds of times larger than the visible web.

Websites on the Dark Web are generally encrypted using the Tor (The Onion Router) open source encryption tool. There are other encryption services (one current favourite is called I2P), but the principle remains the same. The person uploading the material must encrypt it using the tool and the person who wants to view the material must use the same encryption tool to view the content. Sites encrypted using Tor have URLs which are a string of letters and numbers followed by the suffix .onion.

Needless to say, in an environment where people are anonymous there is a great deal of illegal, unpleasant and frightening material, but there are some legitimate uses for this space. For example, conversing anonymously is important for people (such as journalists) who want to share sensitive material. People living in totalitarian or highly regulated states, can also use the Dark Web to communicate with the outside world. Some people simply feel that the most visible part of the web allows large companies and governments to know too much about them. Increasing numbers of ordinary people are using the Dark Web to protect their activity online.

There are numerous online articles explaining how to download and use the Tor encryption. Up until recently, you had to download a specialist browser, such as the Tor Browser. But a new search engine called 'Onion City' has been released which is available easily on the web and searches Tor pages, making them accessible on any computer. As it makes Tor far easier to reach for the average person and of course the authorities, one can only assume those using this part of the Dark Web for illegal activities may begin moving to another space. Be aware also that material accessed via Onion City appears as regular web pages and is not secure.

Whatever your view of the Dark Web, journalists working on investigations into illegal pornography, drugs or weapons deals or terrorism may find material of value to them here. Investigative journalists working undercover or those working with whistleblowers or sources who cannot be identified also make regular use of this encrypted part of the web.

If you work for a large media organisation you shouldn't attempt to access the Dark Web without getting advice from your IT department or a senior member of staff. Not only might your activities raise suspicion, but you may also unwittingly download dangerous or insecure software onto a work computer. If your research is legitimate, then you will be given help and advice to access the material safely and without getting yourself into trouble!

Message boards, discussion groups and web forums

There are a massive variety of places where online discussions and debates take place. Whether you call them message boards, bulletin boards, discussion groups, or web forums, they are all great places to find case studies and interviewees. The simplest way to locate discussions relevant to your story is to use a search engine. Simply type the search terms 'xxxx message board' in the search box (replace the xxxx with your topic).

Internet forums differ from chat rooms in that people on chat rooms all communicate at once, while a forum tends to include posts, which are added one after another. Chat rooms might offer the chance to meet a relevant interviewee or case study, although you will probably need to wade through a great deal of irrelevant rubbish in the process.

Newsgroups are similar to forums, except you need a piece of special software on your computer to read the content. Newsgroup material is distributed via a network called Usenet. You have to pay for access to Usenet. Newsgroups can be useful because they are organised into subject groups and sub topics. Users can maintain their anonymity on Usenet so it can be a useful research tool to discover people who want keep their identities secret or it can offer an alternative option for speaking to sources in confidence. Research using Usenet and Newsgroups is a specialist skill that most journalists would only use for complex and long-term investigations.

Listserves are useful and a less-known way to find case studies and interviewees. They are mailing lists, which allow people to communicate and share material easily by email. A company called L-Soft runs the system. It provides a searchable catalogue of the various mailing lists, which cover diverse subjects, ranging from artisan cheese production to aerospace. There are also several dozen journalism mailing lists. There is a useful mailing list service for UK academics and researchers called JISCmail, which offers a search function. It's a good way to find experts who are actively involved in discussions about specific academic subjects.

Following blogs and keeping your own blog are two other ways to contact and speak to people who share your research interests. If you work for a large news organisation you will need to check their policy on personal blogging before you start, as some may not want you sharing professional work online. Writing about what you do and bringing your work to the attention of people on your patch or beat can be a great way to raise issues, ask for help and even find sources and contacts. Obviously, you should be promoting and sharing your blog posts and those of your contacts by social media.

Alerts and content management

With vast quantities of material posted online, it's important to be able to access the material you want and keep up with new information. It's also vital for a journalist working an online beat to manage and store their research information successfully.

There are a good number of useful alert tools that search the visible web for new material that's relevant to your research area. By far the most popular at the moment is Google Alerts, which sends an email every time a keyword appears online. For example if you cover a physical patch, you can set-up a Google Alert for any material posted online containing the name of your patch. There is a free alternative called Talkwalker and a number of paid-for services that provide a more tailored service.

Remember:

- There is a huge amount of legal information on the web, invisible to search engines.
- Using multiple search engines or advanced search terms can reveal new content.
- Sitemaps are a good way to find material hidden on a site.
- The Dark Web is a large encrypted area of the Internet.
- There is a lot of illegal activity in the Dark Web.
- The Dark Web allows people to work and share material anonymously.
- Message boards, discussion groups and web forums are good places to find interviewees.
- Some online forums require special software and specialist knowledge.

Social media

The number of adults in the UK who are online continues to grow; interestingly though, around 13 per cent of adults have still never accessed the Internet (ONS, 2014). Of those who are online, 54 per cent use social media (ONS, 2014). This actually means that while journalists love social media, almost half of the UK population can't be reached on social networks. So don't forget that the telephone and email remain important research tools.

The use of social media for digital research can be broadly broken into two areas: first, searching for material and people already on social networks and second, soliciting material using social networks. These are skills that most working journalists use every day, to a greater or lesser extent. Social media networks will come and go, but having a good understanding of how they work and who uses them is very important. Looking for the wrong kind of people on the wrong network can be pointless at best and counter-productive at worst. As US social media expert Andy Carvin told *The Guardian* in 2011, 'I'm really agnostic (about social networks), it's a matter of whether the people I want to talk to are on there, about who's using it and what information I can glean from it.' It's also important to understand that social media networks operate very differently from other media. They are very much about community, sharing and discussion. 'Broadcasting' on them in a traditional way doesn't work well and often proves pretty unproductive.

As with search engines, a few big players dominate the world of social networking, but their popularity is in flux. According to the Reuters Digital News Report 2014, Facebook remains by far the most important network for news. Twitter is influential and widely used in some countries, while Google+ and WhatsApp are becoming increasingly important. If people are using a particular social network to access news, then this will clearly be a good place for journalists to make contact with them.

No book can offer an up-to-date understanding of numbers and usage patterns of social media, as it changes daily. As always, this information is available on the web and can be accessed from some of the most reputable analytics companies. Don't expect certainties though. Each of the analytics companies uses different data collection methods and provides different statistics. You need a broad understanding of the social media landscape to draw some general conclusions and help you search social media most effectively.

Practical use of social media

The best way to understand a social network is to use it. You won't be able to build a relationship with your sources, if you are not active on their preferred network, and sharing your thoughts and work are important ways of building trust. The most important aspects of using social media as a research tool are choosing the right social network for your research, building your own credible presence on the network and then using it effectively. Before you start interacting in a professional capacity on any social media, spend some time thinking about the merits and implications: what should you be posting and what might happen if you make an ill-judged post or comment? It's hard to get rid of media posted on social media, so better to consider this from the beginning and don't risk your career or professional reputation. Where relevant check your employer's social media usage policy. I know many journalists who use a simple rule; if you wouldn't want your grandmother to see it, then don't post it!

Here is a guide to some of the most popular social networks of the early part of the twenty-first century and how journalists may be able to use them for research purposes. It is not by any means intended to be a comprehensive guide. It can take several months of usage and experimentation to understand a social network and much of the work you do will need to be tailored to your particular area of journalism. However, this section provides a basic introduction to many of the current most popular networks and will suggest some more areas for research.

Facebook

As already mentioned, this is the most popular social network in current use and is an excellent place to find interviewees and sources. Although Facebook does remain most popular among the young, if you're trying to contact older people, this is also the social network they are most likely to use. It's worthwhile to note that some very young users are beginning to move away from Facebook, as they see it as being the 'uncool' network their parents use. There is a tendency for people to see Facebook as a leisure space, although this has changed in the last few years with the growth in news apps.

When using Facebook as a research tool, it's wise to set-up a private and professional account. There are options to have one profile and tailor who sees material relevant to them, but there are risks to this option. Ensure that your accounts are secure with a strong password. Getting your private social media account hacked is embarrassing and frustrating, but having your professional account hacked could seriously damage your reputation, and you may even lose money.

However you choose to organise your professional Facebook presence, it's important to assure other users that you are a reliable and genuine contact. Facebook itself provides some really useful information for journalists who want to use the network successfully. The emphasis is very much on 'community'; sharing material with your followers, giving them a behind-the-scenes insight into your work and using the site to publish your work alongside finding sources and contacts. The extent to which you do this will vary according to your role. Those working for large professional news organisations may not need to spend much time developing their professional Facebook profile. Freelancers, on the other hand might well spend considerable amounts of time building their online brand. If you do work for a large news organisation, it is very important that you understand how your employers prefer you to use your own professional social media accounts. They may take a dim view of posting breaking news on your own site rather than theirs and this will be doubly important for you, when you are posting while undertaking paid assignments.

Building a network of professional contacts can be done using the 'follow' feature and linking this to your other online profiles and website. As with all social media, the more you create interesting content and share this, the more new contacts will be drawn to your network.

When using material such as images and quotes sourced on Facebook, you must consider the ethical and legal implications. The information may appear in the public domain, but is it legal to take it and use it for your story? Even if it is legal, is it ethical to take material and use it without the source's permission?

Perhaps the most important thing to remember about Facebook is that using it in a professional and personal way are two very different experiences. The way you use Facebook professionally will also differ dramatically, depending on your style of journalism. It's worthwhile spending some time planning how you want to use Facebook for work and doing some research before you start your professional research.

Instagram

According to recent research, Instagram has overtaken Twitter for active users and among some users is more popular than Facebook. (Facebook won't be too worried – they also own Instagram!) It's easy to see why this has happened in a world where mobile Internet access is growing. Instagram users are more likely to be female than in some other networks and they are more likely to live in urban areas (probably because it's easier to upload images where there are fast 3G and 4G mobile networks). Some people have described Instagram as the first truly global social media, because clearly images are not limited by language. Instagram also allows users to edit and share short 15 second video clips, which do not loop.

Instagram's most obvious use for journalistic research is the sourcing of images. This is easy and effective, but there are copyright and ethical implications. There are also benefits for journalists who want to share their work using Instagram, as it allows the rapid and easy uploading of breaking news images, behind the scenes shots and more intimate professional material. Some news organisations are experimenting with uploading short video news updates to be shared on the network. Others are using snippets of video or still images to offer samples of longer work. The network's use of hashtags also makes it a good place to curate material or follow contributions to a particular discussion. So it's an excellent network for following a breaking story and also providing your own live blogging content.

Vine

Vine is a relatively small network compared to Instagram and is owned by Twitter. It too allows the sharing of short video clips. The clips are only 7 seconds in length and the editing opportunities are more limited than on Instagram, but the short videos do loop. One of the merits of using Vine for research is its membership of media creatives and a more 'niche' market. A search for short video clips should certainly start with Instagram, but it would be unwise to ignore Vine.

YouTube

While many of us use YouTube rather like an on-demand video service, its value as a social network shouldn't be overlooked. Broadcasters and individual journalists use YouTube to share their content and the network has its own CitizenNews Channel. YouTube is clearly the most fruitful place to search for video content. It's used by campaign groups of every colour and belief, and has created its own stars.

YouTube's 'News Near You' feature geolocates video by its IP address, which is a great way to ensure the video was uploaded where the user says it was. It's also a good way to locate citizen journalists and user generated content (UGC) in a particular area. Some research suggests using UGC from YouTube can be more productive for journalists than posting their own material. Certainly many broadcasters have had real success soliciting material from YouTube users for their debates and discussions. The 'comments' area below each video is also a fruitful place to search for contacts and post appeals for material.

Twitter

Many journalists would argue that Twitter provides their single biggest source of information and people. It should be remembered, though, that it is not the largest network and some people see it as 'elitist' and unrepresentative.

In order to work successfully on Twitter, it's vital that you have a relevant or eye-catching image with a clear profile that explains who you are and what you're doing on the network. The best way to start building contacts is to begin following people who are relevant to your field of interest and to start tweeting yourself. In recent years Twitter has gained a reputation for nastiness and spamming. So it's really important that you approach people with courtesy and use the network wisely. Remember, your funny political tweet from last week could jeopardise an interview this week. Media-rich tweets tend to generate the most engagement, so it's better to include images and video if you can. You can create collages of multiple images to showcase what you've created and include material from Vine. Don't use loads of hashtags; apart from being a waste of space, they tend to confuse and irritate people. Twitter itself recommends no more than two. Try to take part in online networking events. Once you get involved in a Twitter community you'll soon find people gathering together once a week to share material around a specific hashtag.

Twitter's basic search tool is a great way to start investigating a story, but its advanced search page can help you to narrow down what you're looking for and provides a useful location search feature. If you're looking for eyewitnesses, you may be able to contact someone who was close to an incident, even if they're not currently tweeting about it. If you're looking for older material you can't use the search function on Twitter, but Topsy is a tool that will do that for you. Incidentally, there is a Twitter hashtag #journohelp, which often gets a quick response.

Once you start following large numbers of people, it can be hard to keep track of all the different content. It's a good idea to set-up Twitter lists to divide up the material or even use a dashboard such as Tweetdeck or Hootsuite. It's also worth doing some online research to find other tools for managing your Twitter research, as there are new resources appearing almost daily, for example at the moment Tweetlistmanager is great if you're following a huge number of accounts and need an easy way to keep track of them.

If you're freelancing, then you may need more complex tools to maximise your impact on Twitter. There are some excellent tools, such as Refollow, which allow you to build an audience of the most valuable followers. There are also many great social media marketing tools that enable you to dig down into your Twitter feed and spot your main competitors, find the best time to Tweet and to track down those key influencers in your field. Take a look at advice on marketing websites as well as journalism networks for the latest and try as many free options as you can before paying.

LinkedIn

LinkedIn is by far the most popular network for business. Like many of the other networks it can be used to promote your professional skill and share stories, but is perhaps most useful for making professional contacts and finding interviewees. The network has its own group for journalists called 'LinkedIn for Journalists', which has more than fifty thousand members. It also runs regular webinars to help journalists make use of LinkedIn's research opportunities. The network hopes that by encouraging journalists to share and network on LinkedIn they will be more likely to use the network as a source. This will, in its turn, encourage other users to make more use of LinkedIn to promote their brands and personal expertise.

As with other social networks, the emphasis is on sharing information and joining in discussions. LinkedIn advises users to complete their profiles, providing as much detail as possible, which allows users to maximise their contacts. Using keywords and telling a strong story in your profile makes it easier for contacts to find you and will encourage them to stay with your page. LinkedIn also suggests that journalists join groups to allow them to participate in online conversations. This is clearly particularly relevant for journalists working particular beats or patches.

When searching on LinkedIn don't forget to use the advanced search link. It's a really simple way to find contacts with specific attributes, such as former employees of an organisation. You can also search for people with unusual combinations of skills. Journalists are often asked to find unusual case studies, such as 'a chef who used to work for a hedge fund' and LinkedIn is great for making those sorts of contacts. LinkedIn groups allow people with similar interests to get in touch. The network provides a directory of groups and this can allow you to look for people whose accounts may not appear in a search. If you're running your own blog or have an online brand, consider setting-up your own LinkedIn Group, which will help to attract people who are interested in your subject area. Another valuable use for LinkedIn is to use your expert contacts to confirm a story. Often, by the time a tip reaches a journalist, specialists in that area have discussed it for some time.

LinkedIn only allows you to send messages to others in your network, but in practice you can approach sources by attaching a short note to a contact invitation. Most people forward these invitations directly to their email accounts and will reply fairly quickly. If you want more options for making contacts on the network, you might consider paying for a premium account. This give you access to a variety of additional functions, including access to more detailed profiles and Open Link which allows other members to message you, whether you're linked or not. This could be a valuable function for freelance journalists who may be using the network to find work and source original stories, whereas a journalist working for a news organisation may find they only need the options of a basic account.

Google+

Google+ poses an interesting dilemma for UK journalists: do you need to be on the network at all? Very few people in the UK are active on Google+ (although many will unwittingly have accounts which are opened when you create a YouTube or Google Mail account). The network is more popular in the United States though and is a good place to contact interviewees in the US. Also as Google runs the network and it links up some of their other online features, a presence may well boost your personal SEO.

Google+ does have some specialist features for journalists; allowing them to add by-lines to photos and create specialist profiles, and it offers the opportunity to contact people with private messages (something that can be harder on other networks). Google Ripples is a useful tool to track anyone who has shared your posts or to track how a news story is developing.

By far the most valuable and used tool for journalists is Google+ hangouts. It's a great way to conduct interviews, gather vox pops, and some broadcasters have been using hangouts in live television and radio news. There are a number of options for sharing emoticons and images, but the free videoconferencing option is probably most valued by researchers and reporters.

Figure 3.1 Social media is adapting as smartphones and tablets take over from computers © Esther Vargas

Messaging apps

One of the fastest growing social media trends is the blossoming of messaging apps. These allow people to keep in contact with short text messages, images and, in some cases, videos. They were initially seen as an alternative to SMS text messages, but are becoming increasingly popular with young people and news organisations have begun to see an opportunity to reach new audiences. SnapChat is by far the most popular with WhatsApp, WeChat, Viber and Mxit also increasingly used.

Each of the apps offers slightly different features and that means they lend themselves to different forms of communication. WhatsApp remains centred on messaging capabilities and this encourages users to discuss and comment on content. The Chinese app WeChat allows users to create profiles and also makes it easier to share media. Viber can be easier for publishers to use, as it can be updated on a desktop computer. Mxit works on less expensive feature phones and so is very popular in its home country of South Africa.

At the moment news providers are experimenting with output on these platforms to see how their young users respond. Early findings suggest a more personal approach; brevity and as much simple content as possible seem to work well. There is a clear opportunity to use the platforms to cover live events with brief snippets or news or story updates. SnapChat has launched a service called Discover in partnership with some major news providers. The opportunity for SnapChat users to view a variety of brief story teasers and then choose to access the information in more detail could well be an influential new development in news production. Unlike some other social networks, such as Facebook, there is no algorithm to choose news stories for the user. Instead they are free to choose any story they want from any partner news provider. So once again brand identity could be the key to getting attention. At the moment most SnapChat channels on Discover are being updated sporadically and so it's not a great place to search for breaking news now.

There are clearly opportunities for journalists to share their work via messaging networks, and they are rapidly becoming a rich source of user generated content. As with all social networks, user habits are changing quickly. If young people are using these networks in large numbers and sharing material on these apps, it's likely that the apps builders and news organisations will want to find ways to connect with this audience. It seems very likely that in the next few years more news content will be found on and sourced from messaging networks.

Audioboom and Soundcloud

These are the two best-known audio sharing sites (Audioboom used to be known as Audioboo). Interestingly, for several years the use of audio online had become somewhat polarised, with a widespread interest in podcasts, which tended to be longer programmes, and in contrast, sharing of and interest in short audio clips. Audioboom still restricts those using its free service to three minute clips, but the paid-for service now allows much longer podcast-style content. The advantage of posting longer content on Audioboom is its strength as a social network.

Soundcloud began life more as a music-sharing site, but now hosts a large quantity of other audio content. It restricts the total duration of audio material you can share on its website. Both these sites offer a really rich resource for audio and video producers. There are numerous musicians who may be willing to allow you to use the music copyright free. There are also sound effects and audio recordings of a wide variety of locations and people. The sharing of non-music audio files remains a relatively niche area compared to video, but if your passion is radio, podcasting or the spoken word then these are great sites.

Pinterest

Pinterest is an unusual combination of social network and bookmarking service. It allows users to upload, manage and curate media information known as 'pins'. It's been the great social networking success story of recent years, with women dominating the number of users, although there is a growing number of men. It's also popular among young women, but once again that is changing.

Hard news journalists may find Pinterest less useful than those working in features and lifestyle journalism. Many have described its main strengths as 'fashion, food and weddings' but its reach covers many areas of women's interest and lifestyle. Its other main asset is its ability to save and curate material. Many of the new messaging networks dispose of posts within a few seconds, and on Twitter, a post can disappear after a few minutes, but Pinterest pins have longevity. Some journalists have used Pinterest to offer a new life to archived online material. Others have used it to collaborate with readers and even pin collections of photos on breaking news stories.

For researchers, the undoubted benefit of Pinterest is the ability to reach new audiences. It allows you to share and generate content and contact people who might not be accessible through other social media. It is possible to message people on Pinterest, but they need to be following at least one of your boards, so the key is to build content and allow people to access your profile on other media.

Figure 3.2 New social networks are always appearing. Is Ello a future success story? © Ello

One of the biggest social media stories of 2015 was the network Ello, which claimed to be ethical and advertisement free. It was unashamedly anti-Facebook and received considerable media attention and people were (reportedly) rushing to join. There were also a growing number of small, but successful niche networks, such as Foodie for food lovers and Fitocracy for those keen on sharing their exercise experiences.

Overseas networks

If you're researching stories in other countries, it's worth being aware of some of the most popular social networks that are not in the English language. The user data for these sites comes from Statista (2015). The most popular non-English messaging app is QQ, which is based in China. With more than 800 million active users, it allows you to share text, voice calls and video. If your work covers China or takes you to the Far East, there is also an English version. QZone is China's largest social network and is owned by the same company as QQ (Tencent). The English version of QQ will allow you to access the basic functions of QZone if you don't speak Mandarin. Baidu is a popular Chinese search network and has more worldwide users than Twitter, while the microblogging site Sina Weibo offers an English service. If you're researching a story in Russia you may want to take a look at VK (or Vkontakte). It's the largest social networking site in Russia and although it has only 100 million active users, it can be the best way to contact people in Russia and other eastern European countries. The messaging app LINE is the most popular social network in Japan and there is an English version if you want to contact sources in Japan.

Researching and sharing successfully

One big challenge for journalists when using social media networks is dealing with their proliferation and the sheer volume of information they can provide. With some social networks it's easy to see how they might be used for journalistic research, while others only offer opportunities for journalists working in particular specialisms. Some seem to offer little to the researcher at first glance, but in some respects, that's missing the point. While a network may not initially seem a likely prospect for sourcing and sharing journalistic content, those which prove popular will soon add more features and generate content to attract more users. Journalists who are able to meet these creative opportunities will have early access to these networks, finding new and exciting ways to tell stories and reach new audiences.

One way to make it easier to work alongside your audience on multiple social networks is to use a dashboard. Hootsuite, Buffer, Sprout Social and Sendible are all tools which allow you to post content to various different social media feeds at the same time, schedule posts for the future and monitor other social media content. There are also a growing number of social media management tools, which offer unique and really useful features. ITTT (If this then that) allows you to specify a particular response to an event on social media. TrendSpottr helps you to identify people and content that is becoming influential online. It's a clever way to source new stories and trace possible interviewees. Rignite is a dashboard, which focuses on team working. Viraltag is great for scheduling visual content (particularly Pinterest) and Schedugram does the same for Instagram. Manage Flitter cleverly analyses when most of your social media audience is online and ensures that your posts are likely to get the most attention.

If you're conducting social media research on a breaking story, there are some very useful services that allow you to search real-time social media posts. They swiftly scan a variety of social networks and aggregate a selection of relevant posts. Currently useful are Socialmention,

Addictomatic and IceRocket. Tagboard is useful because it allows you to search hashtags across a selection of social media. These tools are great ways to do a quick trawl of social media comment on breaking news.

Remember:

- Social media can be used both to research material and solicit content.
- The use of social media networks is constantly changing.
- It is important to know what kind of people use which network.
- Social network usage varies across the world.
- Journalists will need to follow their audiences as they move from one network to another.
- It's important to keep access to the best tools to access and manage social media content.

User generated content

UGC is one of the most commonly used terms for material produced by a journalist's readers, viewers and listeners. It's a very loose term, as it can be used to refer to content produced by any person online as well as the work of more professional bloggers and 'citizen journalists'. Other much-used terms are 'Collaborative Journalism' and 'Citizen Media'. UGC is a highly complex world of content. It includes individuals who might post one of two images on social media and people who regularly document their lives through a variety of media. It can also cover highly paid professional bloggers and a multitude of organisations posting content online to support their vested interests, either explicitly or implicitly.

It's often suggested that the concept of UGC began with the advent of the Internet, but again this isn't strictly true. Before the Internet, journalists received letters and phone calls from their readers, viewers and listeners. They were also offered content produced by PR and marketing companies, often in the form of 'Electronic Press Kits' that not only included press releases but also still images and even audio and video footage. However the sheer volume of material now available online is clearly unprecedented. The debates about the definition of the so-called 'Citizen Media', and its impact are not covered in this book. This is intended to be a practical discussion of how professional journalists might use this material and some of the benefits and pitfalls of doing so.

There are broadly two sources of UGC content available to a journalist: material that is posted unprompted online and material that is solicited by the journalist. Much of the material that is posted unprompted can be accessed using the research tools discussed earlier. Increasingly social media content is crawled by search engines. Google in particular is thought to have a preference for newly created content, which leads the search engine to give preferential treatment to blogs and social media content.

Verifying social media

One of the main roles of a modern journalist is to filter the vast quantity of material now available online, find that which is genuine and relevant and then weave this into a reliable narrative. A journalist might be sourcing a brief quote for a print article, or creating an entire social media story using Storify. Whatever the purpose, using UGC without solid checking can very quickly undermine the accuracy of a journalist's work. Most large professional news organisations will have their own system and tools for checking the veracity of social media. Many, however, follow the broad processes outlined below.

- *Does the material look right?*
  This may sound like a ridiculous question, but at first glance some online material can immediately appear suspect. Images appear online very swiftly after an event, but did this picture pop up too quickly? Do the pictures appear overly dramatic or 'artistic'? Does a character in a video appear to be acting? Or does the weather look peculiar? Does the material support the story, as you understand it so far? A journalists' sceptical eye can be by far the most valuable tool.

- *Speak to the source*
  If you can get in contact with the person who posted the material online, this is an excellent way to check its veracity. Ask them the same questions you would ask any source. Chatting informally can provide a wealth of information, which can be double-checked. Where do they live? How did they source the material? What's the weather like now? How did they come to post the material? Remember you may need to maintain their anonymity or ensure their conversation with you does not put them in danger. There are some useful tips for doing this in Chapter 6.

- *Online heritage*
  Take a look at the online profile of the person who posted the material. When did they join the network you are using? Do they have accounts on other social networks? An account which was only set up a few hours or days ago, contains no other posting or any plausible information about the account owner should raise your suspicions.

- *Does the material appear elsewhere?*
  People posting Internet hoaxes often use material already available online. A quick search for video or still images using obvious key terms will reveal the original material. A hoaxer looking for images of a road accident in Derbyshire will search for those images using the terms 'road, accident and Derbyshire' or they might look for the relevant make and model of car or include the words 'dramatic' or 'shocking'. You can use Google Reverse Image Search or TinEye, which is a fantastic tool that can also allow you to 'reverse search' images to see where else they appear.

- *Metadata*
  Take a look at any metadata available from still images or video. It may be possible to open the material with an editing programme and see additional information about when the file originated and whether there's any hidden location data or even evidence of editing. Zooming-in can reveal all sorts of strange anomalies in the image, such as peculiar straight lines or colour changes which weren't immediately visible to the naked eye.

- *Location Data*
  It's often possible to crosscheck a location against the information available on online satellite and mapping tools. Does the area look similar on Google Earth? Have people

posted other images on Flickr of the location? Do these images show the same buildings and geographical features? Social media location search tools like Geofeedia or Ban.jo can also provide assistance here.

- *Weather*
  This is one obvious and really great way to check whether an image is genuine. If the image is supposed to be new, then check contemporaneous weather reports. Alternatively you can use a search engine to find archived weather reports to check whether it really was raining in that location on that day.

- *Foreign language text*
  If there is any text in an image or a post, it's important to get it translated. If you need to, use a character reading tool such as FreeOCR to lift the words from an image and then put them into a translation tool. Take a look at the text in any quotes or re-tweets – do they support the claims about the information or are they critical?

- *Language and accents*
  It can be very hard to track down verification data in some parts of the world, in particular areas where you don't speak the language. One very useful verification method is to ask a contact to check the language being spoken and the accents of the participants. Arabic, Spanish and French are spoken across many countries, but each country will have its own accent, slang and sentence construction. A native speaker will soon spot that a video was not shot in the location it claims.

- *Crowdsourcing*
  Another more unorthodox way to verify media is to ask other members of your audience. Some news organisations might worry there is a danger of undermining their reputation, but others may be happy to share their content with their audience. You might choose to re-post the material on your personal social media feed to solicit comments or verification. Snopes.com is an interesting site, which highlights common Internet rumours and untrue stories that tend to keep popping up.

An alternative to verifying social media content yourself is to use a company such as storyful.com. The social news agency sources, verifies and licenses social media content. While many large news organisations are able to do this form of research themselves, there is a use for the company's services in some smaller newsrooms or among other companies, which use social media content.

Remember:
- UGC can be posted spontaneously or solicited by a journalist.
- Verifying UGC is crucial.
- There are some great verification tools, but careful checking and good judgement are important too.
- Wherever you work, follow a structured process of UGC verification.

Approaching sources online

The digital world is packed with potential news stories, contacts and interviewees, but contacting people online also poses some issues and possible dangers. When you start your professional journalistic career, check back through your current social media accounts and make sure they are appropriate for your professional life.

Always ensure you adapt the tone and content of any requests for help to suit the different social media platforms. It's wise not to set up an account and immediately start contacting people and asking for help or advice. Many social media users value the genuine 'community' feel of their social network. Posting content that requests help and advice without sharing information and joining in a conversation, can feel as rude as walking into a room crowded with strangers and yelling questions in the general direction of people you want to speak to. Show people you're genuine by sharing content, offering your own help and advice and joining in the conversation before you start trying to get them to help you. When using email or social media to approach potential sources and interviewees, it's wise to maintain a professional manner. Using someone's surname might feel a little strange online, but it displays courtesy and you can then change the tone of your message to match your correspondent's response. Remember that different social media may be used for different things. People certainly expect professional contact to be made through LinkedIn; they may not be so keen to be contacted by Facebook. People use Twitter, Instagram and Pinterest for a variety of different purposes and it's useful to take a look at their accounts before messaging them, to see how they're interacting with that particular social network.

When you contact a source or interviewee online it's vital you perform all the same checks and ask all the same questions you would of a contact you speak to on the phone or in person. Use your research skills to ensure they are genuine. You need to be particularly careful about this when offering money or other rewards to potential interviewees. It's natural for some people to be tempted to create or embellish stories when money is on offer.

Interview

Amber Phillips is a freelance television producer, who works in documentaries and programme development. She's currently researching a new television series for Vice Media. Here she describes how she uses digital resources for research.

You're producing video content for Vice, which is a really innovative media organisation. How does that allow you to research and produce news differently?

I work as a freelancer in TV production, and the series that I'm currently working on isn't traditional news. However, saying that, much of Vice's content is very journalistic and their USP is finding a story that either hasn't been told before, or telling it in a new way. In my personal opinion, Vice allows ambitious creatives to tell stories that other organisations would steer away from.

What kinds of research do you do at work and what resources do you have?

No different to any other production company or news organisation, other than having the benefit of asking other Vice offices for local intel. Personally, I rely heavily on social media (Twitter especially) for finding stories and people, blogs, Reddit, Instagram, YouTube, local news and occasionally Lexis Nexis.

Where do you see journalism in ten years' time?

There will be a new generation of citizen journalists, making very impressive content and broadcasting from their own channels. We are already seeing this on multiple platforms, but this will increase as people's consumption changes. I also believe (and hope) that there will be changes in legislation in what people can report. What is considered to be 'in the public interest' is spiraling out of control.

Sourcing quotes and conducting interviews online

It is becoming increasingly common to conduct interviews online or via social media messaging. In many respects this is a highly efficient and useful way to source quick quotes and straightforward interview material. The quotes can often be pithy, well considered and similar to those taken from press releases. There is no reason at all why an interviewee shouldn't send you a few sentences to add to a short print or online news story.

This form of interview is not a substitute for longer research interviews or the more complex and in-depth interviews needed for feature material. If in doubt, it's always better to do an interview face to face or over the phone. A good interviewer needs to gather information from an interviewee's tone of voice, body language and the way they move from answer to answer. You can't do this successfully online. If you do ask an interviewee to send you quotes by email or online message, don't forget to warn them you may well edit or re-order their comments. There is a danger some contributors might feel their honed interview questions should be replicated in full, whereas this may not suit the structure and angle of your content.

Personal security

Whenever you interact with other people online, you must ensure your own personal safety. This may be another reason to have separate professional social media accounts. You don't want people contacting you, or worse making comments or criticisms, in your personal digital space. NEVER meet anyone you've contacted online without taking appropriate safety precautions. If you work for a large media organisation you will probably be required to adhere to safety guidelines and possibly even produce a risk assessment. If you're freelancing you'll need to make these judgements yourself. It's easy when starting out on a new career to take risks and journalists do often go to places that are more dangerous than most work places, but it's still important to evaluate the possible risk and ensure it is mitigated as much as possible.

Remember:

- Keep your personal social media accounts private, or delete unprofessional content.
- Don't just use social media to request or demand material, engage in the conversation.
- Be polite online. It's easy be more informal later, if your source does the same.
- Online contacts should be checked just as carefully as any others.
- Online interviews work well for pithy news quotes.
- Meeting in person is better for longer interviews and profiles.
- Keep yourself safe online.

Crowdsourcing stories

Crowdsourcing has become an increasingly popular way to research journalistic work. Also known as collaborative journalism, it can range from a simple request for UGC, to a wide-ranging and complex digital investigation.

There are several decisions you need to make when organising a crowdsourced story. First, you need to decide exactly what you want your collaborators to do and where in the journalistic process their work will be used. For example, you can ask them to source original content for you by taking photographs, recording video. Or you may get them involved in the editorial process, checking for errors, improving copy or even writing your headlines. Once you have established what you want your crowd workers to do, then you need to decide how you're going to organise and manage their work and what verification process you will put in place.

People are unlikely to work for you for nothing. If you're lucky enough to work for a large media organisation with a strong reputation, then the reward of seeing their content quoted on television or radio may be enough reward. If you're looking for more complex collaboration, then it's important to involve your crowd workers and ensure they understand the process and see a clear benefit either for themselves or society in general. The founder of US collaborative news site MuckRock, Michael Morisy (2015) believes crowdsourcing works best when people feel they are part of the story: 'MuckRock's crowdsourcing of stories has been effective and emotionally engaging for our readers and reporters because it involves them directly in a satisfying narrative arc of challenge, discovery, conflict and change.' It's important to engage with your audience, share your ideas and plans with them. Once they understand your ideas and motivation, they are far more likely to help you.

Be clear on your intended outcome before you start a project. If you're not clear what you're trying to achieve, then it's unlikely people will understand what you're asking them to do. Make things simple and ensure the responses you receive will allow you to create your final story. If you need photographs, for example, give people guidelines about how and where you want them taken and what format or quality standards they need to meet. For example, one of the biggest problems faced by television broadcasters in the infancy of mobile video was the tendency for people to shoot footage with their phones in portrait mode, making the pictures unsuitable for broadcast. Now TV companies advise viewers to turn their phones around before filming to get the best images. Here are some of the most popular current uses of crowdsourcing for journalism:

- *Sourcing original ideas*

  This form of crowdsourcing asks the public to come up with story ideas. This can be something they are worried about, interested in or something they enjoy. In 2014, the BBC sent a team of journalists out across the United States in a project called BBC Pop Up. The team set up the corporation's 'mobile bureau', spending time in local communities, getting to know what matters to them and then sharing those stories with a worldwide audience. The material was published on the BBC's own website and social media. The project was so successful, it moved on to Kenya in 2015.

- *Carrying out research*

  This approach can either involve research alone or combine the generation of story ideas with the next stage of development. In July 2009 a pioneering crowdsourcing website called 'Help Me Investigate' was set up by journalist and academic Paul Bradshaw. Over the five years it was up and running it helped collaborators work on more than a hundred and fifty investigations and many of the resulting stories made their way into more mainstream media. Speaking to News Rewired, Bradshaw (2010) saw a number of benefits in this approach:

  Engagement firstly, previous examples of crowdsourcing show that people are much more interested in an issue if they're part of the investigation. Secondly, access to a wider skillset: we've had a couple of investigations, which involved data analysis by a forensic accountant most news organisations couldn't afford.

- *Processing data*

  In 2009 after a long high-profile campaign, the House of Commons released hundreds of thousands of pages of MPs' expenses details; seven hundred thousand documents covering four years of spending. *The Guardian* newspaper immediately launched a major crowd-sourcing experiment, asking its own readers to work through the documents and analyse what was in them. The project was a massive success and has formed the template for many subsequent crowdsourced research projects. The team behind the website soon realised that it was important to make the experience fun. They included material to show people they were making progress and they even added an element of competition with a 'top users' chart. Developer Simon Willison told Neiman Lab in 2009:

  Any time that you're trying to get people to give you stuff, to do stuff for you, the most important thing is that people know that what they're doing is having an effect . . . It's kind of a fundamental tenet of social software.

- *Checking and verifying*

  As already mentioned, one successful way to check the authenticity of social media posts or conversations is to ask other users to contribute their knowledge or opinion. US journalist and social media specialist Andy Carvin became well known for his work on Twitter during the Arab Spring. One of his most successful techniques was to tweet out breaking stories asking for advice, ideas and corroboration. He was able to verify and aggregate huge amounts of information.

- *Building a narrative*

  The next step from simply gathering information from collaborators is to build that into a story. This can be done in a whole variety of ways, from turning the contributions into text, or plotting them onto a timeline or map. *The Guardian* journalist Paul Lewis used

Twitter to great effect when investigating the death of Ian Tomlinson at the G20 protests in London. Using material posted on the microblogging site, Lewis began to piece together information from the half hour or so before Mr Tomlinson's death. After around six days of working online, *The Guardian* managed to bring together the evidence of about twenty witnesses and plot them on a map. As their evidence built-up and they published their progress online, more people came forward with information and a key witness from the United States provided video of a police officer apparently pushing Ian Tomlinson to the floor (Lewis, 2011).

- *Curating opinion*
  This option allows journalists to work with the general public to curate their thoughts, beliefs and ideas. In 2010 the *New York Times* asked its readers to fix the US budget. On the surface this was an enjoyable financial puzzle and UK newspapers have created a number of similar online financial games. The difference was that the newspaper collated the entries and used them to draw together a number of themes and opinions. Seven thousand people responded and although not scientific, the result did sum up the deadlock over the future of the US economy. Just as in the wider political landscape, participants fell broadly into two categories: those who wanted only cuts and those who wanted a combination of cuts and increased taxation. Just as with the broader political debate, the game showed that the two sides of the argument had widely differing and irreconcilable views (Leonhardt, 2010).

- *Collaborate production*
  The final crowdsourced journalistic form is collaboration in writing and producing the final output. There are dozens of collaborative news outlets, which allow people to write and publish their own news. Reddit is not strictly a news site, but a crowdsourced curated feed, which brings together material from all over the web. Users can vote to make a piece of content more or less prominent. Although much of the material is not news, many people use it as a news source, particularly during breaking stories. Some sites have sprung from other well-known brands such as CNN ireport and Wikinews. Associate Press' Newsvine allows you to link your contributions to Google Adsense, while Digital Report promotes and supports prolific contributors with a reward scheme.

However you plan to use crowdsourcing to aid your research, you must implement a process for verifying the contributions. In 2013 the managers of Reddit were forced to apologise after the site wrongly identified several people as suspects in the Boston bombings. Even with the help of hundreds of hands and the most recent digital tools, the basic journalistic skill of assessing a source and checking the facts remain central to the process.

Remember:

- Crowdsourcing is powerful, but people need an incentive to contribute.
- There are many uses for crowdsourcing throughout the journalistic process.
- You must plan a clear outcome and give straightforward instructions to your contributors.
- Ensure you have a system in place for verifying contributions.

Apps for research

While the Internet provides a fantastic source of information, programmes in the form of apps also offer some great opportunities for researchers. There are relatively few apps designed specially for journalists, but here is a selection of those available at the moment, which can be used to make our job faster, easier or more efficient.

- *Reading and writing*
  Evernote is a very popular app and journalists can use many of its writing functions. Apps that allow you to download information and keep it to read later, are also incredibly useful. Many researchers use a simple app called Pocket, which allows you to download content when you have a mobile signal and then read or watch it later offline.

- *Call recording and transcribing*
  There are a number of apps which allow you to record calls on your mobile phone, which is really valuable when keeping contemporaneous notes or even wanting to record clips for online packages. They each have different features and charging plans, but some of the most popular include iTalk and Tape-a-Call. SkyRecorder can be used for recording Skype and other VoIP calls. oTranscribe is recommended for journalists who regularly need to transcribe recorded content into text as it makes it much easier to listen and type at the same time, while some journalists use Dragon Dictation to automate transcription.

- *Audio and video*
  Among the hundreds of apps, which allow you to record and edit audio and video, are the popular FiLMiC Pro, Videolicious and Voddio. There are also mobile versions of iMovie and for broadcasters, Avid produces ipad and iphone versions of its software Pinnacle Studio. Twisted Wave is popular for audio editing, alongside iTalk.

- *And some others*
  Here's a somewhat random selection of other apps which can be incredibly useful for journalistic research. There are times for legal, regulatory or ethical reasons that you might need to blur someone's face in a photograph and Touchblur can do that very easily. If you don't have a scanner at home to scan documents, then CamScanner or Scanner Pro allow you to take photos on your phone and turn them into .pdf documents. If you're in a massive hurry to file copy and get to your next location, then TypenWalk can make is easier to type and see where you're going at the same time.

The apps that work well for one journalist may be useless for another. As with all digital technology, the best way to find the tools that work for you is to keep in touch with other journalists and researchers through social media, blogs and specialist websites.

Useful web resources

Apps have become the most popular new tools for journalistic research, but there are still some very useful web resources online. Wikipedia of course remains invaluable (although you must scroll to the bottom of each page and check the references to verify the information). 192.com is one of the oldest and most popular web directories. Basic directory enquiry style information is free, but for a small fee (many media organisations pay for subscription) you can also access all sorts of other information such as electoral roll details, house prices and company records. Bear in mind that a lot of this data is available elsewhere without charge, but 192.com is useful for accessing the material quickly in one place.

If you're looking for interviewees or case studies, several journalists have set up online resources. Responsesource.com is a commercial site that allows you to send a direct request for an interview to dozens of PR professionals, marketing teams and charities. It filters the requests and sends them to relevant sources. Sourcewire.com is a similar website, which allows you to access press releases by subject. Casestudylink charges a small monthly fee to allow researchers to search for case studies, share their case studies and tips with other journalists for a fee and sell ideas and stories. If you're a TV or radio researcher Findatvexpert is another commercial site that can help you to track down knowledgeable people who are happy to appear on mic or screen.

Some other useful websites are 10minutemail which beats spam by allowing you to create an email address for just 10 minutes, use it to register for a website or organisation before it disappears and Dictation.io, which is a useful online dictation tool. Finally if you're waiting for a big news announcement, which is due to be posted on a website, often the site will become jammed by users. Coralcdn.org can help you to bypass the traffic and reach the site.

A great site to help you to pitch and sell your work is Online Newspapers. It's an online directory of hundreds of publications from all around the world. If a publication in the UK isn't interested in your pitch, that doesn't mean an editor across the globe won't think it's a brilliant idea.

Organising information

Most offices and newsrooms still have filing cabinets and you'd be hard pushed to find a journalist who doesn't keep at least one drawer crammed with useful bits of paper. Indeed, as we learned in Chapter 2, paper notebooks are often the best way to keep contemporaneous notes. Newspaper offices will often store notebooks from journalists working on major investigations. But how do you keep such digital information safe and properly indexed?

Keeping digital notes

It's perfectly acceptable to keep your notes as a journalist on your tablet or mobile phone, but they must be as detailed and carefully recorded as they would be on a paper notepad. (Take a look at the section on Contemporaneous Notes in Chapter 2). Set-up a filing system with dates and keep all your note-taking records up to date. When you think about how time-consuming this could be, you can see why a reporters' notebook, carefully dated at the top of each page remains a favourite tool. It's small, efficient and doesn't suffer from a flat battery. If you decide to keep your notes for a major piece of journalistic investigation digitally, then assume someone may want to look at them and make sure they can be easily retrieved. It's also important to store details of any email conversations you might have had or social media interactions.

Backing-up your work

Can you honestly say all your most important online content is backed-up? Most of us don't keep enough back-ups of our valuable online data, but this is particularly important in a work environment. It's unlikely you'll keep your contacts book up to date and much more likely that (like most journalists) your contacts, emails and online research content are spread across a number of digital devices. It's strongly advisable to set-up a digital back-up system for all your digital material and ideally one that works across a number of devices. There are a variety of free and paid-for 'cloud storage' options, but don't let your most important work materials all disappear when your phone is stolen or your computer crashes. If someone questions the quality of your work, then your research records are your defence.

Bookmarks and online research tools

Most of us have faced the irritating challenge of tracking down a great website that we saw several months ago or trying to find an online video to show a friend. While you can keep adding a web address to your favourites, that list can soon become unwieldy and difficult to use. If you're carrying out basic online research or have a limited area of interest, setting-up a series of folders within your favourites list can be an adequate way to store your most-used sites. One problem with doing this is that you're missing out on the valuable research resources offered by social bookmarking sites.

StumbleUpon is the most popular social bookmarking site. By telling the site what interests you and what you don't want to see, it builds a home page of material that is tailored exactly for you. The more you use it to navigate around the web, the more it learns what you like. You can either use it to 'stumble upon' things that are recommended for you, or use its toolbar for your browser. Pages you 'like' are saved in your favourites. You can submit web pages that you've enjoyed; follow people in a similar field to you and see what your friends and colleagues have been accessing. This has clear benefits for journalists who can use it to research a topic area or see what others in their field are learning about.

Delicious allows you to save your bookmarks on a personal online site, which you can access anywhere (great if you're in the habit of losing your phone or tablet or work in more than one office). The simplest way to use Delicious is to add its little button to the top of your search page and click it to 'tag' the material when you like content. You can make this decision private or public. Public tags are used to highlight popular material and this becomes a great research resource. You can see the bookmarks of influential people in the field you're researching or find the most popular pages in a particular subject area.

Digg operates a little like a news site where the readers do the editing. Popular material arrives on the homepage and makes the basis of a news feed. This is a great way to see what is interesting or popular among Digg readers and can offer story ideas, but for research purposes the search function can allow you to see material on particular topics that has been 'dug'. It's an interesting way to find alternative material on a subject.

In its simplest form Diigo is a bookmarking tool rather like Delicious, but it offers a variety of other features. You can store a variety of media in an online library and highlight important elements or even add sticky notes. Diigo archives material you have stored and so it can never disappear and the link on Diigo will always work. You can share your bookmarks publically or make them private and there are also opportunities to work collaboratively, with groups adding notes or commenting on the same content.

Remember:

- Stay up-to-date with new and useful research apps and web resources.
- Keeping contemporaneous notes is important – even when doing digital research.
- Ensure you have a system for digital note-taking.
- Back up all your work.
- Bookmarking tools provide a valuable resource for online researchers.

Things to do

Build your contacts

Choose an area of journalism that particularly interests you, such as sports, science or local politics. Using three different social media networks, approach three potential sources to introduce yourself and ask for their contact details. (You will approach nine different people in all.) Which social network was most useful for your specialism?

Using a search engine or engines of your choice, identify five online publications, magazines or blogs, which cover your chosen specialist area. Contact the editors of each, either by email or social media. Ask whether they accept work from freelance journalists and establish their payment rates. Finally encourage them to keep you in mind for any future commissions.

Practise your research

Set-up a social media dashboard for your professional social media accounts. Research several of the different dashboards available and if necessary try a couple out to choose the best one for you. If you already use a dashboard, carry out an audit to ensure it's working well for you. Are you able to manage your work accounts successfully? Are you building the best contacts and interactions? Would another dashboard be more appropriate?

Research in action

Choose five social media networks you don't usually use. Create accounts and use their content to find an original local news story for your area. Write-up the story for your personal blog or a local news website. Then use your new social networks to publicise and share your story. Which of the networks was the most useful for research? Which was best for generating interest in your finished work? Will you continue to use any of these new networks for your journalism?

Issues to discuss

The Internet is full of fascinating and exciting information, but it's very hard to know what is true and what isn't. What responsibility do professional journalists have to help the public filter this information and establish reliable sources of information online? If so, how should we do this?

The Dark Web has received a great deal of coverage in the press. It's often criticised for being a hiding place for criminals and illegal activity. Do you think there is a place online for anonymity? Can the Dark Web play a useful role for journalists who wish to contact their sources secretly?

Places to learn more

Books and journals

Agarwal, S. and Barthel, M. 2015. The friendly barbarians: Professional norms and work routines of online journalists in the United States. *Journalism*. 16 (3) 376–91.

Allan, S. 2006. *Online News*. Maidenhead, UK: Open University Press.

Bradshaw, P. and Rohumaa, L. 2011. *The Online Journalism Handbook: Skills to Survive and Thrive in the Digital Age*. London: Longman.

Cook, C. and Knight, M. 2013. *Social Media for Journalists: Principles and Practice*. London: Sage.

Dick, M. 2013. *Search: Theory and Practice in Journalism Online*. London: Palgrave Macmillan.

Donsbach, W. 2014. Journalism as the new knowledge profession and consequences for journalism education. *Journalism*. 15 (6) 661–77.

Hill, S. and Lashmar, P. 2013. *Online Journalism: The Essential Guide*. London: Sage.

Krumsvik, A. and Skogerbo, E. 2015. Newspapers, facebook and twitter. *Journalism Practice*. 9 (3) 350–66.

Online resources

Casestudylink	www.Casestudylink.co.uk
Copyright Guidance from the Intellectual Property Office	www.gov.uk/government/uploads/system/uploads/attachment_data/file/375953/Guidance_for_creators_and_copyright_owners.pdf
Find a TV Expert	www.findatvexpert.com
Google Webmaster Guidelines	https://support.google.com/webmasters/answer/35769?hl=en
Online Newspapers	www.onlinenewspapers.com
Responsesource	www.Responsesource.com
Sourcewire	www.Sourcewire.com
Verification Handbook	http://verificationhandbook.com/book/
Web Directory 192.com	www.192.com

References

Anderson, M. 2009. *Four crowdsourcing lessons from The Guardian's (spectacular) expenses-scandal experiment* [online]. Massachusetts, MA: Niemanlab. Available from: www.niemanlab.org/2009/06/four-crowdsourcing-lessons-from-the-guardians-spectacular-expenses-scandal-experiment/ [accessed 20 June 2015].

BBC Academy. 2015. *Social media copyright and fair dealing* [online]. London: BBC Academy. Available from: www.bbc.co.uk/academy/journalism/article/art20130702112133512 [accessed 21 June 2015].

Gunter, J. 2010. *Q&A with Paul Bradshaw: Crowdsourcing investigative journalism*. Brighton, UK: News Rewired. Available from: www.newsrewired.com/2010/06/09/qa-with-paul-bradshaw-crowdsourcing-investigative-journalism/ [accessed 21 June 2015].

Heawood, S. 2015. *Jon Snow: 'In the establishment, I'm the most anti-establishment person I know'* [online]. London: The Guardian. Available from: www.theguardian.com/media/2015/apr/12/jon-snow-channel-4-news-interview [accessed 19 June 2015].

Kiss, J. 2011. *Andy Carvin. The man who tweets revolutions* [online]. London: The Guardian. Available from: www.theguardian.com/media/2011/sep/04/andy-carvin-tweets-revolutions [accessed 19 June 2015].

Leonhardt, D. 2010. *How readers chose to fix the defecit* [online]. New York, NY: NYTimes. Available from: www.nytimes.com/2010/11/21/weekinreview/21leonhardt.html [accessed 20 June 2015].

Lewis, P. 2011. *Citizen Journalism*. TEDx Talks [video, online]. Available from: www.youtube.com/watch?v=9APO9_yNbcg [accessed 21 June 2015].

Morisy, M. 2015. *Using narrative crowdsourcing to find and tell stories* [online]. Stanford, CA: JSK Available from: http://knight.stanford.edu/journalism-challenges/2015/using-narrative-crowdsourcing-to-find-and-tell-stories/ [accessed 20 June 2015].

ONS, 2014. *Internet access: Households and individuals 2014* [online]. London: ONS. Available from: www.ons.gov.uk/ons/dcp171778_373584.pdf [accessed 11 July 2015].

Robertson, J. 2013. *Why Google isn't winning in Russia* [online]. Bloomberg Business. Available from: www.bloomberg.com/news/articles/2013–04–26/why-google-isn-t-winning-in-russia [accessed 15 May 2015].

Statista, 2014. *Active reach of selected search engines on laptop and desktop computers as of August 2014, by country* [online]. New York, NY: Statista. Available from: www.statista.com/statistics/284789/active-Online-reach-of-selected-search-engines-by-country/ [accessed 20 June 2015].

Statista, 2015. *Leading social networks worldwide as of March 2015, ranked by number of active users (in millions)* [online]. New York, NY: Statista. Available from: www.statista.com/statistics/279548/market-share-held-by-search-engines-in-the-united-kingdom/ [accessed 6 July 2015].

Statista, 2015. *Market share held by the leading search engines in the United Kingdom (UK) from November 2012 to May 2015* [online]. Available from: www.statista.com/statistics/279548/market-share-held-by-search-engines-in-the-united-kingdom/ [accessed 20 June 2015].

Where not referenced, quotations are from interviews, emails or social media conversations with the author.

4 Data journalism

Introduction

From MP's expenses to the US embassy cables, some of the most influential news stories of the early twenty-first century have been researched and published using data journalism. The deluge of data available to reporters, alongside new tools to source, analyse and disseminate large quantities of information, has dramatically changed the nature of our craft. While some commentators maintain that data journalism will continue to be used by relatively few specialist reporters, more enthusiastic proponents believe that computer aided reporting is fuelling a resurgence in investigative journalism and some go as far as arguing that all journalists must now learn basic data handling skills. The man who invented the Internet, Sir Tim Berners-Lee, is firmly in this camp: 'Data-driven journalism is the future . . . it's going to be about poring over data and equipping yourself with the tools to analyse it and picking out what's interesting.' (2010)

There is little doubt that ability to access and analyse data is providing journalists with the opportunity to scrutinise those in authority in a way never before possible. For decades reporters relied on others (often the stakeholders themselves) to carry out statistical work and were often presented with deeply flawed results.

Attempts to challenge data or the analysis given could be a slow and fruitless process. Few journalists have the skills or persistence to thoroughly investigate the stories presented to them. With growing campaigns for open data, however, reporters are able to acquire entire databases, follow-up paths of investigation and carry out sophisticated statistical analysis with the click of a mouse. An in-depth understanding of the methods and skills of data journalism requires years of study and training on a variety of software programmes. This chapter introduces some of the basic concepts and processes involved in data journalism and points the reader towards further reading and research.

This chapter covers:

- A brief history
- What makes a great data-driven story?
- Sourcing data
- Freedom of Information Act
- Auditing data
- Cleaning data

- Analysing data
- Data visualisation
- The importance of accuracy and context
- Elections

Journalists have increasingly become central figures in the campaign for open data. The Freedom of Information campaigner, Heather Brook, fought a long and highly-publicised battle to access details of MP's expenses, which ended with the leaking of the data to the *Daily Telegraph*. *The Guardian* newspaper has run its own 'Free Our Data' campaign. More controversial, has been the emergence of websites such as Wikileaks. Some have questioned whether the work of such organisations can strictly be called journalism, since the zeal with which huge quantities of data were obtained and published bypassed the journalistic checks of filtering, identifying and researching individual stories. Whatever the current debates surrounding its use, data journalism and the explosion of social media reporting may well become the defining paradigms of our craft in the early 2000s.

So what exactly is data journalism? Experts disagree on the exact definition of data journalism or computer assisted reporting (CAR). The phrase 'computer assisted reporting' appears to have originated first in the United States and can arguably cover all forms of journalism involving computers and so would also be included in this book's chapter on Digital Research. The term 'data journalism' is used more frequently in the United Kingdom and specifically describes the acquisition, analysis and dissemination of data. Over the past few years however, the terms have come to cover most of the same areas of journalistic research and for working journalists it would be fair to assume that data journalism and CAR are now much the same.

A brief history

The very first computers were used in journalism in the late 1950s, and were reserved for large high-profile stories such as the analysis of election results. In 1952 the US television network CBS used a massive UNIVAC mainframe computer to predict the result of the presidential election. It wasn't until the late 1960s that a small group of innovators began to pioneer a method of investigative journalism, which would grow over the next forty years to completely revolutionise journalistic practice. In 1967 American newspaper journalist, Philip Meyer, carried out what is thought to be one of the very first pieces of CAR. Following riots in Detroit, he used an early computer to analyse statistics and show that college students were just as likely to riot as young people who had dropped out of education. Professor Meyer, as he is now known, jointly won a Pulitzer Prize for Local General Reporting the following year. He went on to become a highly respected academic, developer and proponent of CAR.

Over subsequent years microprocessors were invented, computers became smaller and cheaper and journalists began to use them to delve further into government data. A series of high-profile stories researched using CAR methods were published in the United States and journalists using data journalism investigations became regular winners of the Pulitzer Prize.

The next dramatic development came with the spread of Internet access and the World Wide Web in the 1990s. Huge quantities of data became available online and rapidly improving desktop computers were able to access and analyse this data far more efficiently. Software was developed and shared online to analyse, link and display data and data journalism grew to its current prominence in the early part of the twenty-first century. Many of the leading news organisations now have dedicated data journalism teams whose sole role is to acquire, analyse and publish data.

Data journalism has also created its own stars. In the United States, two of the best known are Nate Silver, a statistician who made his name predicting US election results and now edits ESPN's FiveThirtyEight blog and blogger Esra Klein, who edits the website Vox. In the United Kingdom, data journalism has been mostly developed by news organisations such as *The Guardian* and the BBC, but Heather Brook has been a pioneer in the field and other names to watch out for include journalist Simon Rogers, academic Paul Bradshaw and *The Guardian*'s James Ball.

Remember:

- The first computers were used for journalism in the 1950s.
- The first Pulitzer Prize was won for CAR in 1968.
- Smaller faster computers led to the spread of CAR in the 1970s and 1980s.
- The development of modern data journalism came with the growth of the Internet.

What makes a great data-driven story?

Clearly the main prerequisite for a data-driven story is some quantifiable data, but there are particular types of data sets and approaches to analysis that make some data stories more successful than others.

A change in perspective can help in developing an interesting narrative, either allowing the reader to zoom in and examine the information in more detail or widening the scope to allow the data to be seen in context. A good example of this might be a map, which can be explored from a variety of perspectives, giving data at countrywide, citywide and street level. Following data over time is a straightforward and simple way to create a story. The reader should be able to track changes and compare and contrast them within differing timeframes. Think of the rise and fall of a stock market. A graph showing only one day could show that prices may have risen in the last 24 hours, while a graph showing a year's data may illustrate a far longer downward trend. Sometimes the 'outliers' or unusual bits of data can form a story. Why, for example, does one city have three times as many traffic wardens as other cities of a similar size? Contrasting two clear sets of data can prove interesting. This is often seen when comparing data sets for men and women, such as research that shows a gender gap in wages. Finally, combining two associated but different sets of data may provide valuable insights. For example, you may be able to correlate data from a politician's diary with their expense claims, to see which parts of the day they're spending the most public money.

Sourcing data

There are as many sources of data as there are any other story sources. Journalists can collect the figures themselves by carrying out their own research. They can obtain the data by contacting organisations or using Freedom of Information requests, or they can use more sophisticated

Interview

Simon Rogers is a pioneer of data journalism. He created the Guardian Datablog and is now Data Editor at Google in California. He has won many awards and his book 'Facts are Sacred' is considered one of the seminal works in data reporting. Here he talks a little about the current state of data journalism.

Must journalism include an element of analysis and context, or is it enough to simply publish large data sets online?

I think publishing data sets and making them more accessible should be a key part of what any data journalist does. The world out there has a much broader knowledge about what the data actually represents than you do and your work is so much better if you incorporate that knowledge into your journalism. It's also an important verification tool: by making the data open you are making sure your work is correct. It's not enough to be clever; you need to be accessible, too.

Do you feel data reporting is still being hampered by governments' reticence to publish data?

Less than it used to. We can't complain about a lack of data, although I think we can complain about the way it's published: we still see PDFs and other inaccessible formats (which is why it's an important role to republish those data sets in easier to use ways). Having said that, the real gap is realtime and comprehensive election data: this is the very stuff of democracy and it's still proprietary information. The thing that's missing is context though: you can have all the data in the world but without context it's just a bunch of numbers. And that is our job.

Where do you see data journalism moving in the next five years?

It's already becoming a much more mainstream part of reporting. There are so many outlets now, in a way that just wasn't there before. I think it's important that this is still seen as a journalistic exercise: the data journalists I enjoy reading are journalists first, statisticians second. If that trend continues, then data journalism will start to become just what it always should be: just journalism.

methods to find the information online or amalgamate data from a variety of locations using specially written computer programmes.

Opinion polls and surveys

A basic understanding of statistics is important for the vast majority of journalists, and this is particularly true when reporting opinion polls and surveys. There is an important distinction between two different kinds of opinion polls: those where the sample of people questioned is carefully chosen by the polling company and the second where the participants choose to take part and all their responses are recorded. Online polls are a great example of surveys where there is no control over the participants. There has been increasing criticism of journalists who have been guilty of giving badly designed online polls the same prominence as more complex professional surveys. Although to be fair to most reporters, it is hard to tell at first glance whether the results described in a well-written press release are sourced from a good piece of research or a quick chat with a few people in the street.

The British Polling Council represents many of the most reputable polling organisations in the United Kingdom and it has produced its own guide for journalists. It considers polls with controlled samples of respondents and statistical weighting (where relevant) to be 'scientific', and it argues these will generally be more reliable. The President of polling company YouGov, Peter Kellner, has said (2015).

> Just as a stopped clock tells the right time twice a day, unscientific surveys will occasionally produce right percentages. But they are far more likely to be badly wrong . . . Such polls tend to attract people who feel passionately about the subject of the poll, rather than a representative sample.

So it's very important before reporting any survey or poll to do some basic research to establish who did the research, why and how it was conducted. It's also crucial to find out the margin of error. The margin of error is a statistical calculation of the confidence you can have in a poll's accuracy. The larger the margin of error, the less reliable the findings of a poll will be. Tiny differences or changes that are smaller than the margin of error are not significant findings and should not be reported as news stories. If your report is a brief light-hearted piece about people's favourite colour flower, such rigour is unlikely to be important, but for journalists working on important social affairs or political stories, understanding the basics of opinion polling is vital. If your work is likely to include a lot of polls and surveys, then it's worth buying a book on basic statistics and survey design. There are a number of good books that have been written for academic researchers and can give you a solid grounding in how to spot a well-designed survey and come up with reliable findings.

Freedom of Information Act

The Freedom of Information Act 2000 was introduced by the then Labour government and came into full force five years later. The Freedom of Information (Scotland) Act 2002 serves the same purpose for official bodies overseen by the Scottish Parliament. The act gives individuals the right to access recorded information held by public sector organisations. It has proved a very fruitful source of stories for journalists in general and data journalists in particular.

How to make a Freedom of Information (FoI) request

One important thing to do before you make a FoI request is to check whether the information is already publicly available. Start by reviewing some of the searchable web pages that list prior FoI requests in your chosen research area. Also take a look at the resources on the website www.whatdotheyknow.com. Another option is to make a quick call to the press officer at the relevant organisation, or you can search the organisation's website, using one of the methods mentioned in Chapter 3 to see if they've already published the data online. (Using a data file type in your search terms should help to reveal usable data records).

If you have made every effort to find the information you want and not been able to access it, then it is certainly time to make a FoI request. The Freedom of Information Act itself includes a comprehensive list of organisations covered, but broadly you can make requests from:

- Government departments, public bodies and committees.
- Educational institutions (schools, colleges and universities).
- The National Health Service.
- Some of the emergency services (the publicly-owned services, such as the police).
- Publicly owned companies.
- Publicly owned museums.

You can contact an organisation by letter, email or fax or a specialist website such as whatdotheyknow.com. Some organisations also have pages on their own websites that allow

---

FREEDOM OF INFORMATION IN ACTION

In practice, Freedom of Information requests can cover virtually any subject. They range from highly controversial topics such as abuse in care homes to the comic or ridiculous. During 2011 there was considerable media publicity around FoI requests about local councils' plans for zombie attacks!

A great place to start browsing through FoI requests and to get some ideas for your own, is the website What Do They Know (www.whatdotheyknow.com). The site includes hundreds of thousands of requests. Some relate to major national issues, others may seem trivial, but the matters raised may still affect many hundreds of people.

Here's a request about the reliability of a bus service from south London. The request may have been made by someone frustrated by their daily commute, but you can see how the data could form the basis of a local newspaper story. Note how clear and specific the initial correspondence is:

Original FoI Request:

Dear Transport for London,
Could you please tell me for the month of May 2015 for each day between the hours of 0700 and 0900 for the 133 bus route originating Streatham Station?
1. Actual frequency per hour
2. How many buses terminated their journey at Monument
3. How many buses terminated their journey at London Bridge

(Whatdotheyknow, 2015)

The FoI Case Officer at Transport for London supplied the information as an Excel file and the data set can be seen in Figure 4.2. There were a few further clarifications, but you can see some clear themes in the data without carrying out any formal analysis. It looks like there were some serious problems with the route on the mornings of 26th and 28th of May. (The service was stopped before its final destination on numerous occasions.)

Figure 4.1 Freedom of Information in action

you to make a FoI request online. However you send your request, ensure you address your correspondence to the right person. Give your name, address and a clear explanation of the information you want (for example stipulate if you want a detailed data set or a brief summary). It's better to keep your request specific and limited in scope and then follow it up with another request, rather than be over ambitious. You can also specify at this time the format you would prefer for the information. Consider how you plan to analyse the data (more information later in this chapter) and ask for the most suitable file format. You should get a reply within 20 days. In general the request will be free, but there may be a small charge for printing or photocopying. The organisation will tell you if you need to make a payment.

If you are unhappy with the response you have been given, consider whether you can modify your request in a way that would still secure the information you want and satisfy the organisation's problems or objections. If your request was not clear or specific enough, go back and clarify. An organisation can refuse your request for some particularly sensitive information, but it must give you a reason. It can also refuse to retrieve information for you, if it will cost more than £450. (It's £600 for central government). This is one of the reasons why it's best to keep your request clearly defined and relatively specific.

It's important not to give up. Investigative Reporters Guy Basnett and Paul McNamara (2015) have submitted numerous requests:

> FoI is partly a numbers game between over-stretched FoI officers and time-poor journalists. And sometimes it seems some public authorities refuse requests as a matter of course. It's a successful tactic, because many journalists immediately give up. Don't be one of them.

If this still doesn't get the response you want, go through the organisation's own appeals process. If you're still not happy after this, you can make a complaint to the Information Commissioner's Office.

Date	Sched Freq for Hour 7-8am	Sched Freq for Hour 8-9am	No. of Curtailments @ London Bridge	No. of Curtailments @ Monument
01/05/2015	11	15	1	0
02/05/2015	6	6	0	0
03/05/2015	5	5	0	0
04/05/2015	5	5	0	0
05/05/2015	11	15	3	0
06/05/2015	11	15	9	1
07/05/2015	11	15	3	0
08/05/2015	11	15	0	0
09/05/2015	6	6	0	0
10/05/2015	5	5	0	0
11/05/2015	11	15	4	0
12/05/2015	11	15	1	1
13/05/2015	11	15	0	0
14/05/2015	11	15	0	1
15/05/2015	11	15	1	1
16/05/2015	6	6	0	0
17/05/2015	5	5	0	0
18/05/2015	12	13	2	5
19/05/2015	12	13	0	4
20/05/2015	12	13	0	5
21/05/2015	12	13	0	5
22/05/2015	12	13	0	0
23/05/2015	6	6	0	0
24/05/2015	5	5	0	0
25/05/2015	5	5	0	0
26/05/2015	12	13	2	11
27/05/2015	12	13	0	5
28/05/2015	12	13	0	12
29/05/2015	12	13	0	2
30/05/2015	6	6	0	0
31/05/2015	5	5	0	0
Total	283	332	29	56

Figure 4.2 Freedom of Information source file

Sometimes you're not given the information you requested, because the authority doesn't actually have that data. Read the response you get carefully and be reasonable, as the author of FoI Man blog, Paul Gibbons (2015), advises:

> Accept that in some cases, the authority just does not hold the information you've asked for. You may think they should, but if they haven't, you can't use FoI to force them to create it. Often the authority will explain why they don't hold it.

Difficult data

As Simon Rogers explained, one problem often experienced with FoI requests, is that the information you receive is not provided in an easily accessible format. It's common to send files in portable document format (.pdf) and perhaps most challenging of all, scanned images, neither of which can be imported directly into a spreadsheet or database software. This makes it much harder to view and manipulate the data. Sometimes this is done quite deliberately, although an Appeal Court ruling in August 2014 did make things easier for researchers submitting FoI requests. Hearing a case against Buckinghamshire County Council from journalist Nick Innes, Lord Justice Longmore ruled that so far as reasonably practicable a researcher should be able to request data in a specific digital format. In his ruling he said:

> To my mind the words of Section 11(1) of the 2000 Act are not intended to give the person requesting information only a choice between being provided with the information in permanent form or being provided with the information in another (non-permanent) form. That would be a restriction on the requester's ability to say what was or was not acceptable which would be surprising to find a statute intended to open up channels of information in bureaucracies which had hitherto been closed.
>
> (Innes v Information Commissioner and Buckinghamshire County Council. 2014)

Make sure you stipulate what file format you require in your first request. If you don't receive that, go back to your target organisation and ask why. If you believe they're being deliberately obstructive, you may wish to appeal to the Information Commissioner. If you have exhausted all attempts to get data files, all is not lost. There is information later in this chapter on how to deal with challenging data types.

Data scraping

The Internet is a data-rich environment. We use that data every day, whether it's for ordering our weekly shop, downloading a film or booking a flight. The information is accessible and freely available, but it needs some skill to acquire it in a usable format.

Many data files are available on the invisible web, which can be accessed using the skills discussed in Chapter 3. A simple Google search on a specific website, including an Excel or database file format can turn up some fascinating material. More complicated, is sourcing data that is stored across a variety of websites, in images, or needs to be collated over a period of time. This material can be collected with a simple computer programme known as a 'scraper'. There are three ways to do this: employ a professional coder to help you, use one of the tools online to help you create a scraper or learn to write your own code from scratch. There are one or two data scraping tools on the Internet that can genuinely be used easily by an amateur with no understanding of computer code, but there aren't too many, and without some coding experience, those that need minor 'tweaks' to get the right output can be difficult to use. There are plugins for the Chrome and Firefox browsers (Scraper and Outwit Hub), which will do simple scraping. Import-io is straightforward to use and requires no downloading, as is the service offered by Kimono. Which of these you choose to use, will depend on your personal IT skill and the data you want to scrape.

Journalist coders

Competency in using spreadsheets and databases can take a data journalist a long way, but learning to code opens up a whole new area of research. The vast majority of journalists will never need to write code (although its worth remembering that children are now taught the basics of coding at school and when these young people arrive in our industry, the expectation that journalists will have coding skills may well become far greater). Learning to code is not easy and it is time-consuming. For a one-off investigation it is probably worth paying someone else to do it for you.

If you decide to learn to code, two of the most popular programming languages in journalism are Python and Ruby. There are plenty of free teaching resources online and many free code editors, which allow you to write algorithms. It is hard though, to persist with learning a difficult new skill without support and help. The website hackshackers.com provides a fantastic resource for journalists who want to learn to code and lists meet-ups around the world, to allow you to make contact with other journalists working in the same area.

But is it legal?

The legality of data scraping is a hazy area. There is little doubt that companies all over the world use scraping tools to collect information and check out what their rivals are doing. In response, most big organisations also have a team of coders who try to block their websites from scrapers, for a variety of reasons. One being that a great deal of processor power can be wasted answering multiple scraper searches.

When it comes to scraping, UK and European law is complicated and depends very much on the kind of data involved. The two main legal routes for websites seeking to protect their data are enforcing their 'Terms and Conditions', which may prohibit scraping, and using intellectual property law. There have been a number of contradictory legal rulings across the European Union on the status of scraped data and whether it is subject to copyright law. It generally depends on the kind of data that was taken. In addition in 1996 the European Union adopted a Directive on the Legal Protection of databases, but there has been very little case law under this directive testing the possible legality of scraping.

Journalism clearly plays a different role in society compared to private organisations, which might be scraping data for financial gain. But if you do decide to scrape data from a website you should certainly check the terms and conditions and consider whether you might be breaking copyright law. If you do decide to breach the site's terms and conditions, you should be prepared to face legal action, however remote the prospect.

There may also be some regulatory considerations for those who undertake data scraping. Clause 10 of the IPSO Code advises:

> The press must not seek to obtain or publish material acquired by using hidden cameras or clandestine listening devices; or by intercepting private or mobile telephone calls,

messages or emails; or by the unauthorised removal of documents or photographs; or by accessing digitally-held private information without consent.

So scraping that accesses information, without permission or a public interest justification might well break the terms of the code. As with so many issues of ethics, it's wise to consult colleagues and your editor, before beginning a scraping project.

Interview

Martin Belam is a journalist and data expert. He's worked on many of *The Guardian*'s groundbreaking data initiatives and the recent digital projects for Trinity Mirror. Martin blogs about user experience, journalism and digital media at martinbelam.com

What are the most important research skills for aspiring new journalists to develop?

A good command of spreadsheets and of how to manipulate text in them, as well as numbers. Excel is a useful tool, but Google Docs also has some powerful functions that allow it to draw in data direct from the web. And of course, a good dash of common sense and critical thinking. 'If it looks too good to be true, it probably is' holds just as much online as it does offline. Pausing to reflect 'how likely is this?' is a valuable skill when assessing the veracity of information. And learn about statistics.

In a world of digital communication, how valuable are traditional journalistic skills such as using the telephone and interviewing people directly?

For me the old skills are just as important. An investigation might start with digital data, but good stories are always about people, or the effects of data on people. Just putting some pretty graphs together does not engage the audience by itself, unless the graphs are part of a well-researched narrative.

Many would argue that much online journalism is derivative, badly researched and poorly attributed. Is there still a place for great research?

I'm not someone who subscribes to the view that the Internet has driven down the quality of journalism. I think the web has put fact-checking, cross-referencing, and ever available archives at the disposal of an ever-growing army of people who can hold the press accountable for sloppy journalism and that is a good thing. A good young journalist will be writing material that stands out, and stands up, in that environment.

Remember:

- All journalists need a basic understanding of statistics.
- Always check the source and methods used to conduct surveys and polls.
- FoI requests offer journalists a rich source of data.
- Data does not always come in a usable format – sometimes this is done deliberately.
- Learning to code can help you to source online data by scraping.

Auditing data

This is one of the most important stages in dealing with data for journalism. Before spending time and effort cleaning and analysing data, it's worthwhile stepping back and asking whether this data is appropriate for your story and will give you the information you need. This audit stage can prevent a great deal of wasted time and effort. It is entirely possible that data requested or accessed with the best of intentions may not be what you expected. It's also possible that data may be poor quality, or incomplete and so doesn't merit any further work.

Cleaning data

Data is always 'dirty'. However reliable and reputable the source, there will be mistakes, errors and inconsistencies. They may seem like minor things, but even the smallest inconsistency can have a dramatic effect on the final result of any analysis. Organisations that work with a lot of data may have their own software or processes, which a journalist will be expected to follow. If that's not available there are some general areas that need to be covered.

Spreadsheet or database?

This decision will depend on the size of your data set, what you want to do with it and your personal skill. Many data journalists find spreadsheet programmes are more than adequate to analyse smaller data sets and carry out the functions they need to perform. If you want to do more complicated analysis and deal with much larger data sets, you may need to use specialist database software. If you're not a data specialist or are just starting out in the field, it's well worth getting some expert advice and if necessary some database training.

File format

The best way to share data is through a file type known as 'comma separated values' or .csv. The advantage of this type of file is that it can be viewed in a whole variety of software programmes, including popular spreadsheet and database software such as Excel and Google Docs. If the file type you acquire is not suitable for your analysis you will need to change the format into one that will work in your chosen data software programme. There are some tools that can help you to extract .csv data from .pdf files, such as Tabula, but you must check any results thoroughly. For example, it's important to verify that columns and rows contain the same data as before and that figures haven't moved or disappeared. In some cases it may be better to approach a database specialist to ensure this is done correctly.

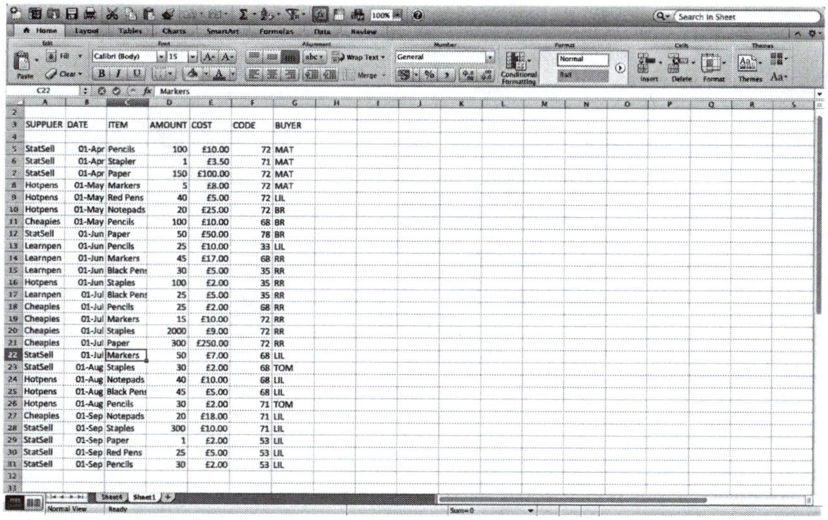

SUPPLIER	DATE	ITEM	AMOUNT	COST	CODE	BUYER
StatSell	01-Apr	Pencils	100	£10.00	72	MAT
StatSell	01-Apr	Stapler	1	£3.50	71	MAT
StatSell	01-Apr	Paper	150	£100.00	72	MAT
Hotpens	01-May	Markers	5	£8.00	72	MAT
Hotpens	01-May	Red Pens	40	£5.00	72	LIL
Hotpens	01-May	Notepads	20	£25.00	72	BR
Cheapies	01-May	Pencils	100	£10.00	68	BR
StatSell	01-Jun	Paper	50	£50.00	78	BR
Learnpen	01-Jun	Pencils	25	£10.00	33	LIL
Learnpen	01-Jun	Markers	45	£17.00	68	RR
Learnpen	01-Jun	Black Pens	30	£5.00	35	RR
Hotpens	01-Jun	Staples	100	£2.00	35	RR
Learnpen	01-Jul	Black Pens	25	£5.00	35	RR
Cheapies	01-Jul	Pencils	25	£2.00	68	RR
Cheapies	01-Jul	Markers	15	£10.00	72	RR
Cheapies	01-Jul	Staples	2000	£9.00	72	RR
Cheapies	01-Jul	Paper	300	£250.00	72	RR
StatSell	01-Jul	Markers	50	£7.00	68	LIL
StatSell	01-Aug	Staples	30	£2.00	68	TOM
Hotpens	01-Aug	Notepads	40	£10.00	68	LIL
Hotpens	01-Aug	Black Pens	45	£5.00	68	LIL
Hotpens	01-Aug	Pencils	30	£2.00	71	TOM
Cheapies	01-Sep	Notepads	20	£18.00	71	LIL
StatSell	01-Sep	Staples	300	£10.00	71	LIL
StatSell	01-Sep	Paper	1	£2.00	53	LIL
StatSell	01-Sep	Red Pens	25	£5.00	53	LIL
StatSell	01-Sep	Pencils	30	£2.00	53	LIL

Figure 4.3 Spreadsheet software like Excel is an excellent tool for analysing simple data sets

In order to understand the labels used in more complex data sets you may need the dictionary, which is the structural design for the database. It's usually a separate file and will explain some of the codes used in complex data sets. For example, when entering gender data, a database may use the digit 1 to indicate male, 2 to indicate female and 0 when no sex data is present. This would be meaningless without the dictionary. It's wise when sourcing data to ask for the dictionary alongside the data itself (for example ask for it specifically in an FoI request). When you've read through the dictionary, don't ignore any unattributed or strange data elements. If something looks peculiar or doesn't make sense, go back and ask for further information. Sometimes practical changes are made after a database is designed and those importing the data are forced to leave out that information or add it to another category, which can distort any findings you come up with.

The data cleaning process

There are a number of basic processes that need to be followed to do a basic clean up of a data set. The complexity and time taken to do this varies dramatically and many modern spreadsheet and database programmes include functions to make this easier. There are also specially designed programmes available to perform data cleaning. Here are some very basic manual steps to follow with simple data sets.

- *Appearance*
  The first stage is to check whether the data 'looks' right. Can you see all the fields easily? Are there any missing columns or rows and are the text or cells in different colours. You will need to check whether this is deliberate or accidental.

- *Blank cells*
  Were these left blank in error, or is the omission deliberate? Blank cells need to be checked and data entered where necessary to allow successful analysis.

- *Spelling*
Where the data includes text, a simple spell check is worthwhile to ensure the text values have been entered consistently.

- *Duplicate rows*
It's important to search the data for any duplicate entries. These are often harder to find where the data has been entered inconsistently or there is a blank cell.

- *Inconsistency*
This is very common in data sets. Take the author's name for example. This can be entered in a variety of ways: Vanessa Edwards, V. Edwards, Edwards – V., etc. It's important before doing any analysis that inconsistencies like this are resolved.

- *Dates, figures and numbers*
It's vital to ensure that all dates, prices and other numbers are labelled consistently. For example, dates can be entered in a whole variety of different ways: 25/12/72, 25 December 1972 or 25th Dec 72. Again without consistency, any analysis of the data will be incorrect.

- *Incorrect entries*
Data is often entered incorrectly, particularly if numerous users have entered it on a large database over a period of time. Material may be placed in the wrong cells or irrelevant information included. Such errors may be visible to the eye, or you may be able to use the search or order functions to throw up inconsistencies.
    There are a number of tools, which can carry out some of these processes for you. Open Refine (formerly Google Refine) is excellent and one of the most widely used. Data Wrangler is another option.

Remember:

- Make sure you choose the best software to analyse your data.
- The format of your data may need changing or modifying.
- All data is 'dirty' and will need some cleaning.
- There are some basic manual processes for cleaning data.
- Programmes are available to help clean large data sets.

Analysing data

Good data journalism is similar in many ways to complex investigative reporting, in that it requires the support and commitment of an editorial team, along with the confidence to allow the reporters to spend time and effort exploring the details of a story. Not every investigation will result in a story. It is quicker and cheaper to examine data with a specific outcome in mind or to look for statistics to support or disprove a particular belief or theory. There are also data sets (such as election results) that themselves form the story and can be presented in their entirety with tools for the reader to choose the elements that are important to them.

It's not just journalists who are faced with trying to tease themes and stories from large quantities of data. With the growing trend of making large data sets available, it's an issue for a whole variety of industries. Stories can be discovered in data by a variety of methods. One is obviously to spend time making a systematic examination of the figures. With very valuable sets of data (such as the UK MP's expenses figures) this kind of meticulous research is very easy to justify, but with more obscure or less newsworthy data, such expensive and time-consuming work can be hard to support.

It's important for all journalists to have a basic understanding of numbers, as a researcher and data specialist from the Christian Science Monitor, Leigh Montgomery, explains:

> An essential skill (is) being able to make sense of metrics. Everything is quantified now, and everyone is constantly data mining, so you'll be doing this in an internal as well as an external capacity. What's great is that topics and issues of urgency and importance will be able to be readily identified and responded to.

More complex data analysis combines a variety of academic specialisms. A journalist who wants to develop a deep understanding of the subject will need at the very least an understanding of spreadsheet software, some training in statistics, and possibly programming.

In its simplest terms, data analysis looks to identify trends or patterns in data and also features that don't fit those patterns. This can be done on a series of levels, starting with the most basic analysis using school level maths, moving on to simple manipulation of spreadsheets, database queries and even using more complex computer algorithms or visualisations for analysis rather than for presentation of the data. As the data becomes increasingly complex, a journalist will need a better understanding of analytical tools. For example, without the relevant skills it's hard to tell whether a stray figure is significant or simply a random error. As with so many parts of our job, being successful is about knowing the limits of your knowledge and being able to find the right person to help check-out a story. What most journalists do need is a basic ability to spot likely trends, changes or patterns in data and the scepticism to question those conclusions and check them, where relevant.

Data interrogation

In many ways, data can be interrogated in the same way you would interrogate an interviewee. Start by asking the same questions. Consider who collected the data. Were they qualified to do it properly? Why did they collect it? Was it for genuine research, or to prove a point or even sell something? How were the figures collected? Was it done in a fair and scientific way? Starting with these questions will help you to look for possible areas of interest in the data. If a local builder produced figures on the number of new houses built in your area, that company might have a vested interest in making themselves look very productive. Did they really produce more houses than any other company? Or have the figures been adjusted to hide the fact that they had more locations and staff than their rivals?

If you can start with one clear question, such as 'How much does the cost of cutting grass verges vary across councils?', then this can form a really strong basis for your data analysis. If you're not able to start with a specific question, then there are some basic ways to analyse your data for possible stories.

The following processes are the very first steps in data analysis and can be performed on relatively small individual data sets, which have been cleaned and prepared. In order to carry out these processes, you need the most basic understanding of spreadsheet software and when working with small data sets, these examinations can even be done by eye.

- *Really big and really small*
  Take a look along each of the rows or columns. Do any look much larger or smaller than the others? Perhaps dozens more people have accidents in one public park compared to another, or a university has spent a very large sum of marketing money on one event. You would need some statistical skill to establish whether these differences were really significant, but if something looks strange, there's nothing to stop you picking up the phone and calling. The dangerous park may be a news story, or of course it may just have a children's playground, which the neighbouring park does not.

- *Sorting*
  If you're having trouble spotting anything that stands out, then most spreadsheet software will allow you to sort columns and rows. You can put similar data together; sort from the smallest to the largest, or by other criteria. Once you have the biggest and smallest cells grouped together, you may be able to spot a trend. Perhaps you've spotted that the councils who spend the most on rubbish collection are all grouped together in one geographical area. Picking up the phone will give more context or help to explain the reasons for this grouping.

- *Filtering*
  Another useful and very basic tool is the ability to get rid of columns and rows, which are not part of your story. You can use this to focus your investigation on sub sets of data or just to check you have counted the rows, columns and cells correctly.

- *Adding things up*
  If nothing stands out at first glance, try adding up some of the columns and rows. You can do this using the simple SUM function in the spreadsheet. Again look for figures that seem unusual or out of place. For example, why did a library spend five times as much on staff as the one in the next suburb?

- *Averaging*
  Again it's really straightforward to look for the average of a column or row. Without getting too complicated, there are different kinds of 'average', but the most familiar to most people is the 'mean' (the sum of all the numbers in a row or column, divided by the number of cells). By looking at the average spent by each local library on each staff member, you might find the library which initially raised your interest is actually very efficient. It's just big and needs a lot of staff!

- *Pivot tables*
  The pivot tool is more complex, but can allow you to do more complicated analysis of your data in both spreadsheet and database software. In its most basic form it's a summary tool, which can automate some analysis for you at the click of a button. It's a great way to simplify large sets of data. You can create a pivot table from any part of your data. The table will allow you to combine and add up different columns and rows very quickly and then sort out information by a variety of factors, such as date.

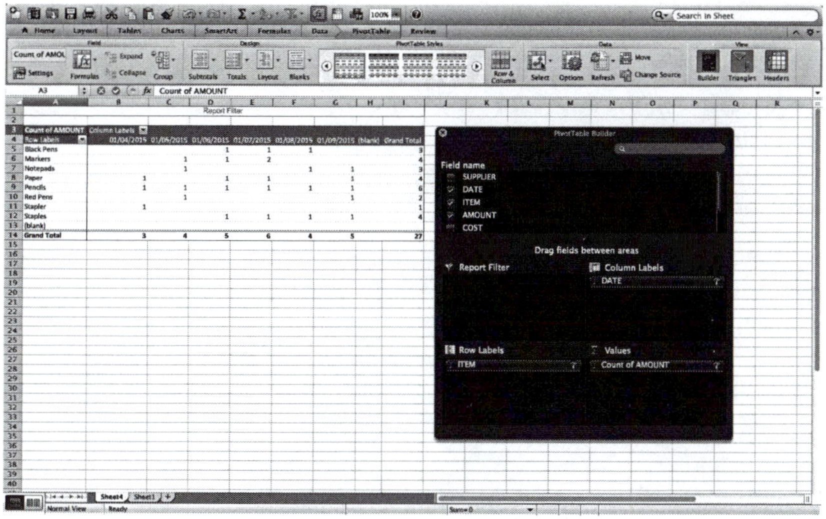

Figure 4.4 Pivot tables in Excel are easy to produce and allow basic analysis of spreadsheets

The processes above are the very first steps in the most basic data analysis and work on single sets of data with very straightforward stories. When you have larger sets of data to analyse, or you want to start combining or analysing two or more sets of data at once, you will need more complex skills.

Queries

The basic process when analysing data in spreadsheet or database software is to write 'a query'. This is the standard way to extract information from a database. As already discussed, it's far easier to make relevant queries of your data if you already have a journalistic question you want answered, but it is possible to start with an area of investigation and make queries on a number of issues and look for points of interest. Queries can allow you to explore specific sections of data or combine information from two different sets of data.

Writing queries and analysing the information they extract is a skill, which requires a solid understanding of spreadsheet and database software. There are some excellent books to teach these basic skills and also a wealth of information on the Internet. If you're really keen to learn more about working with databases, it may be worthwhile investing in a training course. *The Guardian* runs data journalism training sessions, as do the Centre for Investigative Journalism and a number of colleges and universities.

Remember:

- Treat data like any other information, ask the same questions.
- Small data sets can be analysed with basic statistical skills.
- Larger data sets will need specialist analysis.
- When reporting your work, share the process and data if possible.

Interview

Stefano Ceccon is a Senior Data Analyst for News UK. His work appears across a variety of publications, including *The Times* and *Sunday Times*.

What areas of digital research do you find exciting at the moment?

Of course data, the availability of tools and data sets is growing exponentially and journalists can now find interesting stories using data. There is no time to manually sift through this enormous amount of data being released, so it's imperative to learn to use tools to import, manipulate, and analyse data. Obviously journalists do not need to carry out all this work alone, but can benefit from the growing number of data journalists available in the field.

Which app/programme/website do you find indispensable?

Google Sheets is pretty useful. It allows you to collaborate and share documents and spreadsheets internally without having to create multiple versions of the same files and attach them to emails. Another tool, which we use quite a lot in the data team is Abbyy Fine Reader which allows us to convert PDFs into machine readable documents (e.g. data tables). Other useful tools for digital savvy journalists include version control software, which can be used to guarantee consistency and robustness in the process of finding and working on a story, mapping tools (such as CartoDB and Quantum GIS, which is a very powerful open-source software to manipulate geographical data). Also timeline.js is a good tool to build timelines quite easily. There is also a range of tools and programming languages for those journalists who want to become even more technical, for example D3, R, and Python. Regarding social media, I think that Twitter is a key tool for digital journalists for promoting, engaging with the readers and often enriching their stories with new voices.

What skills should new journalists be learning if they want a career in digital research?

Journalists should first of all learn to use basic digital tools like spreadsheets and social media tools. The next step would be then to start learning to use more technical tools, such as data manipulation software and visualisation tools. Being able to find, manipulate, analyse and visualise information will empower journalists and increases the quality of their work and the industry overall.

Data visualisation

In journalism the term data visualisation tends to be used to describe information graphics. However the practice of data visualisation also covers the use of charts and maps to research and analyse data. A data journalist may use these tools to spot trends, patterns or interesting outliers. They might plot the data in several different ways, in order to establish the best way to illustrate a particular story. It's for this reason that an examination of data visualisation techniques is included in this book.

The ability to display data in new and ever-more creative ways is made possible by two different aspects of digital technology: the ability to store and process large quantities of data and the processing power to create complex, interactive graphic images. It might be argued, however, that the real flowering of this new area of journalism has come with the spreading use of mobile technology such as smartphones and tablets. Personalised data sets and interactive graphics work particularly well on touch-screen technology, allowing readers to explore and investigate a story in a way that's unique to them.

The new journalistic skill of data visualisation has developed swiftly both in response to, and in some cases as a leading force, in this transformation of the Internet. Critics have raised concerns that offering large quantities of data for readers to search and manipulate to reflect their own preferences and interests undermines the role of the journalist as editor, but supporters of data journalism argue that this form of journalism has fuelled a resurgence of investigative journalism and provided new and exciting ways for people to consume news.

It can be argued that this new form of journalism requires an even deeper understanding of the information presented. A journalist can no longer get away with pulling out an angle and arranging the information to support that story. The journalist must decide which aspects of the data to present, how they relate to each other and how they can be best illustrated in a dynamic and interactive way. The journalistic skill now lies in seeing a number of possible themes or angles and giving readers the tools and relevant information to develop their own personalised narrative. With this form of journalism, the focus of the journalist has moved 'upstream' with a closer and deeper relationship to the primary source (the data) and less direct influence over how this information is ultimately understood by the reader.

The job of the data journalist may include a variety of skills. In some organisations the journalist will be expected to perform every part of the data analysis and presentation process from sourcing, cleaning and programming to designing and writing text. In other organisations there may be specialists employed to perform each of these aspects of the role. One of the most interesting features of this form of journalism is the growing requirement for staff with a mixture of information technology, editorial and artistic skills. The need for staff who can work with computer software and create engaging visual images may have started with the gaming industry, but the requirement is now spreading to other aspects of the media.

The job of a data visualisation specialist is most likely to begin with a reliable, clean data set and a clear purpose for the visualisation; whether that's to illustrate a specific theme or story or to provide the readers with the tools to manipulate the data themselves. The work of creating graphics or visualisations is an art as much as a science and the same data sets will produce completely different visualisations, depending on the journalist working with them and their final aims.

Journalists now have access to a wide variety of visualisation tools and some larger organisations have their own programmers who work with journalists to produce bespoke graphics. As with other areas of online journalism, the digital world changes very swiftly and any journalist working in the field of data journalism needs to keep up with the latest tools. There are hundreds of interesting and innovative data visualisation tools, which allow the journalists to aggregate and present information. The following is a selection of those which are currently most popular.

Figure 4.5 Tableau is typical of many visualisation programmes that can help you tell stories with data © Tableau Software

Maps

Google Fusion Tables, Maps and Tour Builder, can often be the most obvious choice when representing data with mapping tools, but there are other options. StoryMap has been created by Knightlab and allows you to embed geo-tagged images into a map. Geocommons is a public community based on the software GeoIQ, which allows journalists both to analyse and visualise data. QGis is a powerful open source tool, which can be downloaded onto your computer and also has a beta android version for mobile devices. TileMill from Map Box is described as a 'design studio' which accepts data from a wide range of sources and allows you to publish to desktop and mobile devices. BatchGeo is a tool which claims to make mapping as simple as 'cutting and pasting' from a variety of diverse data sources. CartoDB is a simple tool used by some UK newspapers and offers a free version for limited amounts of data. ZeeMaps is another great option, which allows you to place data on a Google Map and embed the results or download them as a .pdf or .jpeg. Tableau is very popular visualisation software and includes a wide variety of options, including maps.

Graphs and tables

Tableau also provides a fantastic range of graph and table options for reporters. Google Sheets is very popular, and another straightforward option is Infogram. Datawrapper allows you to create a variety of visualisations and embed them into a website or blog. ManyEyes is one of the older visualisation tools and designers say its visualisations can appear somewhat dated, but it still works well for some stories. Piktochart claims to make really attractive graphs and table visualisations quickly. Infoactive allows you to design interactive data visualisations through a simple online interface. Zoho Reports does not offer the most creative visualisations, but does allow real time analysis from online sources. Plotly is one of the more complex options but offers a lot of opportunities to customise graphics.

Interview

Claire Miller is a data journalist for Media Wales. She's worked for the publisher for five years and runs the Wales Online datastore, where all the data and graphics used on the website are stored.

How have you developed your career in digital journalism?

I started out in journalism just as digital was starting to become more of a focus for newspaper companies, which has given me lots of opportunities to experiment with telling stories in different ways online. There are lots of free tools and tutorials online to help learn to do things like making interactive graphics, or video and so on. So it's mostly a combination of teaching myself and experimenting with what's out there and being able to tap into online communities. Those working in digital journalism are pretty good at sharing ideas and ways of doing things, and if you spot something that looks good and works, you can try to apply some of the things to your own work.

Some of your data journalism stories are really accessible and fun. Do you think data reporting can be made to work for every audience?

Yes, our focus, because of the type of newspaper we produce content for, is much more tabloid and local. There can be a misconception that data journalism needs to be focused on the detail of the analysis or needs to have complex graphics that show lots of information, and that can work for some audiences, but we focus more on telling an interesting story that comes from the data and making it easy for people to explore the data if they are interested. Often people won't even notice that the story is a data story, it's just an interesting story that tells them something about their lives or the area where they live.

What's your favourite digital research tool at the moment?

I'm finding Tableau really useful for analysing big data files, managed to search through and find what I was looking for in a file with 30 million rows the other day in minutes, which is useful for finding potential stories in big open data dumps. Open Refine is also great for analysing data, useful for cleaning up files, particularly where you've combined FoI responses from several places and ended up with lots of different variations for the name of the same thing, and for scraping in data from websites.

More about coding

When there's no 'off the shelf' option for sharing your data stories, then the best option may be to learn to code and create your own visualisations. This book is about research and so the opportunities and challenges offered by learning to code aren't really within its remit. But it's important to point out that the more you know about coding, the more you will be able to check your work and analyse it in an intelligent way. Coding allows you to customise tools that are already available, and where required, create your own. The ability to develop interactive online materials will help you and your audience share and analyse your work. More complex and detailed research can even be used to create an online or downloadable app.

Not only does coding offer a variety of ways to develop your journalistic skills, it can really improve your job prospects. A growing number of companies have identified a shortage of creative people who are also able to programme. If this chapter has whetted your appetite for coding then Codeacademy is an excellent place to go next. As groundbreaking data analyst and US businessman, Nate Silver, said in 2014 'If you're an aspiring journalist who knows how to code really well, you are in a very hot market.'

Remember:

- Data visualisation is not just a way to share your work; it can be used for analysis too.
- Understanding visualisation tools will help you choose the right one.
- Data journalism can be fun and entertaining.
- Coding skills make you a better data journalist and improve employability.

The importance of accuracy and context

Although cleaning, analysing and presenting data properly may seem incredibly time-consuming and complicated, it's absolutely vital. The data can't give you the information you need if it isn't comprehensive and consistent. In fact, there's a real danger it will give you a totally wrong answer. If the analysis isn't done correctly or the presentation of the conclusions drawn is not done with the relevant context, then the audience has been misled.

When you write-up or record the story you have developed from the data, it's always wise to share the process you used if possible. Increasingly online news organisations are also posting the original data or data sources online to allow readers to review the figures themselves. You must ensure the language you use to write-up the story correctly reflects the complexities of the data and does not encourage the audience to draw incorrect conclusions. Many data journalists argue that learning to analyse data correctly and report the findings responsibly is an ethical requirement of our profession.

In 2013 the Texas Tribune website in the United States took down a very popular piece of data journalism. For several years it had provided a database of the prison population in Texas, allowing the general public to search for information about inmates and crimes committed. It was only when the paper began to get complaints about the accuracy of the information (in particular that some criminals were recorded as being guilty of crimes they did not commit) the journalists realised that some of the data they had received was incorrect. A government department supplied the information and when it was contacted, it became clear there were problems with the way some criminal offences had been categorised. The newspaper posted an explanation on its website 'When we heard the agency's acknowledgement of errors in its data entry process, we pulled the database from our site. We're not comfortable publishing information whose accuracy is in question.' (Grissom, 2013) The database was altered and was subsequently put back online, but the journalists took the accuracy of the information as seriously as they would have done with any other story.

In the United Kingdom the Ofcom Code covers accuracy in section 5.1. The BBC Editorial Guidelines give more specific advice on the importance of presenting data accurately. It says:

> When we report the results of any research, especially when information is being summarised, the audience must be able to trust that the journalism behind what they see and hear is robust, the research is reliable and meaningful and the language used is both consistent and truthful. This accuracy, clarity and credibility is as important when we report on 'polls' and 'surveys' as it is in the rest of our journalism.

It is also important to put data into context. The best analyst may misunderstand or misinterpret figures if they don't understand where they come from or what outside factors affect them. Data can't be gathered in a vacuum and it can't be reported in one either. In 2014 US journalist Greg Satell claimed it was time to 'rethink data journalism'. He wrote:

> In truth, it's the data journalism model itself that falls short when confronted with complexity and nuance . . . Traditional journalists could benefit from more data literacy and objective analysis, while data journalism would be much improved by real world context.

Although some data specialists might disagree with Satell, there is little doubt that most journalists would benefit from a better grasp of figures.

Elections

One of the largest data sets the average journalist will ever deal with is the result of an election. Print and online journalists tend to have an easier time when reporting such votes, as they're not expected to be unbiased. For broadcasters, election reporting is a minefield, as the regulators require their impartiality. Broadcast journalists should keep detailed records and monitor all their output to ensure they meet this requirement.

Law and regulation

Most election reporting is covered by the Representation of the People Act 1983. For print or online reporters this stipulates that they must not make false statements about election candidates. Doing so could be a criminal offence. All reporters are also covered by the Representation of the People Act 2000, which prohibits the publication of any exit poll results until after polling has closed. Broadcasters are required to remain impartial under the terms of the Ofcom Code. Both the code and BBC Editorial Guidelines give detailed advice on how this should be achieved.

Opinion polls

As already discussed at the start of this chapter, it's important to check out how any survey is conducted before reporting its findings. This is particularly important when reporting opinion poll results during election coverage. Broadcasters should steer well clear of any poll, which has not been conducted by a reputable polling organisation. Without detailed information about how the research was carried out there is little way of knowing whether it's reliable and could lead to claims of bias. Using findings from established polling companies is fine, but all the results should be put into context, ideally with details of the sample size and margin of error.

One of the big shocks of the 2015 General Election was the repeated inaccuracy of opinion polls, which suggested the race was much closer than the final vote showed. Investigations were launched and many reasons have been suggested for why the pollsters got it wrong. Whether a media organisation is regulated or not, giving its audience misleading or inaccurate information makes it look incompetent and undermines audience trust. On a wider level the reporting of opinion polls, right or wrong has an impact on the democratic process by influencing the way people vote. The best journalists can do is to research the quality of the polling thoroughly, report the findings fairly and accurately and wherever possible put the results into context.

Things to do

Build your contacts

Research the contact details for the people responsible for FoI requests at three public organisations in your local patch. Have a look on their websites to see if they maintain a database of previous FoI requests and if so, bookmark the pages in your online bookmarking system.

Practise your research

Using any method you like, examine the websites of your three chosen organisations for useful data. You may want to look back at Chapter 3 for some advice on identifying data files on websites. If you are unable to find a data file, search instead for data as a .pdf and find a piece of software online to help you convert this to a suitable file type.

Choose one of the organisations you have researched and make a FoI request. Ensure you choose some information that is not readily available and that has not already been requested.

Research in action

Take either the data set you obtained from the website or the result of your FoI request and choose a method of visualisation to display your research. Does the visualisation make it easier to understand the data or spot interesting trends? What other forms of visualisation could you have used?

Issues to discuss

Data has formed the basis of some of the biggest UK news stories of the early twenty-first century; yet some argue that publishing large sets of data without analysis and context is not journalism. Do you agree?

Critics of data journalism claim its weakness lies in the lack of specific subject expertise of those carrying out the analysis. How might this be addressed in the working newsroom?

What ethical challenges do journalists face when sourcing, analysing and publishing data?

Places to learn more

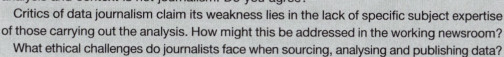

Books and journals

Bradshaw, P. and Rohumaa, L. 2011. *The Online Journalism Handbook*. London: Longman.

Buckingham, A. and Saunders, P. 2004. *The Survey Methods Workbook: From Design to Analysis*. Cambridge, MA: Polity.

Felle, T. 2015. Digital Watchdogs? Data reporting and the news media's traditional 'fourth estate' function. *Journalism* [online]. Available from: http://jou.sagepub.com/content/early/2015/07/10/ 1464884915593246.full [accessed 5 January 2016].

Keeble, R. and Mair, J. (eds). 2014. *Data Journalism*. Suffolk, VA: Abramis.

McCandless, D. 2012. *Information is Beautiful*. (New Edition). Glasgow, UK: Collins.

McCandless, D. 2014. *Knowledge is Beautiful*. Glasgow, UK: Collins.

Rogers, S. 2014. *Facts are Sacred*. London: Guardian Faber.

Online resources

British Polling Council	www.britishpollingcouncil.org/questions.html
Centre for Investigative Journalism	www.tcij.org/resources/handbooks/ data-journalism
Code Academy	www.codecademy.com
Data Journalism Handbook	http://datajournalismhandbook.org/1.0/en/ index.html
Data Journalism Heist – Paul Bradshaw (.pdf edition)	https://leanpub.com/DataJournalismHeist
Finding Stories in Spreadsheets – Paul Bradshaw (.pdf edition)	https://leanpub.com/spreadsheetstories/
Five Thirty Eight Blog (Edited by Nate Silver)	http://fivethirtyeight.com
Freedom of Information Act (Full Text)	www.legislation.gov.uk/ukpga/2000/36/ schedule/1
Guardian Datablog	www.theguardian.com/data
Help Me Investigate Project (Currently not in use)	http://helpmeinvestigate.com
Information Commissioner's Office	https://ico.org.uk
ProPublica Data	www.propublica.org/data/
Scraping for Journalists – Paul Bradshaw (.pdf edition).	https://leanpub.com/scrapingforjournalists
Vox Blog (Edited by Ezra Klein)	www.vox.com
What do they know?	www.whatdotheyknow.com
Wikileaks	https://wikileaks.org/index.en.html

References

Arthur, C. 2010. *Journalists of the future need data skills, says Berners-Lee* [online]. London: The Guardian. Available from: www.theguardian.com/technology/organgrinder/2010/nov/19/berners-lee-journalism-data [accessed 13 July 2015].

Basnett, G. and McNamara, P. 2015. FoI at ten: How all journalists can use the Freedom of Information Act to find great exclusives [online]. London: Press Gazette. Available from: www.pressgazette.co.uk/FoI-10-how-all-journalists-can-use-freedom-information-act-find-great-exclusives [accessed 21 June 2015].

BBC Editorial Guidelines. 2015. *Section 10: Politics, public policy and polls. Opinion polls, surveys and votes* [online]. London: BBC. Available from: www.bbc.co.uk/editorialguidelines/page/guidelines-politics-practices-opinion#Reporting%20Opinion%20Polls [accessed 15 May 2015].

Gibbons, P. 2015. *FoI Man's Guide to Making FOI Requests* [online]. London: FoI Man. Available from: www.FoIman.com/resources/FoIguide1 [accessed 15 June 2015].

Grissom, B. 2013. *T-Squared: Why we unpublished our prisoner database* [online]. Austin, TX: Texas Tribune. Available from: www.texastribune.org/2013/07/22/tdcj-data-errors/ [accessed 15 May 2015].

Innes v Information Commissioner and Buckinghamshire County Council. 2014. [2014] WLR(D) 358, [2014] EWCA Civ 1086, [2015] WLR 210, [2015] 1 WLR 210 [online]. Available from: www.bailii.org/ew/cases/EWCA/Civ/2014/1086.html [accessed 15 May 2015].

Kellner, P. 2015. *A journalist's guide to opinion polls* [online]. London: The British Polling Council. Available from: www.britishpollingcouncil.org/questions.html [accessed 14 May 2015].

Satel, G. 2014. *This is why data journalism is failing* [online]. Jersey City, NJ: Forbes. Available from: www.forbes.com/sites/gregsatell/2014/06/01/this-is-why-data-journalism-is-failing/2/ [accessed 25 June 2014].

Soper, T. 2014. *Nate Silver's advice to young journalists: Learn to code now* [online]. Seattle, WA: Geekwire. Available from: www.geekwire.com/2014/nate-silver/ [accessed 21 June 2015].

UK Government. 2014. *How to make a Freedom of Information (FoI) request* [online]. London: UK Government. Available from: www.gov.uk/make-a-freedom-of-information-request/the-freedom-of-information-act [accessed 21 June 2014].

Where not referenced, quotations are from interviews, emails or social media conversations with the author.

5 Non-digital research

Introduction

As we've been discovering in the last two chapters, computers, software and the Internet have become central to successful journalistic research. They have made it far easier to track down sources, check background information and analyse and present data. However, computers are not the only resource needed to produce great journalism. A wise researcher should have a variety of other tools at their fingertips to ensure they get the most accurate, comprehensive and relevant information in the shortest time possible. It's often the ability to use these other research tools and techniques that can give a journalist an edge.

This chapter focuses on an admittedly mixed bag of non-digital research tools and resources, which can be used by professional journalists to investigate and develop stories. It takes a look at the importance of using the telephone effectively; the services offered by professional researchers and the future of librarians and library services.

Clearly some of these tools and resources will be used more frequently than others and their relevance will depend on the type of journalism concerned. While a daily news journalist spends much of every day on the phone (or 'phone bashing' as it's called in many newsrooms); an investigative journalist could spend hours searching out an obscure piece of medical research, while a television documentary maker may take days to hunt down the sole portrait of a historical figure to illustrate their new biography. Much of this work can now be done online, but that doesn't mean these other resources aren't extremely useful and well worth knowing about.

As with all the other skills discussed, the key to all these research techniques is curiosity. In the words of journalist and presenter Jeremy Paxman: 'If your natural response is not to ask who, what, why, where and when, then journalism may not be the career for you . . . It's a great life if you are curious about how things work and why.' (2014)

This chapter covers:

- Telephone technique
- SMS and app text messages
- Letters and notes
- Making sense of academic journals
- Using libraries and working with librarians
- Other libraries
- Copyright
- Risk assessments

Telephone technique

Nobody who followed the long-running saga of British newspaper reporters accused of hacking into the voicemail messages of victims of crime, celebrities and politicians could doubt that the telephone remains a vital tool for journalists. As more and more personal communication moves to email and social media, it's easy for early career journalists to overlook the importance of using the phone effectively, but when it comes to getting great personal information the telephone can only be bettered by meeting a source face to face.

The telephone has one big advantage over email. It's far harder to ignore. While many of us feel no guilt when deleting an unsolicited email, an insistent phone call demands to be answered, and a friendly, well-informed voicemail message can be equally hard to overlook. A telephone call can demonstrate interest, empathy and understanding in a way that can't be matched online. Consequently, a journalist who knows how to approach a potential source by phone can often be the first to secure an exclusive interview

A common scene in many newsrooms used to be the sight of a reporter systematically ringing numbers from a telephone book. That practice continues although the numbers are now more likely to come from websites or an online directory. In a daily news environment, this can be the only method to track down the victim of a crime, relative of a criminal or eyewitness to an event. When producing longer features, researchers are often asked to track down unique case studies, and this can also take hundreds of telephone calls. BBC Producer Gill Blackwood describes the challenges of booking guests for Radio Five Live on the College of Journalism website:

> If you can't get the interviewee you really want you'll need to come up with alternatives. You could be working on several stories at once, so need to be able to prioritise your tasks. Get your calls in early and be prepared to chase them.

When making numerous research calls like this, it is vital to keep notes and be systematic. Traditionally, journalists used their notebooks to keep track of numbers dialled and possible leads generated. Increasingly, this information is being stored in smartphones or laptops, while in larger organisations colleagues and fellow researchers may keep the notes in a database where the information can be accessed. Whether your employer maintains records online, or you're expected to keep your own, it's well worth developing your own call log. On days when you're expected to make dozens of phone calls, it can be a great way to ensure you don't miss an opportunity or forget a call-back. You should also remember to transfer your new contacts into your contacts book or database for later use.

SMS and app text messages

When chasing a big breaking story for daily news outlets, phone calls will be the most obvious option, but it is worthwhile remembering that people involved in such dramatic events may well be on the phone to relatives and friends or even other news organisations. In cases such as these, it is well worth sending an SMS, WhatsApp or Snapchat text message to your potential interviewee.

Text messages have an additional advantage when trying to contact interviewees overseas. Many people speak English well enough to understand a simple written message, but may not be able to deal with a highly pressured interview over the phone. A text message in English will let them know they may be receiving a call from an English-speaking journalist, giving them the chance to prepare or put you in touch with someone who speaks English well enough to help.

Remember:

- Great telephone skills are central to good journalism.
- Keep track of your calls with a methodical system.
- Persistence generally pays off.
- Text messages can be useful, particularly during a breaking story.

Letters and notes

It seems almost ridiculous in this age of instant digital communication to suggest that a letter might be the best way to contact the occasional source or interviewee, but some journalists would still argue that paper can be among the most effective ways to get someone's attention. A piece of paper sits on your contact's desk and demands attention. It can also show your determination and keenness to speak to them. Additionally, while it can sometimes be hard to find an individual's email address online, a letter can be sent to them directly at a general postal address. On most occasions a typed letter will appear most professional; on other occasions, a hand-written note or card with some personal content can grab a potential contact's attention, when popped through the door.

There is one particular group of potential interviewees who might be best approached by letter, and that is the very elderly. Despite the rise of the 'silver surfer' many much older people don't have access to the Internet. Approaching a frail elderly person directly by telephone or knocking on their door might also prove intimidating or insensitive. However, a polite letter of introduction will appear courteous and allows the potential interviewee to consider your request in advance or approach a friend or relative for advice. You can include samples of your other work or a note from a mutual contact to reinforce your good intentions. Such an approach will depend on the journalist's employer and timescale; many daily news editors would laugh out loud at such a tactic! However, a formal letter of introduction may prove particularly fruitful for those working on documentaries or longer print features, where they need to build up a long-term relationship with a contributor.

Making sense of academic journals

Journalists who work in specialised fields, such as medical or scientific reporting, are often required to transform dry academic studies into more accessible journalistic articles, but academic journals can form a rich source of stories for all journalists. They don't only cover the latest academic findings but also offer areas of debate and discussion and potential future subjects of concern; all these could form possible new angles for a story. A basic understanding of these publications can often put a reporter ahead of the field when coming up with new stories and ensure they have a good understanding of the context and background of topical issues. As we saw in Chapter 4, there is also a growing call for journalists to develop a greater knowledge of mathematical analysis and statistics, particularly those who hope to work in the areas of computer assisted reporting (CAR) and data analysis.

Many young journalists now train at university and are familiar with the organisation and publication of professional or academic journals and the papers they publish; however, for those who joined the journalistic profession from other fields, a first encounter with an academic article can prove a confusing or even frustrating experience. Writing stories from academic research provides an additional challenge, since it can often be difficult to translate the detailed nuances of academic writing into clear and succinct prose that is easy for the layperson to understand. It's this mismatch that lies at the heart of many disagreements between journalists and academics, who may feel that their work is being misrepresented.

Journals are the prime outlet for new academic research. They may be published by an academic publisher, a university or non-profit organisation. Journals are generally 'peer-reviewed'. This means the papers are assessed for quality by other professional researchers in the same field before they are included for publication. Academics write and submit unsolicited papers, and for many, their professional success and reputation is measured by the number of articles they have published and the quality of the journals concerned. The most prestigious journals, such as 'Nature' and 'Science' are widely known, although there are thousands of other journals each covering their own area of research. Some of the biggest journals have their own press offices, which publicise papers of national or international interest, but smaller journals can often provide a fruitful source of stories for those journalists working in the relevant beat or patch.

Academic papers are written in a very specific style with an abstract at the beginning and a discussion of the results at the end. These two sections are the best places to start when deciding whether a paper might form the basis of a journalistic article; but don't stop there, it's really important you read the whole paper. Then ring one of the authors and interview them. They will be able to bring their work to life and explain its significance. Try also to talk to other academics named in the references at the end of the paper, as they will be working in the same field. Many universities offer searchable databases of staff on their websites, which make this easy to do.

It is wise to treat academic papers with some caution. A single paper may be one part of a wider discussion, or a close examination of one element of an argument. Papers are also sometimes published as part of a developing debate and shouldn't be quoted as the final word on a subject. Again, it's often best to ring the researchers involved to get their advice before finalising your story. As Harvard University's website Journalism Resource advises: It is crucial to avoid what some call the 'single-study syndrome': basing a story entirely on the results of one study, without exploring alternative research angles. While the peer-review process should ensure that only the best and most reliable research is published, some studies can be 'outliers'.

It's also worthwhile double-checking who funded the piece of research you are reporting, since there can be questions of bias in some academic work. Vested interests should be stated at the end of the paper, but do some digging. Academics receive funding from diverse bodies.

Remember:

- If you have time, a traditional letter can make a good impression.
- It's worth taking time to understand the basics of academic journals.
- If you don't understand academic research, seek specialist advice.

Using libraries and working with librarians

During the latter part of the twentieth century, the job of the researcher was closely linked to the environment of the library. News organisations were no different. They maintained large cuttings, picture and video libraries staffed by professional librarians. These hugely knowledgeable and talented people worked alongside journalists, but in their own distinct physical environment, building knowledge, archiving developing stories and providing a wealth of advanced research skills.

With the advent of the Internet, the role of libraries and librarians was clearly destined to change. Many news organisations were keen to save money. They argued there was no longer a need for professional librarians, and many news libraries were closed altogether. Those with a keener interest in investigative journalism or new journalistic methodologies held back, and in many cases, this has proved a wise decision. As the complexity of research opportunities offered by the web has become apparent, it's become clear that librarians and professional researchers still have a valuable role to play, even if they are doing their jobs in different environments. At the start of the twenty-first century, professional librarians are now working alongside digital researchers and online journalists to pioneer new ways of investigating stories and presenting the information they find. Many of the news organisations, which had the foresight to retain their professional research teams are leading the world in online research methods and breaking stories that have changed the world. For example, in *The Guardian* newsroom, members of the Research and Information Department write background material and post on the Datablog.

There has been increasing discussion and collaboration between journalists and librarians, as both professions share two key aspects. Both jobs are about sharing information and both are facing a frontline challenge from the expansion of the Internet. In 2009 The National Union of Journalists joined a campaign to save public libraries. Writing in 2011, Barbara Jones of the American Libraries Association wrote:

> Newsrooms and libraries produce information essential to the healthy functioning of democracy. Ironically, they are also threatened by the same social media that help them thrive: It is harder to verify 'facts' . . . The definitions of who is a 'real' reporter or a 'real' librarian are getting murkier every day.

For many daily news journalists, it's true the Internet is the only research tool they will need; but for reporters carrying out complex investigations, those working on data projects and journalists producing long-form material both for print and broadcast, the library and their professional research colleagues provide vital support. Professional researchers have advanced skills that allow them to access and track down information far faster than a jobbing journalist or writer. Katy Stoddard is a Senior Researcher and librarian at Guardian News and Media. She says if you're lucky enough to work with professional librarians, you should make use of their skill: 'Make friends with your librarian! It's not just a case of getting someone to do the research for you; they can show you how to improve your own search skills, so you're not relying on Google for everything.'

A librarian with a particular area of interest will not only know where to look for information but will also know the significance and context of the information and be able to suggest further contacts and potential interviewees. They may also have an advanced understanding of data analysis or statistics, which will allow them to spot crucial errors in a complex story.

Interview

Leigh Montgomery is a US Data Journalist and professional librarian, based at the respected Christian Science Monitor. She is a pioneer blogger and is an expert in collaborative online tools.

Many news organisations no longer employ media librarians. How do you think this has affected the quality of modern journalism?

There are more errors when experienced researchers are not part of the process, which is the most serious issue. Information professionals are adaptive and networked with others in their field. They have the ability to locate information and apply it where needed or share their knowledge to help their editorial team produce their best work or enhance their colleagues' knowledge. These professionals research, classify and manage information in multiple formats, even creating it directly and ensuring its accuracy at multiple stages in production to transmit to aggregators and other external outlets, as well as repurpose it internally. For these reasons, it affects journalism's accuracy, efficiency and profitability.

How is the role of the professional media researcher changing in the new digital environment?

It is changing in that more of us are closer to the pipeline. We are producing content directly in the form of short online articles, repurposing content in galleries or archival blogs and making use of the organisation's most valuable asset: content. Some of us are using those skills in what we're told is a growth market: the fact-checking of allegations, statements and slogans.

Others that are doing advanced work include data projects and analysis, working with developers, or are on other collaborative teams drawing upon talent across the newsroom. Working on taxonomies and ontologies, classifying content and delineating relationships between related terms so that the audience can get at the meaning, not just the article, is something librarians are expert at. This is becoming huge in the digital space, and I think it is going to change the business once it is automated, and some standards emerge.

How do journalists benefit from working alongside professional researchers?

As opposed to a search engine, I think, I feel, I empathize, I evaluate and I criticise. These lend added dimensions to what it means to research. I observe sources of information, denote them in my daily experience or media diet, their bias, their quality, where they are appearing on the Internet and may have come across them before, so I'm able to make recommendations about online sources as if I was referring to books on a shelf in the library. I also analyse data for some of the smaller or unusual details 'outliers' that could be something to consider or a story on its own. This is beyond analysis – it's insight.

Remember:

- If your publication or broadcaster employs specialist librarians, you're lucky!
- A professional new researcher can help you save time and effort.
- Many news librarians are experts in data analysis and statistics.

Figure 5.1 The British Library has highly qualified research teams and an excellent website

Other libraries

Libraries of all descriptions are changing. There is a growing debate about whether they will retain their physical buildings or become purely online resources. However most researchers will agree that there is still a need at the moment for information resources, which are maintained and catalogued by humans rather than computer software. The semantic web may be developing at a rapid pace, but computers will have a long way to go before they can interpret significance and meaning as well as a human being.

Public libraries

The services offered in public libraries are sadly less useful for journalists than they used to be. A general decline in visitors and budget cuts mean the resources on offer have been greatly depleted, but they can still offer some useful assets, particularly to journalists hoping to develop their knowledge of a local news patch. Most local libraries still keep newspaper archives (particularly of local papers), and increasingly, these are being moved online. Some libraries employ librarians who specialise in local history and family research, while others may have been working in the same library for decades and can offer a wealth of general local knowledge.

Perhaps even more useful, in many areas a local library card can give you free access to a variety of excellent online research tools, which would usually require a membership fee. These can include collections of national newspapers, encyclopaedias, events calendars, along with legal and picture archives. The service will differ depending on where you live but is certainly well worth investigating.

The British Library is the UK's national library with a collection of more than 150 million items. Wales and Scotland each have their own national libraries while Northern Ireland has the Northern Ireland Publications Resource. These libraries collate and catalogue information, which is made available to researchers (Figure 5.1).

Figure 5.2 For a specialist science researcher, London's Wellcome Library is a valuable resource

The British Library, in particular, receives a copy of every publication produced in the UK and Ireland. Once again it would be a rare occasion for a journalist to visit one of the national libraries, but their resources are still incredibly valuable. The libraries' experts offer a wealth of useful information with free advice and more in-depth research services available on a scale of charges. Many of the staff at the British Library are also experts in research practice and are pioneering some of the most exciting methods of digital investigation and research projects in the world.

Specialist libraries and archives

Perhaps least used by working journalists are the remarkable variety of specialist libraries and private archives around the UK. Many of these, such as the National Art Library housed at the Victoria and Albert Museum in London or the medical library at the Wellcome Collection, focus on a particular area of knowledge (Figure 5.2).

Interview

Ross MacFarlane is the Research Engagement Officer at the Wellcome Library in London. The library is part of the Wellcome Collection, a huge resource of medical science artefacts funded by a global charitable foundation.

What can specialist libraries and archives such as yours offer professional journalists?

What we offer in the Wellcome Library are friendly, knowledgeable staff able to assist with all manner of enquiries. We offer though an enabling service, so we will point you in the right direction and leave the thrill of the discovery to you! Our facilities are conducive to detailed research: Wi-Fi-enabled reading rooms and a mix of rare materials and contextualising secondary sources. We also offer to all registered library readers remote access to a range of around 60 online resources, many of which are only otherwise available through university libraries. So members of the Wellcome Library can access from anywhere in the world: online resources such as the The Times Digital Archive, a large suite of Nature titles and the riches of Early English Books Online, Eighteenth Century Collections Online and the complete back run of *Punch* magazine.

Do you think journalists make the most of the help you can give?

This varies! It's all down to the individual journalists: how much time they have, how specific their enquiry is and their expectations of the service we can offer. However, we really believe that the more time and research a journalist can invest in our collections, the more ultimately they (and their readers) will gain from the experience.

What would be your advice to a journalist hoping to improve their research skills?

My advice would be to keep an eye out for new developments offered by research libraries which would aid their work, whether training sessions, new resources or 'meet the librarian sessions'. It's always worthwhile signing up to library e-newsletters and following libraries through Facebook, Twitter and their blogs.

How do you see the future of libraries such as your own in a digital world?

The Wellcome Library is involved in a large and ambitious digitisation project, opening up our unique collections to a worldwide audience and providing a global resource for the study of the history of medicine and the wider medical humanities. As much as library content, notions of physical library space are changing in a digital world. For some researchers, the silent air of a traditional research library still provides an inspirational environment for thinking and writing. Increasingly though, we may see more attempts by libraries to use physical spaces to engage with audiences in more interactive ways, as we are attempting with our new Reading Room.

However, even given the changing demands of our readers, expertise on guiding users to reliable and relevant resources – whether print or digital – will still be necessary. We'll also have to cope with the changes of acquiring, assessing and preserving so-called 'born digital material' – the archives of the future, which will have a life cycle which won't include a paper copy!

University and independent libraries

Another valuable and often free resource is that offered by university libraries. These libraries house extensive specialist collections, and the buildings are generally open to the public with differing arrangements for membership and study. The University of London's impressive Senate House Library is open to the public, as is the John Rylands University Library in Manchester and the Queen's University McClay Library in Belfast. In many smaller towns and cities, university libraries may well house the most extensive reference collection in the area and should not be overlooked.

There are also a large number of unique independent libraries and collections across the UK. Some, like the London Library, charge a membership fee but can also provide temporary membership to allow researchers to use material which is not accessible anywhere else. Particularly useful are the postal services offered by many specialist collections. This means journalists working across the country can take advantage of their resources.

Some of the most unusual independent libraries are members of the Association of Independent Libraries. Stretching from Penzance to Crieff, these unique collections house an eclectic mix of research materials ranging from personal diaries and ships' logbooks to photographs and engravings. Many would prove particularly useful for journalists writing on local history or researching niche areas.

Picture libraries

There are dozens of picture libraries and agencies throughout the UK. Some are public bodies, while others are private organisations whose sole income comes from licensing the images they own. Unlike online stock shot collections, which simply aggregate millions of images,

Remember:

- Public libraries are a great place to visit if you're working in local news.
- Your local library may provide a digital newspaper library.
- National Libraries have their own researchers and great resources.
- Working on a feature or documentary? Specialist and private collections may help.

traditional picture libraries act as curators and agents for visual images and provide an invaluable service for working journalists. Most picture libraries now provide access to their catalogues online and can supply their images digitally. One of the biggest advantages of using the services of a reputable picture library is the knowledge that the pictures can be copyright cleared, verified and used legally. For public-spirited journalists, there is also the knowledge that the fees paid for images not only provide salaries for professional photographers and photojournalists but are also a valuable source of income for many public libraries and collections.

Most of the major UK picture libraries are members of the British Association of Picture Libraries and Agencies (BAPLA). The organisation is a trade body and campaigns to ensure that photographers and agencies are paid for use of their images. It provides a useful online search engine, which allows journalists to track down agencies offering pictures from a particular subject area. Journalists can also use the website to request images to illustrate their work. BAPLA's website also offers advice on copyright.

While large online stock shot libraries offer fast access to cheap digital images, many smaller picture agencies still provide expert researchers to help journalists find the best image to illustrate a story. Such help and advice can be worth its weight in gold, as finding the right image can really make a print or online article stand-out. Smaller agencies often concentrate on a particular subject area and purchasing an image from their libraries will also give a journalist access to yet another valuable research resource.

Interview

Tom Gillmor is Head of Content at the Mary Evans Picture Library, a fifty-year-old independent library in south London, which holds more than a million images, specialising in historical material.

With so many pictures available on the Internet, many journalists may wonder why they should use a traditional picture library such as Mary Evans. What are the benefits for the journalists who work with you?

The Mary Evans Picture Library is unique in its diversity of content, covering all aspects of the past from portraits, events and topographical imagery to large content sections on book illustration, social scenes and the paranormal (to name but a few!). The wealth of wholly owned content available in our archive beyond the material currently online allows researchers the option to find highly specialised imagery and unique and unseen content.

All of our staff are historically trained and any researcher contacting the Library can feel at ease that their requests will be understood, and researched and that every option will be investigated (through both the online and offline collection) to satisfy their enquiry. The most successful picture is often not the most commonly-seen image, but a new take on a popular theme, individual and topic. We have worked hard to make our website simple, intuitive and in keeping with the collection, yet with all the specialist features any researcher would require or expect. With our direct download facility, clients can access and download high resolution files at any point of the day with only a few clicks. We provide imagery to researchers with the guarantee they will not have to clear copyright elsewhere, again simplifying the working process for our clients.

Wouldn't it be better though, if images were simply shared for free?

The simple answer from our perspective is no. Maintaining the rights-managed system in relation to our business is vital as it generates income that we can channel back into maintaining the service we offer to our clients, providing access to unique and easily accessible content and helping to preserve cultural heritage.

The copyright law exists to make sure creators gain just benefit for the work undertaken to create an image. We have agreements to represent copyright holders and own copyright in the versions of original imagery in our wholly-owned collection. Making images available online is also a very expensive business, especially when undertaken in the specialised and academic way we operate. We invest heavily in scanning archival items, researching the provenance and content of imagery and providing a top quality service to our clients, none of which would be possible without the revenues generated from picture sales.

We see part of our role as educating clients and users on the laws of copyright and always strive to get the best return for providing the unique material in our archive and which we represent for our contributors. If every image were free, there would be no incentive for the creative process.

What sort of other research services do you offer journalists?

Beyond the facility of our searchable website, we have a team of dedicated picture researchers, providing research services through our online and offline archives free of charge. We have a vast offline archive of prints, books, magazines, photographs, journals and ephemera items covering all aspects of history, all categorised by subject, date and provenance, available for use and accessible to the research team on-site and not available for searching online. We see the offer of this service as vital, and it is one which is not universally found across the picture library industry.

The library has a specialist focus on history, and we will not diversify the picture content into areas beyond this specialisation, retaining clarity in content and not pretending to be anything other than ourselves. We always encourage researchers to come and work directly with material here at the library. Visiting and viewing the collection first-hand is by far the best way of understanding the breadth of content we have available and is always rewarding for both parties.

Cuttings services

Those of us who practised journalism in the latter part of the twentieth century will be familiar with the work of cuttings libraries. Before the age of digital research, they were often the only way to track down an individual news article or follow the history of a developing story. Larger news organisations maintained their own libraries of newspaper cuttings, while smaller publications used the services of external libraries. Cuttings were kept in box files or on microfiche under subject areas and catalogued with card indexes.

While journalists now rarely use such news libraries, the Information Manager at Guardian News and Media, Richard Nelsson (2013) says they do still have a role:

> The cuttings file will still sometimes be the most useful resource available. The revelations about Jimmy Savile illustrate the point. Newspaper groups such as *The Guardian* that kept their old cuttings in storage were able to go back and look at the coverage from the 60s and 70s.

The vast majority of this material is gradually being digitised and will be far more easily accessible. For example, the British Film Institute had a remarkable library of film reviews and features stored on microfiche from the 1970s, but by 2014 around four million articles had been digitised and made available to film journalists, researchers and fans through the Reuben Library.

There are still a number of press cuttings agencies that monitor press coverage for clients on a daily basis, and a few of these are able to provide older cuttings to order, but clearly the best way now to access newspaper articles is via an online database. If your employer doesn't subscribe to one of these, then they can often be accessed at public libraries or with your library membership card. Newspaper databases cover different groups of publications and varying time periods. Once again it may well be worthwhile seeking the assistance of a specialist librarian to help you find the material you need.

If you don't have enough time to complete your own research, you might consider paying a professional research service. There are a number of online portals, which offer journalists direct contact with freelance researchers. Any journalist should be very hesitant to use the services of such a person without proof that they have successfully carried out journalistic research before and without following up relevant references.

Remember:

- Specialist picture libraries can help with finding obscure images.
- You know an image from a specialist service has been checked and verified.
- Images from picture libraries can be copyright cleared.

Copyright

The implications, restrictions and challenges of copyright law could have been included in pretty much every chapter of this book. Most journalists get frustrated and irritated by the challenges of dealing with copyright issues, although in some respects, we should be passionate about the issue, as it's what protects our work and ensures we can still make a living.

For those writing and preparing online text stories it can be a real minefield, as they are often asked to research and source material online and include multimedia content from other websites to enhance their work.

As always, when you work in a larger organisation, there will be a copyright policy and even a team to help you clear copyright on the material you use. When you're working with a small team or as a freelancer, things can be far more complicated. There is also a confusing distinction between what is strictly allowed under copyright law and what has become common practice, particularly on the Internet.

A good starting point when considering this issue is to think about how you would like your work to be treated. If you're happy to give your journalistic work away for free, share everything you do and allow others to earn money by using your content, then you're probably in a small minority. Most professional journalists need to earn a living, and they need to balance that with the opportunity to share and promote their work online. You also need to remember that some content is extremely valuable indeed. If you consider the huge sums of money paid by organisations to cover high-profile sporting events and musical events, then you can understand why they are dogged in pursuing people who access that material for free.

As a very rough guide, copyright law in the UK covers all written content such as articles, documents, poems, lyrics, plays and novels. Musical and sound recordings are protected. Still images and video recordings are covered by copyright law, as are most art works and drawings, maps, diagrams and logos. Some typographical designs are also copyrighted. The law starts covering the material from the very moment it's created, and the creator of the work generally owns the copyright (unless they have sold it or given it to an organisation such as a publisher). Content is covered for a specific period of time. This can be from between 25 and 70 years, depending on the nature of the material. Practically, this means that the vast majority of the material on the Internet is covered by copyright, and you can't use it for anything without permission. Tom Gillmor is an experienced picture librarian:

> The basic risk of using an image without clearing copyright is to face legal action from the copyright/estate holder of the image/creator under UK copyright law. The penalties and costs of this will obviously vary, but will always be more than those involved with correctly arranging a licence to use an image legally.

There is a provision under law called 'fair use', which is intended to allow some reproduction of material without permission. This was extended in 2014 to include all quotations as long as they are used fairly and properly attributed. Journalists may also use material under the 'fair use' rules for news reporting when they are covering a current event or for criticism or review. Photographs are excluded. Beware that when using material produced by large international organisations, you may have to defend your judgement of fair usage in court. Organisations which have paid a great deal of money for content (such as sports rights) or those which have a very strong brand image centred around their content (such as film production companies or food chains) may be prepared to go to great lengths to protect their intellectual property.

When taking material from social media, these decisions become more complex. Using the material for a news report may be justified as fair use, but is this ethical? How did you obtain the material? Did the person posting it understand that it was being made public? What impact might its use have on their life or that of their friends and family? The BBC's College of Journalism (2015) offers some useful advice:

For many people, social media tools are just an effective means of sharing personal content with a relatively small group . . . a decision on whether to use that content must be balanced against the responsibility of the user to ensure that appropriate levels of security are applied to their networks.

All this must be weighed against the benefit many of us gain from having our work shared and promoted online. In 2014, the Court of Justice of the European Union ruled that embedding material from another website in your own online pages is not an infringement of copyright. Interestingly you are not even infringing copyright laws when the source material is uploaded without the permission of the copyright holder. However, you should weigh up this freedom against the danger that if the source material is removed, an important element of your online content could just disappear. This is not uncommon when embedding YouTube video in a website. If YouTube subsequently decides to remove the content, then you are left with an ugly black hole in the middle of your work.

You can't copyright news and information, and you can't copyright an idea. So it's perfectly acceptable to produce a feature that is similar to one that's been written before (although it may be much harder to sell a familiar or derivative story to an editor). It is occasionally possible to accidentally include material that you think is entirely novel, but actually repeats material you have read during the research process. If you've been inspired by a piece of work, check before you file your copy to make sure you've not accidentally replicated material. You cannot deliberately repeat or replicate material written by another journalist without their permission or permission from the copyright holder.

Remember:

- Copyright law is there to protect your work and income.
- Fair use does allow limited use of some material.
- Photographs are not covered by fair use.
- Embedding copyright material is not an infringement of copyright law.
- Using copyright material is not only illegal, but raises ethical issues.

Risk assessments

The term journalism covers a wide range of activities. You may spend your day writing in your home office in your underpants, reviewing luxury hotels or trekking through a war zone. Many journalists are natural risk takers and see little point in considering health and safety, but when you pause for just a moment to consider the impact an injury or worse may have on your family, friends or career, it really is worth spending time considering how to do your job as safely as possible.

The culture of health and safety in your organisation will depend on its own history and the activities it expects you to perform. It's often assumed that print journalism offers fewer hazards (a pen and notepad are powerful weapons, but only if used as intended). Journalists who work in audio and video production often work in teams, with bulky equipment and are required to spend more time thinking about health and safety issues. If you work for a media organisation, it will probably have its own health and safety policies and a system of risk assessment and approval. It is important you take this seriously, as it will be part of your contract of employment and of course you don't want to be responsible for hurting a colleague or contributor.

If you are working as a freelancer you may either be entirely responsible for your own health and safety procedures or be required to follow the guidance of your employer or commissioner. If you are responsible for your own working practices, you should complete a risk assessment for any project which involves another person in any respect. Ideally you should get into the habit of completing a brief risk assessment for every project. If you're not prepared to do that, you should at the very least take a few minutes to consider the journalistic point of any project and whether any risky activity really is necessary. The charity The Rory Peck Trust (2013) points out:

> The time to ask yourself 'why am I doing this?' is before you set off, not when you are in the middle of an unfolding crisis. Your reasons may be clear in your head, but writing them down can help you focus on the motivations behind a project.

If you think of nothing else, consider whether you would be able to earn a living if you get hurt.

If anyone else is involved in your project, then you could be legally responsible for him or her and should undertake a formal risk assessment. If you are paying the person involved, you may be classed as their employer and are certainly in charge of their safety (Health and Safety Executive, 2014), and if you are asking a member of the public to work with you, then you should make their safety a priority.

If you want to complete a risk assessment, for whatever purposes, The Rory Peck Trust provides some excellent resources online, including a risk assessment template and advice on insurance.

Things to do

Build your contacts

Visit your local public library and introduce yourself to the staff. Once you've joined, familiarise yourself with the library's non-digital and online resources. Which of them might be useful to you in the future?

Use the library's resources to come up with three ideas for news stories or features. You could find inspiration in old newspapers, ask about local authors or check out some of the events advertised on notice boards.

Practise your research

Take one of your story ideas from above and conduct the research needed to plan and film it as a video news story. You can use any video production equipment you have to hand. A smartphone and editing app will be fine. Look online for advice on using a smartphone to shoot and edit news reports.

Research in action

Produce a risk assessment for your video story assignment. Take a look at some of the risk assessment guidance on the Rory Peck Trust website. Finally film and edit your story and upload it to your personal blog or any other website you prefer.

Issues to discuss

Older people may use the telephone to chat, but young people increasingly use social media to interact. Will the phone be as important for journalists in twenty years time as it is today?

Most news organisations have dramatically reduced their professional research teams. What impact do you think this might have on the future of journalism? Do you believe the rise of online research and CAR might change this trend?

It's easy to download images from the Internet, but what impact does the use of free images have on picture libraries and photographers? Would you be happy to share your journalistic work for free?

Places to learn more

Books and journals

Maxwell, D. 2005. *Phone Skills for the Information Age*. Boston, MA: McGraw-Hill/Irwin.
Seely, J. 2005. *Oxford Guide to Effective Writing and Speaking*. 2nd Edition. Oxford: Oxford University Press.
Shopflin, K. 2008. *A Handbook for Media Librarians*. London: Facet.
Wolf, C. 2006. *Basic Library Skills*. Jefferson, NC: McFarland.

Online resources

BBC Health and Safety Guide	http://downloads.bbc.co.uk/mundo/pdf/safety-journalism_safety_guide_second_edition-v1.pdf
BFI Reuben Library Website	www.bfi.org.uk/education-research/bfi-reuben-library
BT Online Phonebook	www.thephonebook.bt.com/publisha.content/en/search/residential/search.publisha
Yellow Pages Online	www.yell.com/
Online Database 192.com	www.192.com/
find it! – guide to library collections throughout the UK	http://findit.org.uk/

The British Library	www.bl.uk/
The National Art Library	www.vam.ac.uk/page/n/national-art-library/
The Wellcome Collection	www.wellcomecollection.org/
Society of College, National and University Libraries	www.sconul.ac.uk/
Association of Independent Libraries	www.independentlibraries.co.uk/
British Association of Picture Libraries and Agencies	www.bapla.org.uk/
Mary Evans Picture Library	www.maryevans.com/
British Film Institute Library	www.bfi.org.uk/filmtvinfo/library/visiting/resources.html
Guardian Library Twitter Feed	@guardianlibrary

References

BBC News School Report. 2014. *What makes a good journalist – Jeremy Paxman's Tips* [online]. London: BBC. Available from: www.bbc.co.uk/schoolreport/25807998 [accessed 21 June 2015].

Blackwood, G. 2015. *Producer in radio: 5 Live* [online]. London: BBC College of Journalism. Available from: www.bbc.co.uk/academy/journalism/skills/researching-and-producing/article/art2013070211 2133494 [accessed 30 June 2015].

Health and Safety Executive. 2002. *Health and safety in audio-visual production. Your legal duties* [online]. London: HSE. Available from: www.hse.gov.uk/pubns/indg360.pdf [accessed 5 July 2015].

Health and Safety Executive. 2014. *Health and safety law. What you need to know* [online]. London: HSE. Available from: www.hse.gov.uk/pubns/law.pdf [accessed 5 July 2015].

Jones, B. 2011. *Is the line between librarianship and journalism blurring?* [online]. Chicago, IL: ALM. Available from: http://americanlibrariesmagazine.org/2011/07/27/is-the-line-between-librarianship-and-journalism-blurring/ [accessed 15 May 2015].

Journalists' Resource. 2013. *Academic research and studies: How they work and why journalists should care* [online]. Cambridge, MA: Journalists' Resource. Available from: http://journalistsresource.org/tip-sheets/research/introduction-studies-academic-research-journalists [accessed 27 May 2015].

Nelsson, R. 2013. *The head of The Guardian's library on . . . nostalgia for press cuttings* [online]. London: The Guardian. Available from: www.theguardian.com/commentisfree/2013/feb/10/nostalgia-press-cuttings [accessed 30 May 2015].

Rory Peck Trust. 2013. *Get the documents and get started* [online]. London: Rory Peck Trust. Available from: https://rorypecktrust.org/resources/safety-and-security/risk-assessment/Get-the-Documents-and-Get-Started [accessed 30 May 2015].

Where not referenced, quotations are from interviews, emails or social media conversations with the author.

6 People

Introduction

Without sources to share information with us, the work of journalists would be impossible. People are at the heart of what we do, whether they're verifying a minor fact, sharing their personal experiences or providing confidential documents to reveal widespread wrongdoing. An effective reporter knows that facts and figures generally mean little to their readers, listeners or viewers, unless those facts are related to their own lives and experiences. Of course information needs to be verified and attributed, but it's also important to include human context. *Guardian* editor Alan Rusbridger explained in 2014, 'The use of people who are prepared to tell the truth . . . they are vital to what we do and they are vital . . . to the public understanding of issues'.

This chapter leads on from Chapter 2, to focus on the relationship between journalists and their sources. It looks at some basic challenges of dealing with people, including finding good contributors, reacting to tip-offs and the problem of dealing with 'off the record' information. It then goes on to discuss some of the more challenging and complex issues raised by modern journalistic practice.

Some of the material covered in this chapter is at the very heart of how journalists are working now, at the start of the twenty-first century. It's a rapidly developing story, which changes day by day, with new and modified laws and a shifting political environment. This chapter will give new journalists an introduction to some of the current challenges and offer some tools and advice to help them improve and develop their practice.

This chapter covers:

- The power of persuasion
- Tracking down a great contributor
- Managing and protecting sources
- Sources and digital security
- Undercover research
- Making mistakes

The power of persuasion

Journalists spend much of their time speaking to people, gaining their confidence and persuading them to reveal information. Dealing with people from all over the world and from a variety of backgrounds is central to the life of a working journalist, but these skills can sometimes be the most challenging to learn.

A successful researcher will often unwittingly share many of the skills of a great sales or marketing professional. When dealing with people, you need the ability to form a relationship swiftly, explain yourself clearly and encourage them to confide in you. Here are some of the basic skills that can help you to do this via digital communication, telephone or in person.

Body language

This may seem obvious, but if you're approaching someone face to face and you look bored or anxious, you are far less likely to get a positive response. When speaking to someone in person, do your best to behave professionally. If you're struggling, learn to take control of the situation, by offering your hand and introducing yourself. If necessary, prepare a few words of introduction. Many professional people overcome their natural anxiety when meeting new people, by putting on a 'professional persona'. They learn to behave in the way their clients or contacts expect, even if it's completely different to their natural personality. US Journalist Beth Winegarner offers some great advice on Poynter.org (2012). She says,

> Your role as a journalist gives you special permission to be nosy. Police, legislators and everyday citizens might think it's weird if a stranger starts asking them questions, but if you whip out your reporter's notebook . . . they'll usually accept that it's your job to cross-examine them.

Journalists aren't generally noted for their fashion sense, but it's clearly important to be clean and relatively tidy if you want people to trust you and spend time with you.

Vocal tone

There are few more valuable skills for a researcher than a friendly, confident vocal tone. When speaking over the phone, it's important to overcome nerves and inject a 'smile' into your voice. This can easily be done by genuinely smiling while making the call. Think about the person you are calling, do they work in an office, a busy shop or do they travel a lot? Tailor your approach accordingly. Take the very first opportunity to listen to the person's tone of voice and react to that. If they sound happy or tired you might want to refer to that as it immediately personalises the call. Also remember that flattery goes a long way. You may have made fifty calls already, but it's important to make your contact feel special. Make it clear that you chose them for a reason and would really value their contribution.

Many contributors are now approached online via social media or email. Take some time to inject a little friendly personality into these messages too. A brief enquiry about someone's health, clear information about what you're asking them to do and a genuine message of thanks can work well. It can also save you a time-consuming follow-up call. If you're approaching a number of guests via email, take some time to draft a friendly and informative structure and add personal details such as their name and the name of their company wherever possible.

Preparation

Many telephone sales staff work from a prepared script and it's not a bad approach for journalists to take, particularly on the telephone. If you're contacting someone by phone, think about preparing a few clear and simple sentences to introduce every call. You don't have to read them word for word, but it will help you to start a call clearly and confidently. You should try to give the person who answers the phone as much information as possible without intimidating them or demanding an interview. If you work for a well-known or prestigious publication, make sure you include the name in the first few words. Knowing what you're going to say can really ease nerves and put you in control of the conversation that follows. Typical opening lines might be:

> Hello there. My name is Vanessa Edwards. I'm a freelance researcher and I'm currently working on a television documentary about cheese making. I know your company is one of the most respected in the industry and I wonder if you might have a few moments for a chat?
>
> Hello. I'm ringing from *World Choir Magazine*. My name is Vanessa Edwards. We're currently researching an article on choirs in South America. I understand you're an expert on the subject.

Claire Edwards is a journalist for a successful trade publication. She says it's important to try to have a conversation, rather than speak 'at' your contact.

> Remember, the person on the other end of the phone is not judging you – I promise! Always talk slower than you think you should. I guarantee you're probably speaking way too fast. Asking leading questions is also good because then you're engaging with them instead of talking at them. One of my biggest tips though, is to remember that person on the other side of the phone is human too! They could be having a bad or stressful day so don't ever take a phone call too personally.

Research

The Internet has made it relatively straightforward to find out a little about the person you're contacting. It will be much easier to build up a relationship with your potential source if you know the basics about their job and their organisation. It also builds their confidence if you show that you have a good grounding in their area of expertise. Asking thoughtful and well-researched questions may well encourage your source to continue chatting to you and give a formal interview. Another tip is to check images of your contributor online, photos can often give you a good indication about the person's age and the kind of image they like to generate. You can tailor your approach accordingly.

Overcoming objections

You'll be surprised how many times you hear the same excuses for avoiding giving a formal interview. Always plan some tactics in advance to deal with such refusals. If you can change your plans or arrangements to accommodate your contact, then this might well be the point to do so. It's also worthwhile pointing out any personal advantages to them, such as avoiding further contacts from the media or getting the chance to put forward their point of view.

If you work for an organisation that can offer a contributor free transport to and from the newsroom or studio, you may be surprised how many people are tempted by a free trip home in a taxi rather than a cramped journey on a bus or train. Don't be over-pushy though. Someone who has been bullied into speaking to the media will rarely give a good interview; besides, hounding someone is not ethical.

Once you're convinced your source is genuinely unable or unwilling to help you, your line of research should not end there. Always ask if they know anyone else who might have the information you need. Some of my best leads have come from potential contributors who felt guilty about turning me down and were happy to help with further advice.

Forming a close and trusting relationship with your sources will pay off. For journalists working across a small patch it gives the opportunity to source original stories, which are relevant to their target audience.

Interview

Dawn Robinson-Walsh is a hyperlocal community journalist who runs the successful news website 'Bude and Beyond' in north Cornwall. She's discovered that her passion for working with her local community has given her a unique role and responsibility.

What is your experience when researching content for your site? Do you feel you have enough time and resources?

People love getting anything for free, so most people are happy to talk to me for free business promotion or to promote community events. It is much harder to get them to write anything themselves or to encourage them towards actually adding content to the site. I now find that people contact me if there is an issue (almost expecting me to resolve it) so I have become quite integral to the community.

Do you think the traditional media are doing an adequate job in covering your area with well-researched news?

The area I cover is mainly Bude in North Cornwall. The area is covered by *Cornish Guardian* (weekly and online), *Western Morning News* (daily and online) and the *Bude and Stratton Post* (weekly and online), the latter being the most locally produced paper, with a focus on Bude.

The issue is that none of them are based in Bude. They don't know local people, how things work, or the local dynamic here. They have awareness of the big issues, which are local discussion but maybe not news, local businesses, and they don't spend their time in the town, so they do not truly share in people's successes and upsets. Bude is small and therefore, local knowledge is a bonus. I'd say the vast majority of *Bude and Stratton Post* readership (very Launceston based) is among the older population among whom it is well-respected and has a strong following; mine is younger and more community-focused. Different markets. The larger papers are obviously much more commercially orientated and have large teams of staff to fund.

Did you have any journalism training or experience before starting your site?

I have never trained as a journalist, but have worked as a freelance feature writer for magazines, and in local publishing (books). I am also a published author. My main background was in education but my career prospects within HE were severely curtailed when I moved, 5 years ago, to the SW. My previous role was with Northcliffe Digital working for a now defunct website, called Bude People, itself a hyperlocal. So, it has been a learning curve getting to grips with Wordpress, writing content, doing all the associated social media, and so on. Pretty self-taught!

Making that very first contact is always difficult. There are very few people who genuinely enjoy approaching complete strangers, but it's a vital skill for a successful journalist. Perhaps the best advice is to get started quickly and be persistent. The longer you put off making the first call, the harder it will be to wade through twenty or thirty more potential leads.

Remember:

- Most journalists need good 'people skills'.
- Dealing confidently with sources is hard, but will improve with practice.
- Consider developing a professional 'persona'.
- Preparation and research will help you to explain yourself more confidently.
- Be persistent and expect to be turned-down.

Tracking down a great contributor

Real people and their contributions bring journalism alive. They're essential to create colour, atmosphere and character in a piece of work. Indeed in some cases, they're the entire point of a story! It's important to remember that even when a source won't give you a formal interview or allow a camera to be switched-on, the information that they share can still be included as colour or may provide the basis for further research. There are a variety of contributors and sources.

Key players

These are the first contributors you should seek when researching a story. They are the central characters. Their comments may form the basis or angle of a story, or may be needed to stand-up (validate) the report. For news journalists, the pressure to get these key contributors is intense. This has on occasion led to some of the more unacceptable excesses of reporters, desperate to gain access to their most important source. Under no circumstances is it acceptable to hound or stalk a member of the public, but one of the common errors made by new journalists is to accept the first 'no' they receive. There are perfectly ethical ways to seek an important interview, and perseverance is important.

Wherever possible, your first call to an organisation should be to a named member of staff. For many new journalists the obvious first place for a call might appear to be the press office or public relations team; however this can be a mistake. In many respects press officers and PR professionals do an excellent job, but they are often briefed to keep journalists away from key staff or offer bland statements or denials.

There is another reason to hold off from calling the press office. It may tip-off an organisation about your interest in a particular interview. This gives the contributor time to discuss the pros and cons, decide to prepare a statement or refuse to speak at all. It can completely spoil your chances of getting those exclusive comments.

One method is to start with the Internet to track down the name of the person responsible for the area you are researching. Then call the main switchboard and ask to speak to them directly. Although it is clearly unethical to lie, it is possible to limit the amount of information given about the nature of the call to the person who immediately answers the phone. This may help you to avoid being directly put through to the press office.

Many senior officials and politicians have secretaries, researchers and personal assistants who answer their personal telephone lines. These people act as professional 'gatekeepers'. You should never underestimate the importance of being polite and friendly to such people, as it's valuable to have them on your side. If they tell you their boss isn't free, be polite and persistent and ask them when might be a good time to call. By all means leave a message, but don't expect to be called back. You should always ring again and remind the person you spoke to that you were disappointed they didn't call you back as promised as their comments and input were important to you. (A little shame can't hurt!) Even if the secretary can't put you through to their boss, he may be happy to suggest another valuable contact in the organisation.

As already mentioned, whenever making phone calls for research you should always ask whether the person you're speaking to knows anyone else who might be able to help. Successful telephone research is often about developing a 'chain' of contacts. Your first call may not be able to assist you, but they might suggest another local company in a similar line of work. Your named contact at that firm could be on holiday, but their personal assistant might have a friend who works at a third company and so on and so forth. A former colleague managed to secure an interview with an eminent but reclusive retired politician, by persuading the secretary at his former school to pop a note through his door. It was only by lateral thinking and some clever persuasion that he discovered the politician was still regularly in contact with staff and students at the school and only lived around the corner.

Dogged persistence is often the only way to get the right information or interview. Many new journalists will give up a lead after one or two calls because they feel uncomfortable, but an editor will generally want to see far more effort made to contact a source. Very few people find making repeated and determined telephone calls to be an easy or pleasant experience; however it should always be remembered that the journalist who attempts to hold a person in authority to account, is doing their job well and should not feel ashamed of making a nuisance of themselves. Also the praise and respect received for getting a great interview is often more than enough to make up for any initial discomfort. As academic and digital expert Paul Bradshaw points out on his blog (2012)

> What makes a person persevere? It's not just their stubbornness, surely, but the perceived chances and rewards of success. It is about the support behind them, and the pay-off . . . It is about their belief that they can overcome obstacles, based on repeated experience of (and pleasure in) overcoming obstacles.

However keen a journalist might be to get a story, they must be governed by privacy law, ethical practice and the editorial guidelines of their employer. Section 4(ii) of the IPSO Code states that journalists 'must not persist in questioning, telephoning, pursuing or photographing individuals once asked to desist; nor remain on their property when asked to leave and must not follow them. If requested, they must identify themselves and whom they represent'. The Ofcom code has a similar requirement in its Section 8: 'The means of obtaining material must be proportionate in all the circumstances and in particular to the subject matter of the programme'. This recognises that there is a fine line to be drawn between determination and harassment. Judgements will differ depending on the person and their role in a news story. There is a practical difference between repeatedly contacting a public figure whose job involves being in the media spotlight and an ordinary person who has unwittingly become involved in a big news story. One other point to bear in mind is that alienating a potential source can jeopardise the likelihood of their helping you in the future.

If you're in any doubt about the ethics or legal implications of chasing a contributor, you should always seek the advice or a more senior or experienced reporter, a relevant trade union or professional body or even a media lawyer. In short, some editors will expect a reporter to push further than others and it's up to the journalist concerned to decide how far they're happy to go and what they're prepared to do to secure an interview.

Eyewitnesses

It's a sad fact of life that disasters, accidents and crimes are the bread and butter of news journalism. When a reporter starts researching a breaking story, the people at the top of their contact list will be eyewitnesses, the people who can give personal testimony and describe what happened from the ground.

Sometimes it can be very straightforward to track-down eyewitnesses. If a reporter arrives soon after an incident they may well find potential interviewees milling around, trying to help or having injuries treated. This can be an extremely difficult time for new reporters who are faced with speaking to people in the most challenging and embarrassing circumstances. How and when you approach people at the scene of an accident or crime is an ethical minefield and can often mean that new journalists return without the material that is most needed to tell a story.

The IPSO and Ofcom codes both have guidelines on how to approach people in traumatic circumstances. Clause 5 of the IPSO guidance says: 'In cases involving personal grief or shock, enquiries and approaches must be made with sympathy and discretion and publication handled sensitively'. While Ofcom's Section 8 requires that: 'People in a state of distress should not be put under pressure to take part in a programme or provide interviews, unless it is warranted'.

The amount of effort you are expected to make to find eyewitnesses and the pressure you are expected to place on them will differ dramatically depending on your employer. Often local newspapers and broadcasters will be the most sensitive and least intrusive, knowing that they will be judged by their local community and may have to return to the location of the incident in future. The record of some tabloid newspapers when trying to contact interviewees is well known, although recent scrutiny has reduced some of their reporters' most extreme behaviour when it comes to speaking to ordinary people caught up in extraordinary circumstances.

One thing, which new journalists sometimes find surprising, is some eyewitnesses' willingness to speak about what has happened to them and the people around them. There are people who want to share their experiences for a whole variety of reasons; whether it's to praise the emergency services, pay tribute to people who may have suffered or died, or simply to release some of their own grief and distress. There is nothing wrong in approaching someone with courtesy and offering them an opportunity to share what they know, as long as you move away immediately when you are asked to.

If a journalist arrives at an incident late and people have moved on or dispersed, finding eyewitnesses can prove more complicated. An obvious and well-trodden route is to knock on doors or visit shops and businesses. This can again prove quite a challenge for an inexperienced reporter, but repetition and practice will soon make things easier. In fact the endless repetition of the same polite enquiry at every door in a street can soon become routine.

Social media networks provide another excellent way to find eyewitness contributors. People who use social media to share images and comments or let friends and relatives know they are well or safe have willingly posted their views and can be contacted online to arrange a conversation in person or on the phone. Many online and broadcast news organisations will use their output to call for contributions or user generated content (UGC). Some people may also ring newspaper and broadcast newsrooms, because they feel a connection with the reporters or presenters or sometimes to ask for money for their story. However online material is sourced, it's important to verify any content using some of the methods discussed in Chapter 3.

With the continuing squeeze on budgets, many journalists are faced with the difficult task of finding eyewitnesses from the newsroom. This is often also the case when covering foreign news. Social media networks again prove a valuable tool, but it can still be a daunting task, tracking down eyewitnesses many thousands of miles away in a second language. In the UK it's easy to spot relevant social media posts, but if you're working on a story in another country, it's important to identify relevant hashtags and use online translators to provide an idea of what the tweets might be saying. Never rely on material translated online as the source of a story or angle. It's vital to contact a native speaker to identify detail and nuance and use verification methods to validate the information.

Google Streetview can prove invaluable when tracking down eyewitnesses from the newsroom. A quick virtual tour of the area will show immediately any local shops or businesses whose contact details can be found using online directories or search engines. It might also show places where English might be more readily spoken such as tourism businesses, schools, universities or even hospitals. If you're working in a second language and don't have a native speaker in your organisation, consider contacting other journalists in the region or even organisations such as English schools, clubs, newspapers or 'ex pat' communities who might be able to help you with your research. An online translation service can be used to send simple email or social media requests asking for contacts from English speakers. The recipient may not speak English, but might be able to pass the message on to a friend.

Finding key players and eyewitnesses is one of the most challenging parts of a news journalists' job, but can also give the reporter a chance to stand out and really shine. The case study on p. 113 shows just how much time and effort a major news organisation will put into chasing interviews for a big breaking news story. It takes two senior staff just to keep track of all the lines of enquiry and calls being made!

Case studies

Case studies are generally 'ordinary' people who can explain how their lives have been affected by a news story or event. Sometimes they are relatively easy to track down, such as someone who has voted for a particular political party or lives in a specific kind of home.

Journalists at work

Nicholas Gibbon is an experienced broadcast journalist who works in the BBC television newsroom. He was on duty at the BBC News Channel on the day that a Norwegian, Anders Breivik, carried out a bomb and gun attack to kill seventy-seven people in July 2011.

'We got the first reports of the initial explosion via Twitter at around 2.35 pm. Although I was working with a team that would be on air later, it was all hands to the pump and I immediately dropped what I was doing and joined the team that was on air at the time. It was a massive story with around six journalists involved in calling government offices, television and radio stations and newspapers in Norway, along with police, hospitals and even hotels. We have a grid for recording guest bids. It saves duplicating effort and is a useful guide to see who other journalists at the BBC News Channel have spoken to already.

The team found it impossible to get anything for the first thirty minutes. Interestingly there were plenty of pictures via Twitter, but those posting on Twitter weren't checking their messages and didn't respond. The first breakthrough came when a colleague gave us the email address of someone at the Norwegian Broadcasting Corporation (NRK). The reporter at NRK said they couldn't tell us exactly what was happening, but then gave us the mobile number of a reporter who'd witnessed the bombing near the government buildings. Things started to move from there. Because of the popularity of the BBC News website, many people were contacting my colleagues in our User Generated Content team.

By about 4.00 pm four more producers joined the hunt for interviews. By now more names were appearing in agency copy, so it was simple to just get their contact details after a quick Internet search. In these circumstances each producer would be making dozens of individual calls. I think we actually tracked down around a hundred potential contributors – ninety in Norway and ten UK-based terrorism experts. Of these only a few were put on air'.

Others can be trickier, in fact it can be the very rarity of the person that makes them a great interviewee, for example a centenarian who's just learned to fly a plane or a woman whose cat plays the guitar.

One place to start is by contacting charities and support groups. They often value the publicity and may have lists of people who are happy to speak candidly about their personal feelings. In some cases, those who set-up charities or support groups may have had such experiences themselves and may be happy to speak. Another way to make contact with case studies is through online chat rooms or social media sites. If you have time, you can post requests for interviews or speak to people online and ask them individually whether they might become contributors. As with all contacts made online, it is vital to check the person is who they say they are. There are some commercial websites designed to help journalists track down case studies, such as Responsesource and Casestudylink. There is more on using the Internet for research in Chapter 3.

Persistence does pay off when searching for such interviews, but it's certainly not a good idea to be forceful. A friendly and persuasive manner either by phone or through email or social media will be much more successful. Charm and kindness are often greatly underestimated in journalism, but when dealing with people in these particular circumstances they can be invaluable. When contacting someone to ask them to be a case study, put yourself in their shoes. What incentives can you offer them to help you?

There are a great many people in the world who are motivated by altruism. They may be happy to share their experiences if they feel people might benefit from their expertise or reassurance. Sometimes they might be equally happy to help a new journalist at the start of their career. There are also some people who really enjoy the idea of a brief period of celebrity. These contributors are often excellent, cooperative and helpful. Beware of anyone who is too keen to help, particularly if they are interested in appearing on radio or television. There is a danger that some contributors may be tempted to embellish or dramatise their stories to gain further attention. It's tempting to encourage these case studies as they can make great content, but ultimately they undermine your credibility and that of your publication or programme.

New journalists often underestimate the value of exploiting personal and family contacts. Ringing a father or aunt can sometimes feel like 'cheating' and yet it can often be the easiest way to contact a potential source or contributor. A quick phone call of introduction from a friend or family member will often help to open doors. Equally, friends who work in a variety of industries can provide fantastic contacts. It doesn't take many emails or social networking posts before you can soon find someone, who knows someone, who knows a vet, economist or snake charmer!

Experts

Journalists ring experts on a daily basis. They can be among our most valued contacts. Their expertise helps us checkout stories, validate data and of course they make great contributors. An expert adds credibility and authority to a journalist's work. They come in a whole variety of metaphorical shapes and sizes. They vary from academics, through people employed in specialist industries, authors, campaigners, and some are self-taught professional commentators.

One of the best places to start searching is a university website. Many now have searchable databases of their academic staff, organised by subject and research interests. Universities often

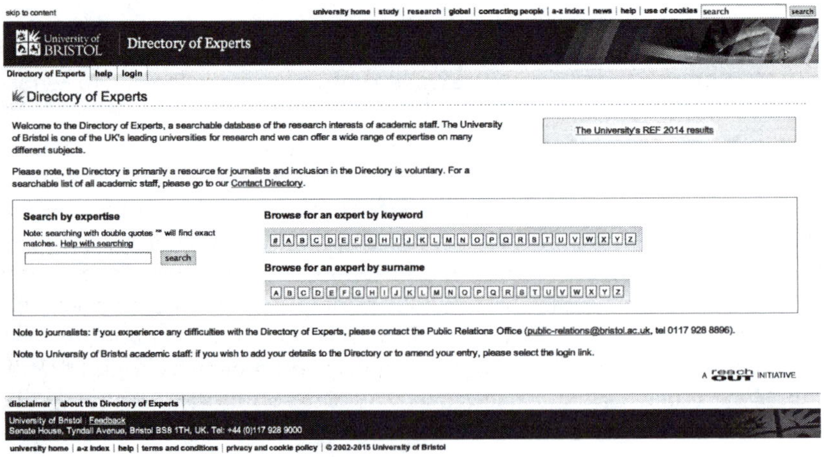

Figure 6.1 Many universities now provide searchable staff databases © University of Bristol

develop areas of expertise, which are related to their geographical location. Coastal universities may have experts in marine ecology, boat design or tourism. Those in big cities may have specialists in industrial history or engineering. While older universities tend to teach traditional subjects, such as mathematics, languages and history, many of the newer universities have developed specialisms connected directly to industry or practical applications of theoretical knowledge.

A very easy way to find authors who have written about your area of research is to use Amazon. It's a great way to search key terms relating to your chosen area. It will throw up a variety of books and one can then see immediately whether someone might have written a few on a particular topic or in a specific style. Try looking at the writer's Amazon page, which should list all their publications and the section which recommends other books as this can flag-up other potential interviewees. Once you've identified an author's name and some of his/her publications, it's relatively straightforward to Google them to find their personal website or agent's contact details.

Finding a really good expert contributor can be harder than it might first appear. There are some researchers who make articulate and willing commentators; however they may not be the most prominent expert in their field and they may certainly not be as credible among other specialist researchers. A journalist needs to give careful thought to the context and audience for their report. A few sentences from any science expert might be perfectly acceptable for a short story about cleaning chewing-gum from a pavement. It would be far more important to find a credible and authoritative expert for a complex piece on global warming for a broadsheet newspaper. These aren't always easy judgements to make and it can be worthwhile ringing a few people in a particular area of research or specialism to establish a contributor's credentials, before using their comments.

The choice between the best 'informer' and 'performer' can add an additional layer of difficulty for journalists working in the broadcast media. The world's greatest expert on a particular topic may be a poor communicator who is unable to simplify their expertise for an average person. They may speak indistinctly or look nervous and uncomfortable in front of a camera. A less renowned academic may be a great communicator, with a friendly approachable style and an ability to make difficult concepts easy to understand. There are ways to work with a less-good performer, particularly in a pre-recorded interview, which can be practised, repeated and edited. When booking guests for live programmes this is a more difficult decision. It's this problem that can sometimes lead to misunderstandings between the academic world and journalists who can be accused of overlooking the best-qualified experts.

Medical experts

When choosing medical experts, journalists have a particular ethical responsibility to their audience. No decent person would want to give misleading or dangerous health advice to a member of the public, especially since in some areas of journalism (such as broadcasting) there remains a considerable degree of trust in our work. It is absolutely vital when interviewing doctors or other medical professionals that you check out their credentials and qualifications. This can be done relatively easily online by contacting their regulating or registering body. If necessary make a few extra calls to ensure they're qualified to speak about the area of medicine you are covering.

Qualified doctors agree to abide by the principles of good medical practice, as defined by the General Medical Council. But particular care should be taken when speaking to those promoting alternative or complementary therapies. While the vast majority of practitioners are safe and have the best intentions, there is always the risk that some are less ethical. The quality of their training and their regulating bodies can vary dramatically. If in doubt, ring a qualified doctor to get their advice on any risks or dangers posed by covering a complementary therapy.

There are a growing number of experts who have developed their specialisms over a number of years and now make their careers as 'media pundits'. Some do this as an add-on to another job, while others are now able to promote themselves directly on the Internet. Expertise from particular industries can be extremely valuable; some contributors make a career out of previous work experience – former pilots, military staff and police officers are particularly sought after. Bloggers and vloggers make a rich new source of potential pundits, but they should be treated with caution. Some blogs offer a mine of genuine expertise. Many finance and politics blogs can be excellent, as are some that represent particular areas of society. Mumsnet has been a real success story. YouTube vloggers are a phenomenon and have credibility and access to a much younger audience than many other experts. Other web writers have weaker credentials and are little more than self-appointed experts. It can be hard deciding whether to pay a fee for a pundit's expertise. Many are professional journalists and it seems only fair to recompense them for their time and expertise, but some might argue that the extra publicity for their website or YouTube channel should be enough reward for their time. If in doubt ask your editor.

Protagonists and antagonists

The requirement for balance and impartiality can pose some real challenges when researching interviewees. This is an issue for all news reporters, but it's a particular problem for journalists working in broadcast media news who are required by Ofcom to be impartial. Section Five of the Ofcom Code says 'News, in whatever form, must be reported with due accuracy and presented with due impartiality'. This can make finding contributors for reports or live discussions difficult, for a variety of reasons.

First of all, short news reports or studio discussions lend themselves to stories, which have distinct and opposite opinions. It can be hard in a very short news report to express nuances or complexities of opinion, and in a live debate, speakers who obviously disagree with each other make a more entertaining piece of television or radio. So the producers finds themselves either ignoring this aspect of a story altogether or generating a polarity of opinion where there isn't one. This simplification and generation of conflict in broadcast news is often the subject of criticism. As media commentator Martin Campbell wrote in *The Guardian* in 2011 'Good-guy, bad-guy angles and personality-led, confrontational interviews are the easiest forms of broadcast news output. But they are neither investigative nor revelatory'. Many newsrooms do try to take more complex stories and investigate them with detail and subtlety, but it's always worth reviewing your approach to researching and planning stories and considering whether you are over-simplifying or creating a false conflict unnecessarily.

Another problem caused by the stipulation for balance is the challenge of being forced to reflect two points of view, even when the vast majority of people, including the experts best qualified to judge, believe one opinion is far more valid. This has caused particular problems for broadcasters when covering issues such as climate change, or the risk of a combined measles, mumps and rubella vaccination. In 2014 the House of Commons Science and Technology Committee published a report called 'Communicating Climate Change' which was critical of the media's approach to the issue, calling its attempt to show two sides to the argument 'false balance'. It said,

Submissions to our inquiry commented on a tendency for the media to approach climate science as an argument about two equally valid points of view, rather than discussion about scientific facts, and on the false balance of views being presented as a consequence.

Hoc Science and Technology Committee, 2014

The report recommended that alternative ideas on climate change should be presented, but the BBC should be careful not to present the opinions of lobbying groups as disinterested experts.

Interviewing other journalists

It's becoming increasingly common for journalists to interview each other. This can be for a whole variety of reasons; sometimes it's because a journalist has a particular area of expertise; sometimes the journalist is a celebrity; often the reporter might be talking about a story they've written or researched or they might be taking part in a newspaper review. However good the reason for interviewing other journalists, it can often alienate and irritate the general public. It's often worth challenging a decision to interview another journalist and asking yourself whether there might be another option. The growing tendency for journalists to speak to other journalists has certainly led to the criticism that they're cut-off from the real world and part of a so-called 'metropolitan elite'.

Remember:

- When tracking down contributors, start with the 'key players' central to your story.
- Approaching eyewitnesses needs sensitivity and tact.
- Patience and determination are key to finding great case studies.
- It's important to research credible experts who are also good communicators.
- Beware of creating false conflict or over-simplifying a story.
- When considering interviewing a journalist, always ask if there is a better interviewee.

Managing and protecting sources

A journalist's sources are at the very heart of their research. Put in the simplest terms, a source is anyone who provides you with information. There are as many different types of source, as there are people. A source can be anyone from a member of bar staff, who has some gossip about a celebrity they've served, to a senior member of government. For all journalists, the protection of sources is a fundamental obligation. The IPSO, Ofcom and NUJ codes all recognise the vital important of protecting confidential sources of information.

Most of your sources will be regular contacts who give you relatively uncontroversial material. Their names and contact details will be in your contacts book. Your commitment to them is to store their personal details safely within the requirements of the Data Protection Act 1998 and keep their identity confidential when this has been requested. You should deal with your contacts fairly and always be explicit about how you plan to use their contribution. When a source is happy to be named (and of course this will be so in the vast majority of cases) you should make the source of your information explicit to your audience too.

The best way to build a relationship with your sources is to be friendly, polite and most of all, honest. If you're working for a large news organisation remember you are also responsible for maintaining the reputation of your colleagues and employer. Many contacts will forget your name, but they won't forget your programme or publication. It's easy for one bad telephone call to taint the reputation of an entire team.

Off the record?

The phrase 'off the record' must be one of the few bits of journalistic jargon that is widely known among the general public. In practice though it can be one of the most difficult aspects of a journalist's job to master and is highly controversial. It can easily be misunderstood.

To most journalists 'off the record' means information given can be reported, as long as the source is not identified, but what does 'identified' mean? Does that commitment mean simply not reporting a source's name? Should the journalists ensure any contact with the source is totally secret? Should they consider the possibility of an astute researcher finding out who made the comments? What about the danger of the same comments being made to more than one journalist and the source being identified by combining information in a variety of reports (sometimes known as jigsaw identification)? Perhaps most importantly, has the source thought about all these possibilities? And does the journalist have an ethical obligation to ensure they consider the possible outcomes before they speak? Of course, the answers to these dilemmas are never simple. The care taken to hide the source's identity will be decided with reference to both the possible risk to the contact's personal life and career and the importance of the news story. It's something that needs considerable thought and discussion both with the source and your editor.

Legally 'off the record' means nothing and has no legal implications. However agreeing to an 'off the record' conversation could be covered by the laws on breach of confidence and/or privacy. If the case reaches the court, the judge would be expected to decide whether the information disclosed by a source could be considered confidential and weigh that against the journalist's assertion that the information was published in the public interest.

In practice, most sources can probably be assured that a few brief comments to a journalist on an everyday story will not lead to further follow-ups, but however carefully a publication or programme works to protect the source of a major news scoop, journalists following-up the story are under intense pressure and they've made no such commitments to protect their source. As former Daily Mirror editor Professor Roy Greenslade wrote in his Guardian Blog (2013): 'If the story is big enough . . . then there will be insistent pressure to expose the source by those who went un-briefed'.

Paying for information

There has been a long tradition in the British newspaper and magazine industry of paying sources and contributors, called disparagingly 'chequebook journalism'. It's such common practice in print journalism that it seems almost moot to discuss the ethical issues raised by these payments. It is clearly relevant whether money could be seen as damaging the credibility of the source, undermining the story at a future date. There's a danger a large payment to a source may also influence the news judgement of the journalist. A publication may be more likely to try to use a story, which has cost it a lot of money.

Whistleblowers, leaks and protecting sources

The protection of journalistic sources is one of the most controversial areas of debate in modern journalism practice. Many highly regarded journalists argue that governments' ability to monitor and record communications presents a real and active challenge to journalistic freedom. Leaked documents and information have been at the centre of some of the biggest news stories in the past decade, notably the publication of a leaked file of MPs expenses by the Telegraph Group in 2009 and the scandal surrounding the Mid Staffordshire NHS Trust in the United Kingdom. The organisation Wikileaks was at the centre of a number of major international news leaks including the release of classified documents by US army private Bradley Manning (now called Chelsea Manning).

Edward Snowdon became perhaps the most notorious source of all, when he leaked hundreds of thousands of National Security Agency records to the journalists Laura Poitras and Glenn Greenwald. The documents revealed widespread international surveillance programmes. Chelsea Manning was prosecuted on multiple counts in the United States and is now serving a 35-year sentence. Edward Snowdon was granted asylum by the Russian government and is thought to be living in Moscow.

Men and women who release confidential information have some legal protection in the United Kingdom, in some circumstances, as do the journalists and publications that distribute the material. How much (if any) protection there is and how much it can genuinely shield the individual parties should be considered in depth before beginning work on a major story based on leaked information. This book is not intended to be an in-depth legal text, but here is a brief discussion of some of the issues raised by such stories.

The law covering the protection of sources in the United Kingdom is varied and complex. The overarching law, which protects both journalists and their sources, is Article 10 of the European Convention on Human Rights (Freedom of Expression). Through a number of rulings, judges in the court have clearly indicated that the article protects the anonymity of sources, unless there is an overriding requirement to reveal their identity, which is in the public interest. In 2014 the court provided a factsheet for journalists outlining the implications of the court's rulings.

In UK law, it is important to distinguish between someone who leaks information and the legal definition of a person who is a whistleblower. A leak is the release of confidential information without permission or consent. People leak information for a variety of reasons, but a whistleblower is defined for legal purposes as a worker who discloses wrongdoing in the public interest.

Employment law in the United Kingdom protects whistleblowers, as long as they meet certain legal criteria. Under The Public Interest Disclosure Act 1998 whistleblowers must be acting in the public interest. According to the UK Government Wesbsite (2015) the following areas are covered:

- A criminal offence, for example, a fraud, has been committed.
- Someone's health and safety is in danger.
- Risk or actual damage to the environment has been caused.
- A miscarriage of justice has occurred.
- The company is breaking the law, for example, when it doesn't have the right insurance.
- The whistleblower believes someone is covering up wrongdoing.

In order to be protected, the whistleblower should raise the issue with their employer or a relevant body prescribed by the government. The process is slightly different in Northern Ireland.

Journalists and news organisations are not prescribed bodies. The whistleblower may be protected, however, under the Public Interest Disclosure Act 1998 if they go to the media only in the most exceptional circumstances. They should reasonably believe they would be victimised if they contacted a prescribed organisation or regulating body. Or they should believe there would be a cover-up or evidence would be destroyed or concealed.

There is a further issue to consider when dealing with leaked material: The Official Secrets Acts. The two acts of 1911 and 1989 have very rarely been used in legal cases against journalists, but they have been used to prosecute the officials who supplied them with confidential information. There is no public interest defence in official secrets cases.

Sources who do not meet the legal definition of being whistleblowers have other protection in English law. In general, a person in authority may not request or demand that a journalist reveal the name of a source, however powerful or influential they might be. There are some exceptions. In common law, a judge has the right to demand the name of a journalist's source. A senior official, such as the chairman of an enquiry or tribunal may also be able to do this. The police and security services also have the right to request details of a journalist's sources.

Some authorities may also approach a judge for permission to search premises to secure information and until recently they usually required a judge's permission to do this. With the introduction of the Regulation of Investigatory Powers Act 2000, known as RIPA, this requirement to contact a judge changed. The police and security services still need a judge's permission to access the content of communications, but investigators only need the permission of a senior member of staff to access the basic data; such as the date calls were made or the phone numbers of people called. This has become one of the most hotly debated topics in journalism practice. The implementation of the powers given in the act is overseen by the Interception of Communications Commissioner's Office and there is an ongoing and heated debate between the office and various publications and campaign groups. In addition, the Conservative government elected in May 2015 is reportedly seeking to extend the powers given to security services to monitor and intercept communications data.

Any protection provided by the UK law is irrelevant in an international context. While a UK court might decide the leaking of information is in the public interest a court in the United States might decide the actions of the source could prove a serious challenge to national security. Added to this, is the possibility that police and security forces in any part of the globe may be able to intercept or monitor a journalists' communication with their source. The international nature of many important stories and the ability of governments to act across national boundaries in the unregulated digital environment, make it incredibly difficult for a journalist to anticipate any action that may be taken against them and protect themselves, if necessary.

A journalist must also consider the implications when they approach the subject of their story for a response. This is particularly relevant for broadcasters. The IPSO code only requires a right of reply when there are inaccuracies in a piece of journalism. There is no specific guidance in the Ofcom Code to cover the use of anonymous sources or whistleblowers. Section Seven: Fairness and Section Eight: Privacy both contain relevant information. There is one aspect of the code, which is important when researching such stories. According to Section Seven 'If a programme alleges wrongdoing or incompetence or makes other significant allegations, those concerned should normally be given an appropriate and timely opportunity to respond' (2015). While it is clearly good journalism to secure a response from any organisation or individual criticised in a story sourced from the evidence of a whistleblower, this regulatory requirement can pose a problem, in that contacting an organisation will given them prior notification of a controversial story and may allow them time to take preventative legal action.

In contrast to the legal issues posed, journalists face difficult ethical decisions when dealing with sources on a personal level. Few sources in high-profile cases would say their decision to leak information was an easy one. For many, losing their job is just the start of the problems they face as a result of their disclosure. Deciding how much to discuss the implications of publishing leaked material and/or revealing the identity of a source pose some complex ethical choices. Giving a source a blow-by-blow prediction of the problems their disclosure may bring them and their family could dissuade them from passing on their story and doing significant public good. Equally, not warning them about the possible implications of your story could be very unfair. There is a reputable organisation called Whistleblowers UK, which serves as an advocacy group for whistleblowers in the United Kingdom and provides free legal advice and a useful website.

Having read all this, it would be reasonable (and wise) to think this is a complex and difficult area with a profusion of legal subtleties to consider. For most journalists, the decision to use leaked material or publish the allegations of a whistleblower will require considerable thought, discussion and careful research and planning. For new journalists, the importance of seeking advice and guidance both from a more senior journalist and, where relevant, a lawyer cannot be stressed enough.

Remember:

- Protecting your sources is a fundamental professional requirement.
- If a source speaks 'off the record' check what they mean and respect their wishes.
- Paying for information can distort editorial decision-making.
- Whistleblowers have very limited protection when speaking to journalists.
- When dealing with a major leak ensure you and your source have considered the risks and legal implications.
- Controversial stories need editorial support and good legal advice.

Sources and digital security

The days of meeting sources in public places or holding whispered telephone conversations are long gone. Whatever the debate surrounding the powers of the police and security services, they have more and easier access to communication data than ever before. An official investigator may not be able to directly establish the identity of a source, or access what they tell a journalist without the direct permission of a judge, but they may well be able to find out the phone number or social network used by the source, how often they spoke to the reporter, when they spoke and where. This 'metadata' is more than enough to allow the investigator to establish a source's identity. If journalists want to protect their sources they need to understand communications technology and how to protect that vital metadata.

What this means for a new journalist is that it is very important indeed to be aware of the issues raised by secure communication. Before starting on a controversial investigation, get advice from experts and implement a security policy. Don't promise sources you can keep their identity secret. They have to be as committed as you are to communicating securely and human beings make mistakes. Bear in mind that you might have to maintain a security plan for months or even years.

Meeting in person

When meeting a source in person, it's wise to make a secure travel plan. The measures you take will depend on the content of the story. One of the most powerful tools for those wanting to track a journalist's location, is the reporter's mobile phone. Location data provided by mobile phones can help to pinpoint where you are at pretty much any time of day. One simple way to make it harder for someone to find out where you have met a source is to leave your phone at the office and advise your source to do the same. Consider the presence of CCTV cameras and remember the United Kingdom also has a network of automated number plate recognition cameras. The data from these cameras is stored in the National Automatic Number Plate Recognition Data Centre for two years. There are regulations that restrict who can see this data and when it may be accessed, but if you travel to meet a source by car, there is clearly a possibility that your route could be tracked or accessed using this data. Avoid visiting websites to plan routes online or buying tickets for transport online, as your actions can be tracked. Equally don't use your credit or debit card to buy tickets or pay for coffee en route. Ensure you take enough cash.

Online and storage security

Before a source approaches a journalist, they may already have accessed confidential information or used digital communications in an insecure way. The journalist can't be held responsible for this, but ethically they should do all they can to help the source avoid detection. Given the vast number of uncontrollable variables involved in keeping communications secure, it's really important that you don't make unrealistic promises to your sources.

When speaking to key sources online many journalists also use the open source Tor network (see Chapter 3). It is also possible to use commercial encryption software. Speaking to journalism.co.uk in 2013, investigative reporter James Ball said it was better to use open source software rather than buying a commercial encryption programme:

> Commercial platforms may be in a position where they have voluntarily or been compelled to make deals to create 'back doors' and you will not be in a position to know . . . open source security software has vulnerabilities, but it's a lot harder for these conscious back doors to exist.

When using encryption software, it is important to remember that it may be illegal in some countries.

Data and documents can also be shared more securely through encrypted networks, but remember don't then discuss this material with colleagues on the office email system! If you're planning on storing large quantities of confidential material, you may need to buy and set-up a specific secure piece of computer hardware, but making such storage is totally secure is pretty much impossible.

One golden rule to consider: no conversation or material shared on social media is EVER secure.

Detection tools

There are some detection tools, which can help you to establish whether there is any commercial surveillance spyware on your computer. Detekt is a particularly useful tool, which has been developed specifically with journalists and other free data campaigners in mind. It can be used to check your computer for some surveillance software.

Taking solid security precautions is hard and takes time; however, it's not an excuse for behaving recklessly with a source's information and exposing them to unnecessary risk. In the vast majority of cases, basic security measures consistently applied will provide a reasonable level of protection.

Remember:

- Keep up to date with basic security and surveillance issues.
- Do your utmost to protect a source, but don't make unrealistic promises.
- Ensure your source understands the risks and takes their own security measures.
- If your source contacts you by an insecure means, change to secure communication as quickly as you can.
- When meeting your source in person make a secure travel plan and ensure they do the same.
- Review your digital security procedures before starting a major investigation.
- If you need to, get professional advice.

Undercover research

Of the many hundreds of journalists employed across the United Kingdom today, only a very few will ever work undercover. The decision to hide your identity and immerse yourself in a story poses a host of challenges, legal, ethical and in personal security. An undercover report may only take a few hours as the journalists goes into a shop to buy an illegal product, or may take many years. Some journalists make a career out of undercover investigations, such as award winning British newspaper reporter Mazer Mahmood, known popularly as 'The Fake Sheikh'. Others may spend just a few days working undercover, when appropriate, on a specific report.

With the public outrage and extreme publicity surrounding the Phone Hacking Scandal, the journalistic environment has changed in the early part of the twenty-first century. Journalists are under more scrutiny and there is more public questioning of their methods; both of their justification and ethics. There is a fine line to be drawn between undercover reporting and entrapment and that line will be drawn at different points depending on the news organisation involved.

Clause 10 of the IPSO Code says: 'Engaging in misrepresentation or subterfuge, including by agents or intermediaries, can generally be justified only in the public interest and then only when the material cannot be obtained by other means'. This forms a good basic ethical test for undercover assignments. If this is the only possible way to expose wrongdoing or secure vital information and that material is in the public interest, then the use of subterfuge can be defended. How this works in practice can be more complex. As in law, what constitutes public interest can be difficult to establish and at the time of writing IPSO is a relatively new regulatory body, which has made a limited number of rulings. Ofcom requires similar standards in Section 7.14 of its code, which stipulates that contributors to broadcasts must not be deceived, unless it is in the public interest.

Channel Four (2015) provides some particularly useful advice in its Producers' Handbook. It points out that any undercover filming or reporting may well form evidence in a future 'criminal prosecution, in a libel or privacy action or in an Ofcom investigation'. Considering the possibility that you as a journalist may have to defend your work under this kind of scrutiny can help to focus the decision-making process. The website goes on to advise: 'The way in which the footage is obtained must not, therefore, be open to criticism as to its authenticity or for the methods used to obtain it'. Increasingly the media itself reports and debates the process used to secure undercover material and without a clear defence the journalistic process can become the story, rather than the report itself.

Most organisations have strict procedures for approving and planning undercover reporting. This would usually require the approval of a senior member of the editorial staff. Having decided that undercover work is justified, meticulous planning is needed, with a detailed risk assessment. If you are working as a freelance reporter you may want to consider the ethical and regulatory requirements of any publication that might buy your work. You don't want to go to the trouble of producing a complex undercover report, when it may not be acceptable for anyone to publish or broadcast. It's natural for new journalists to be keen to undertake difficult and challenging assignments, but it should always be asked whether the risk taken could be justified by the expected output.

After an assignment has been completed, further editorial decisions are needed. Does the undercover work provide the information required? Does it breach any laws or regulatory requirements? The BBC's Editorial Guidelines require two stages of approval. They advise journalists that undercover reporting may well be a valid research method, but that does not justify the publication of the material: 'Secret recording can lead to an infringement of privacy when it is broadcast with identifiable individuals. However, the actual recording of the material can also be intrusive, regardless of whether or not it is broadcast'.

Even if your plan to work undercover satisfies all the legal and regulatory requirements, it's important to consider the plan from an ethical standpoint. There is little point carrying out an investigation, which appears unjustified or alienates your audience. The wrongdoing to be uncovered must seem worthy of your drastic action and the logic behind the investigation must be explained clearly and transparently. As Stephanie Chernow says in an article for the Ethical Journalism Network (2014) 'In the end it is the audience that must decide whether the action was appropriate, but in order to do that, they have to be informed that it has happened in the first place'.

Remember:

- Working undercover poses legal, regulatory and ethical challenges.
- Undercover recording may be an invasion of privacy, even if it is for research purposes only.
- Refer to your employer's editorial guidelines before starting work.
- Conduct a thorough risk assessment.
- Review your work before publication/broadcast. Can it still be justified?
- Remember you may need to defend your subterfuge in court.
- Be transparent with your audience, explain why you went undercover and how.

Making mistakes

One of the hardest aspects for a journalist to cope with is when we make mistakes. This happens because we are human beings dealing with other human beings and sometimes there are misunderstandings or things simply go wrong. Journalism is a very public profession and a mistake can be very visible and embarrassing. If as a researcher, you make a mistake, then what should you do about it?

Small errors happen all the time. Generally they don't lead to an incorrect copy or an inaccurate broadcast. If necessary own up to your error in the newsroom or office, apologise to anyone who was affected and do your best to ensure it doesn't happen again. In some newsrooms there can be shouting or aggressive behaviour when someone makes a mistake, but this is becoming less common. Obviously if you are concerned you may have been bullied then you should follow your employer's procedures to deal with this. It's easy to dwell on errors, but this can often lead to more mistakes. The best way to detract from a small mistake is to correct it where possible and go on to produce much more good work.

On rare occasions a serious error may be published or go on air. Clearly anything that breaks the law should be dealt with immediately, with the advice of a lawyer. It's important not to rush into broadcasting or printing a correction, which may run the risk of repeating any offence. In other cases, the print and broadcast industries' regulatory bodies have guidelines for correcting mistakes. Clause 1 in the IPSO Code of Practice requires that 'A significant inaccuracy, misleading statement or distortion once recognised must be corrected, promptly and with due prominence, and where appropriate an apology published. In cases involving the Regulator, prominence should be agreed with the Regulator in advance'. Section 5 of the Ofcom Code advises, 'Significant mistakes in news should normally be acknowledged and corrected on air quickly. Corrections should be appropriately scheduled'.

Web copy can be corrected online, so that the original error no longer appears, although there is a possibility that any cached copy of the page may still contain the mistake. Every web publisher has a slightly different approach to correcting errors online, but there is a growing consistency in good practice. In general, minor typos and spelling errors should just be corrected. Any significant factual error should be corrected and a note clearly added to explain the change. There can be an issue when doing this in larger organisations with apportioning blame. A reporter's name may be on an article, when the error may have occurred during subbing or another part of the production process. Ideally the correction should make this clear without being too complicated. The founder of the blog 'Regret the Error', Craig Silverman, believes the public's faith in journalism is bolstered by well-made corrections. Speaking to Poynter.org in 2007 he argued that keeping good records can also help to avoid future errors.

> Store the error in a database that captures where it occurred, how it occurred, and who discovered it. Then use that data as the basis for a prevention programme. And if a reader or other outside party brought that error to the organisation's attention, they should be thanked.

Things to do

Build your contacts

Focusing on an area of journalism, which particularly interests you, such as celebrity or environmental journalism, put a call out on your own social media networks for potential contacts. Ask friends, relatives and workmates if they can help you build your contacts book, by introducing you to possible sources.

Find three universities that are relevant to your patch or beat. They may be local to your area or have particular specialisms. Familiarise yourself with their media pages. Do they have a searchable database of expertise? Ring and introduce yourself to the public relations team.

Practise your research

Research some of the technology that may help with undercover reporting in your chosen journalistic field. Take a look at the work of other journalists online and get advice from tutors or more senior staff at work. If you are able to access some of the technology, familiarise yourself with the basics and practise recording or filming discretely. Remember to follow the law and any relevant ethical or regulatory guidelines.

Research in action

Undertake your own undercover investigation. Don't be too ambitious or put yourself in danger. Consider a simple report on a company's customer service standards or a product review. Ensure you get the full permission of a tutor or senior member of staff at work. If possible use some of the technology you already tested.

Issues to discuss

Many journalists have been extremely vocal about UK government attempts to increase digital surveillance. Where do you think the balance should lie between national security and privacy?

Under what circumstances (if any) might you be prepared to reveal the identity of a source? At what point does human interest override a source's right to anonymity? Would revealing the identity of a source under some circumstances irreparably damage your journalistic reputation?

All journalists make mistakes. Aside from those, which break the law, which errors do you think are most serious? What measures do you take to check your journalistic work? How do you think online publishers should correct mistakes?

Places to learn more

Books and journals

Carlson, M. and Franklin, B. 2013. *Journalists, Sources, and Credibility: New Perspectives*. London: Routledge.

Dix, R. and Slade, M. 2014. *Protect Your Tech: Your Geek-free Guide to a Secure and Private Digital Life*. Kindle and Create Space.

Greenwald, G. 2014. *No Place to Hide. Edward Snowden, the NSA and the Surveillance State*. London: Hamish Hamilton.

Kroeger, B. 2014. *Undercover Reporting: The Truth About Deception Illinois*. Evanston, IL: Northwestern University Press.

Lashmar, P. 2013. Urinal or conduit? Institutional information flow between the UK intelligence services and the news media. *Journalism*. 14 (8) 1024–1040.

Silverman, C. 2009. *Regret the Error: How Media Mistakes Pollute the Press and Imperil Free Speech*. New York, NY: Union Square Press.

Online resources

Case Study Link	www.Casestudylink.co.uk
Detekt Security Tool	https://resistsurveillance.org
European Court of Human Rights Factsheet: Protection of Journalistic Sources	www.echr.coe.int/Documents/ FS_Journalistic_sources_ENG.pdf
The Future of Investigative Journalism (House of Lords Report)	www.publications.parliament.uk/pa/ ld201012/ldselect/ldcomuni/256/256.pdf
Information Security for Journalists.	http://files.gendo.nl/Books/InfoSec_ for_Journalists_V1.1.pdf London, CIJ.
IPSO Editors' Code of Practice	www.ipso.co.uk/IPSO/cop.html
NUJ Conference – Protecting Journalists and their Sources	www.nuj.org.uk/campaigns/safeguarding- journalists-and-their-sources/
OFCOM Broadcasting Code	http://stakeholders.ofcom.org.uk/broadcasting/ broadcast-codes/broadcast-code/
Prescribed Person List for Whistleblowers (UK Goverement)	www.gov.uk/government/uploads/system/ uploads/attachment_data/file/404330/ bis-15–43-blowing-the-whistle-to-a- prescribed-person-list-of-prescribed.pdf
Response Source	www.responsesource.co.uk
Rory Peck Trust	http://low.rorypecktrust.org
UNESCO Report – Building Digital Safety for Journalism	http://unesdoc.unesco.org/images/0023/ 002323/232358e.pdf
Whistleblowers UK	www.wbuk.org

References

BBC Today [Radio Programme] BBC Radio Four. 27 June 2015. 08:10.

Bradshaw, P. 2012. *Soft Skills: Can you make a 'born journalist'?* [online]. Birmingham, UK: Online Journalism Blog. Available from: http://onlinejournalismblog.com/2012/02/15/soft-skills-can-you-make-a-born-journalist/#more-15813 [accessed 18 June 2015].

Campbell, M. 2011. *If Ofcom shines a light on BBC news, it should wake up Today* [online]. London: The Guardian. Available from: www.theguardian.com/media/organgrinder/2011/jul/03/ofcom-bbc-news-impartiality [accessed 9 June 2015].

Channel Four. 2015. *Secret Filming Handbook* [online]. London: Channel Four Producers' Guidelines. Available from: www.channel4.com/producers-handbook/c4-guidelines/secret-filming-guidelines [accessed 9 June 2015].

Chernow, S. 2014. *The ethics of undercover journalism: Where the police and journalists divide* [online]. London: Ethical Journalism Network. Available from: http://ethicaljournalismnetwork.org/en/contents/the-ethics-of-undercover-journalism-where-the-police-and-journalists-divide [accessed 9 June 2015].

Greenslade, R. 2013. *Why speaking to journalists 'off the record' doesn't guarantee anonymity* [online]. London: The Guardian. Available from: www.theguardian.com/media/greenslade/2013/may/20/thetimes-dailytelegraph [accessed 19 May 2015].

House of Commons Science and Technology Committee. 2013. *Communicating Climate Science* [online]. London: The Stationery Office Ltd. Available from: www.publications.parliament.uk/pa/cm201314/cmselect/cmsctech/254/254.pdf [accessed 19 May 2015].

Human Rights Act. 1998. Available from: www.legislation.gov.uk/ukpga/1998/42/contents [accessed 8 June 2015].

IPSO. 2015. *Editors' code of practice* [online]. London: IPSO. Available from: www.ipso.co.uk/IPSO/cop.html [accessed 19 May 2015].

Marshall, S. 2013. *Protecting journalist sources: Lessons in communicating securely* [online]. London: journalism.co.uk. Available from: www.journalism.co.uk/news/protecting-journalist-sources-lessons-in-communicating-securely/s2/a553653/ [accessed 9 June 2015].

OFCOM. 2013. *The ofcom broadcasting code* [online]. London: Ofcom. Available from: http://stakeholders.ofcom.org.uk/broadcasting/broadcast-codes/broadcast-code/ [accessed 20 May 2015].

Regulation of Investigatory Power Act. 2000. Available from: http://www.legislation.gov.uk/ukpga/2000/23/contents [accessed 9 June 2015].

Rory Peck Trust. 2013. *Risk assessment notes* [online]. Available from: http://low.rorypecktrust.org/Resources [accessed 9 June 2015].

Rusbridger, A. 2014. *NUJ Conference: Journalism in the age of mass surveillance* [video, online]. Available from: www.nuj.org.uk/campaigns/safeguarding-journalists-and-their-sources/ [accessed 9 June 2015].

Scanlan, C. 2007. *We stand corrected: When good journalists make stupid mistakes* [online]. St Petersburg, FL: Poynter.org. Available from: www.poynter.org/news/media-innovation/85908/we-stand-corrected-when-good-journalists-make-stupid-mistakes/ [accessed 7 June 2015].

UK Government. 2015. *Whistleblowing for Employees* [online]. London: www.gov.uk. Available from: www.gov.uk/whistleblowing [accessed 20 May 2015].

Winegarner, B. 2012. *5 ways journalists can overcome shyness during interviews* [online]. St Petersburg, FL: Poynter.org. Available from: www.poynter.org/how-tos/writing/170873/5-ways-journalists-can-overcome-shyness-during-interviews/ [accessed 29 June 2015].

Where not referenced, quotations are from interviews, emails or social media conversations with the author.

7 Interviews

Introduction

A journalist will speak to many people in the course of their career. Only a very few roles, such as reviewing or writing opinion pieces, will allow a journalist to avoid doing interviews.

In their broadest sense, interviews fall into two basic forms: those that are meant to get practical information about a subject and those that are meant to elicit a person's thoughts or feelings. Whichever interview you are doing you need to prepare in advance, build a relationship with your interviewee, ask the right questions and then listen and respond. The amount of preparation and research you need to do in advance of an interview can be easily underestimated. It generally takes far longer than doing the interview itself.

Interview skills seem straightforward when written down and yet learning to be a confident and successful interviewer can be complex and time-consuming. It's as much an art form as a skill. This chapter focuses on the nuts and bolts of researching and preparing for interviews: different types, ways to prepare and some different approaches, but none of this can be substituted for plenty of practice.

This chapter covers:

- Different forms of interview
- Doorstepping and death knocks
- Interviewing vulnerable people
- Planning an interview
- Writing the questions
- Managing your interviewee
- Planning a court case

Different forms of interview

Research interview

The research interview is an informal interview, often carried out over the phone prior to conducting a more focused interview with a source. There is not always time to do a research interview, and they are often more appropriate for long-form journalism or broadcast interviews, but they are a great way to calm nerves on both sides and ensure the interview itself is well focused and covers the most relevant and interesting material. In broadcast newsrooms, a researcher or production journalist may carry out these preparatory interviews in order to write a brief for a reporter or presenter.

Most basic news interviews can be carried out without much preparation, especially if you're only looking for a few quotes over the phone. If you're planning to speak to someone in person for a longer piece, you should try to do a research interview in advance, although this can be easier said than done. It's often such a relief to get someone to talk to you that it seems an imposition to ask them to speak to you twice, but a good research interview is as important for your contact as it is for you. It can help the interviewer and interviewee gather their thoughts and choose the most salient points. This is the chance to ask all the basic 'where, what, why, when and how questions'. This information can be used to form the basis of your story and decide how to frame your main interview questions.

A research interview serves another purpose. It allows you to make the most of your formal interview time. New journalists often start their first few interviews with questions such as: 'Tell me all about your new project' or 'Tell me about what you're doing here'. These questions rarely get good answers and can make you seem unprepared. A research interview allows you to explore every possible line of discussion and gauge where your interviewee is hoping to lead the conversation. If your interviewee is an expert who is providing valuable background information and context, of course you want to follow their lead and cover the material they consider to be most relevant. In contrast, if your interviewee is a figure of authority, you may well wish to challenge them and move the interview away from the subject matter they consider to be safe.

Key player

These are often the first interviews conducted when writing about a breaking or developing news story. They are your primary sources, who provide the backbone of your story. For news reporters, they are often police officers, emergency service workers, eyewitnesses and victims of accidents or crime.

There may be little time to prepare for these interviews, and this is when even the most experienced journalist will resort to using the basic factual questions 'Who, what, when, where, why and how'. If you're under pressure in difficult circumstances, jot these questions down in your notebook to ensure you don't miss any of the basics. We've all walked away from an interview and realised we've forgotten something important, so always ask at the end whether you can take contact details of the interviewee. That way if you have missed anything or come up with other questions later in the day, you can call or email. If you get time, it's always wise to explore a story further where possible. As with all journalistic work, the more rapport you can build up with an interviewee, the more information you are likely to gain from them.

Increasingly, your first contact with a key player in a breaking news story will be at a news conference. It's always a difficult challenge deciding which questions to ask at a news conference. Unless you're quick off the mark, many of the most obvious questions are asked early and you may be left unprepared. It's good practice to listen to other journalists' questions. If they are following a specific line of questioning or are focussing on a specific topic, this may be something important that you can follow yourself. Broadcast journalists are often given the opportunity to record an interview after the main news conference. TV and radio reporters sometimes find print journalists will hang around to listen to their interview or even record what they're saying. There's no shame in giving them an opportunity to ask a question at the end. It may help you to cover an area you hadn't considered or get a better soundbite. There is more information on news conferences in Chapter 2.

Eyewitness

Eyewitness interviews are as varied as the stories that bring them about. Some will be straightforward and enjoyable, such as an elderly woman who has waited many hours to see the Queen in her hometown or an excited child who has witnessed his first New Year's Eve firework display. Some eyewitness interviews can be very practical in nature or be somewhat separated from the action, such as the person who saw a getaway car but didn't realise until later or someone who heard a bomb go off but didn't see any of the resulting damage. Sometimes though, the reporter might be speaking to someone who has experienced a horrific or traumatic experience and could well be suffering from shock or even physical injuries.

When dealing with straightforward eyewitness accounts it's important to listen and give the interviewee the chance to work through their recollections in detail. Sometimes, it can help to ask the same question twice, to allow the person to remember more clearly. As police officers will often tell you, witnesses sometimes see key parts of a story without realising their significance. Yet again, the more understanding, friendly and patient you are, the better the material you will secure. Even if you have watched another journalist interview a witness, do go ahead and do your own interview too. You may ask a more relevant question or have a manner, which elicits a more frank answer.

When speaking to eyewitnesses, it's always important to remember that memory plays tricks. One of the most high-profile cases of eyewitness error was that of the shooting of the Brazilian man Jean Charles de Menezes who was killed by police at Stockwell Tube station shortly after the 7/7 bombings in London. Eyewitnesses told journalists that the young man had vaulted over the ticket barrier and run from police. They also claimed he was wearing a bulky jacket which might have concealed an explosive device or gun. Closed circuit television footage and photographs subsequently showed this information was incorrect. Much has been written about these errors, but it's clear that people under stress can sometimes misremember events. They may embellish their accounts with information heard from other witnesses and even material from the media. Some may also be tempted to enhance their stories to satisfy you. Their stories are truthful in their own eyes, but it's not always possible to treat them as fact until they are corroborated or proven. Eyewitness material should always be attributed.

When dealing with the most difficult and distressing interviews, print and broadcast journalists are required to follow their relevant code of practice. The wording of the Ofcom and IPSO codes requires that people in distress should not be put under pressure and that they should be treated with sympathy and discretion. This advice makes perfect sense on paper, but can be very hard indeed to put into practice. Journalists themselves are under intense pressure when dealing with difficult breaking stories and so may sometimes behave in ways they would not do in ordinary life. For more advice, take a look at the section on working with vulnerable people, later in this chapter.

Expert

Once you've established the basic facts of a story and spoken to the main people involved, the next challenge is to delve deeper. As most of the basic factual information is easily available to your audience on social media networks, these interviews provide the first opportunity for a professional journalist to provide the 'added value' that makes their work important. Expert interviews are often seen or heard on rolling broadcast news networks and provide the kind of in-depth analysis seen in the broadsheet newspapers.

An expert interview requires considerable preparation and a solid research interview can be extremely valuable. A good expert interviewee should be able to explain why something might have happened (or give a variety of possible reasons), outline the context to an event (What were the circumstances that allowed this to happen? How frequent are events like this? Might it happen again?) And perhaps most importantly allow the reader or viewer to understand why these events might be important to them. Not all expert interviewees will be able to answer all these questions, and you may need to speak to more than one person.

One of the biggest challenges when speaking to expert interviewees is the depth and complexity of their knowledge. They may often know far more than the average reader or listener can take in, and some experts may find it hard to edit out the key points. Again, a research interview may help you to work with them to tease out the most interesting or valuable points to make. You may also need to be firm and explain that you have an overview of the entire story and need to focus on one particular aspect or area. Even if your interviewee is more experienced and knowledgeable than you, you still understand how you intend to present your material and also have a better understanding of what your reader or viewer wants to know. Their answers may be too complex for some audiences, but equally they may be too simplified for others. It's your job to ensure the interviewee understands who they're speaking to and what will be important and understandable to them.

Case study

We've already discussed in Chapter 6 how hard it can be to track down good case study (or character) interviews. As with speaking to an expert, a case study interview requires good preparation. It may have taken some time to find the best contributor and persuade them to speak and so empathy and patience will also be needed to get the best responses. It may be worthwhile sharing some information in advance with the interviewee about why and how they may be featured in your report. It can often help them to marshal their thoughts and express their ideas in advance.

Many interviews like this will be conducted at home or work, but one technique that can get great material is to take someone to a location that's relevant to your story. Video journalists often do this to make their pictures more interesting, but it can work well for other reporters. For example, you might ask a parent who has chosen a private school for their child to show you their local state school and explain why they feel it was not suitable for their youngster. Someone who has had a gender reassignment operation may be able to speak with more passion and clarity if they are outside the hospital where the operation took place. Of course, this can only be done where there is enough time, and the journalist must consider any ethical issues; in particular any distress caused to the interviewee.

People will often share more information with reporters who show empathy and an interest in their experiences. There is however a line to draw between remaining professional and becoming too involved in someone's life. Every reporter will draw this line in a different place, and with the growth of advocacy journalism (sometimes known as the journalism of attachment), some journalists and commentators argue that it's more honest for a journalist to express sympathy and in some cases get involved in the lives of those they feature in their reports. In practice, this decision remains a personal one for the journalist involved, under the guidance of their editor.

Confrontational

When asked to name the 'best' journalistic interviewers, the public will often pick out the names of the most dogged and confrontational interrogators. Broadcast journalists such as Jeremy Paxman and John Humphrys have become famous for this type of work, and the set-piece political interview remains a highlight of many news programmes, but this approach must be carefully planned and justified in the eyes of the audience. Tough, unrelenting questioning provides great copy and some excellent television and radio, but it doesn't always reveal much information.

In 1997 Jeremy Paxman became notorious for asking the Conservative politician Michael Howard the same question twelve times. He told Cambridge University's *Varsity Magazine* (2015) his approach stems from a commitment to the audience:

> I think a journalist's job is to ask questions, and, if you ask questions, you should get an answer ... The only difference between a journalist and everyone else is one of opportunity. If you have that opportunity, you owe it to your viewers to get an answer.

Despite the focus on one or two specific issues, this type of interview still requires research and preparation. You need to be sure the question you are preparing to hammer home is the right one that gets to the very heart of the issue in question. There would have been little point in Jeremy Paxman challenging Michael Howard to answer the question 'Did you threaten to overrule him' if he was not entirely sure that this point was at the very heart of the matter in question.

Choosing to tackle the wrong person too aggressively can leave the journalist looking like a bully and let the interviewee off the hook. As Newsnight presenter Evan Davies explained in 2013, tough questioning can genuinely be unjust:

> I think adversarial interviews are unfair when politicians have difficult decisions to make. I think sometimes it can sound like you are blaming them for the fact that they have to make a difficult decision. We live in a second-best world and you need to be careful about that.

There are a number of other ways to tackle such confrontational interviews and it's not always about being forceful and repetitive.

- *Don't bother!*

  This might sound very poor advice, but it is the growing belief of some journalists that there is little point in challenging politicians or senior figures who have no intention of answering difficult questions. They are often given professional 'media training', which makes them experts at diverting tough questions. The methods they use vary from the very inept to those so clever they can appear incredibly frank and open without sharing a single relevant fact. Often, the time given to conduct an interview and the circumstances available may be so carefully stage-managed, it's almost impossible to break through the façade and learn anything new or revealing. This is not to say that you should give these interviewees an easy time, but you may choose simply to flag up an unanswered question and move on or simply accept that sometimes a journalist can do nothing better than report whatever they're given.

- *Be friendly*

  In some respects it's far harder to deflect a friendly, chatty interviewer than an aggressive one. Cheerful good nature and a few jokes may even be enough to put the less experienced interviewee off guard. A better-trained subject probably won't fall for your charming smile, but they will still have to avoid being too dogmatic, or they may come across as being rude and unsympathetic. Some of the best interviewers use these tactics to great effect. They may challenge an interviewee without them even noticing; lull them into a false sense of security and finish with a killer question. This can work particularly well for print journalists who may have time to develop more of a rapport and is suitable for broadcasters whose audience may be expecting a more familiar, natural approach. The danger of this interview approach is that you may come across as being weak or even badly prepared.

- *Be strategic*

  A good tactical interview requires some time and planning. All good interviews should have a point, but in this case, you need a clear idea of where you want to lead the interviewee, and at what point you hope to challenge them. You will need to do significant background reading to find an inconsistency in their opinion or an incident when they have acted in direct contradiction to their policies or stated beliefs. You must also be confident that you know how they will answer most of your questions, as this will allow you to direct the questioning to where you intend to expose this error or inconsistency. The BBC's Stephen Sackur conducts long-form interviews on the programme HardTalk. During an interview on the BBC College of Journalism Website (2013), he advised: 'It is hugely important to think through, not just the beginning of the interview, but think through where you want it to end up.'

Celebrity interviews

Celebrity interviews have a style and an approach all of their own. In the modern age of journalism, most are little more than an exercise in public relations; it takes an interviewer of unique skill to draw out something new or revealing. Celebrity encounters tend to come in a number of set forms.

- *The profile*

  There are two kinds of celebrity profile interview. The first is a genuine interview that the journalist has arranged at their own expense and will include a series of well-researched and revealing questions. The second is organised by the celebrity's publicity team to promote an event or product. These may appear the same to the audience, but in the second case, the reporter will be under considerable pressure to produce a favourable piece of journalism. Any scandal or negative material will be carefully planned with the publicity team to ensure the interview is worthwhile and achieves the required number of column inches. The first interview will be researched and planned much as any other (there is plenty of advice further in this chapter). The second is very much a contract between the celebrity and the journalist. Interviews like this fill the pages of glossy celebrity magazines.

- *Press junket*

  This is a common type of celebrity interview. It is generally organised by a public relations or marketing team to promote a film or other media product. The leading actors, director and other key players in the film production will gather in a hotel and journalists will be herded in and out of rooms to speak to them for a few minutes. Each interviewee will have spoken to dozens of reporters; faced the same questions over and over again and will probably be accompanied by a publicist. If a celebrity interview has a poster in the background, then it's probably from a junket. US entertainment journalist Gary Sussman (2001) says:

  It is easy . . . for journalists to be cowed into submission. There's always an army of publicists hovering over our shoulders . . . if you ask the star about his ex-wife, he'll walk out, and you'll have ruined the interview for yourself and your colleagues; or worse, you'll be blackballed.

- *Down the line*

  Radio journalists may be offered a so-called 'down-the-line' interview. The celebrity will sit in a radio studio at the end of a high quality telephone line, and the journalist will interview them at an agreed time. These are the kind of celebrity interviews often heard on radio news magazine programmes. They are generally longer than a junket interview and can be more personal, but it takes a talented celebrity and interviewer to make them sound genuinely natural and friendly. Similar interviews will be offered to print journalists, although these will more likely be on the telephone. A little extra preparation for an interview like this may be worthwhile as you can develop some original and interesting questions, which may entertain or energise a very bored interviewee.

- *Celebrity news conference*

  Celebrity publicists will sometimes organise a news conference to launch a film or book. A news conference can be a sign the production didn't go well, and there's a need to get the interviews over swiftly, or equally that it's gone incredibly well, and there are far too many interested journalists to organise a junket. A celebrity news conference is not like a normal news conference. The journalist again faces the danger that any difficult questions might bring the event to an early end and attract the ire of the other reporters. Equally, a star who loses their cool and storms out can make great copy. Publicists generally know the reporters they can trust to ask positive questions, and they will often be chosen from the audience to speak.

  The culture of modern celebrity journalism raises a number of ethical challenges. When your audience is fascinated, or obsessed with a current celebrity, it can be very hard indeed to challenge their public relations team and risk losing coverage for your publication. Some journalists and newspapers insist on paying for their travel and accommodation in order to maintain their independence, but often in reality they are under the same pressures as the other reporters. They will have to write broadly positive stories to ensure access to the celebrities in future. It's most likely the case that the readers of these interviews understand the surrounding circumstances and enjoy the glamour and image presented. The manicured and controlled world of the official celebrity interview has also created the journalistic world of celebrity gossip. One could not exist without the other, and both fill millions of Internet pages and employ thousands of journalists.

Sport interviews

Sports journalists face many similar challenges when interviewing sportsmen and women. Aspiring athletes or those in less popular sports may be keen to do genuinely open interviews, but those in high-profile sports will often have the same publicity entourage as major celebrities. Most sportsmen and women are generally happy to talk about their sports and will respond well to a journalist who is well briefed and prepared to ask knowledgeable questions. This is a good way to start an interview, which may move on to more personal material later on.

The 'post match' news conference is generally open to most media outlets, and it tends to focus on the practicalities of a match or contest, but there has been an increasing trend for reporters who ask more controversial questions to be banned from these conferences, and as with celebrity interviews, this encourages more anodyne questions. More worryingly for professional journalists, large football clubs now have their own television stations and online media content and have less need to promote their work through the traditional media. Local newspapers have been barred altogether from interviews and even matches for writing critical copy or failing to 'support' their local team.

In general, it would be fair to say that wherever there are large sums of money involved or reputations to be lost, the desire to control the media will become ever stronger. This has made it doubly difficult for journalists, when it's easy for organisations to bypass traditional media and publish their own content directly online. How much you choose to challenge this will depend very much on your own view of your journalistic role and that of your employer.

Remember:

- If you have time, do a research interview.
- Make sure you take an interviewee's contact details, in case you've forgotten anything.
- Treat interviewees in traumatic circumstances with the utmost respect and sensitivity.
- Expert and confrontational interviews need extensive planning.
- Celebrity interviews are rarely what they seem!

Doorstepping and death knocks

Doorstepping

These two very challenging forms of interview are generally the preserve of the news journalist. Doorstepping is an interview secured by knocking on someone's door or waiting outside a building such as a place of work or police station. It can be anything from knocking to ask for an eyewitness account of a robbery or road accident to a large media scrum outside a politician's house. People at the heart of a large news story can often face a road packed with satellite trucks and cameras, as reporters wait outside their homes for developments.

It is very important before starting to doorstep potential interviewees that you familiarise yourself with your employer's policy on approaching people in their homes or places of work.

These will differ dramatically. The BBC's Editorial Guidelines acknowledge that doorstepping is an infringement of privacy and should 'normally be a last resort.' They advise however, that when a figure is in the news, they should expect to be the subject of media interest. They warn that a media scrum can sometimes be intimidating or unreasonably intrusive. Broadcasters will sometimes share or 'pool' material to avoid this. Section 8.11 of the Ofcom code is more specific:

> Doorstepping for factual programmes should not take place unless a request for an interview has been refused, or it has not been possible to request an interview, or there is good reason to believe that an investigation will be frustrated if the subject is approached openly, and it is warranted to doorstep. However, normally broadcasters may, without prior warning interview, film or record people in the news when in public places.

In the UK, most roads and pavements are considered to be public spaces although it's wise to check this, particularly in city centres where land to which the public has access can be privately owned; shopping centres are a common example. It's also virtually impossible to doorstep someone on property that has a long private driveway. The IPSO code does not mention doorstepping specifically, but Clause 4 states: 'Journalists must not engage in intimidation, harassment or persistent pursuit.' It adds: 'They must not persist in questioning, telephoning, pursuing or photographing individuals once asked to desist; nor remain on their property when asked to leave and must not follow them. If requested, they must identify themselves and whom they represent.' It also stipulates that editors should not publish material obtained in this way, even if they are not the original source.

Knocking on a stranger's door is never easy, but it becomes less stressful and embarrassing with practice. As with an unsolicited telephone call, it can be worthwhile preparing a brief script to explain who you are and why you're there. It makes it much easier when that face appears at the door. Journalists from radio and TV stations often find it easier to get people to talk to them initially as they may be interested in meeting someone from a well-known broadcaster, but the reporter then faces the additional challenge of getting the contributor to speak on camera or microphone. A print journalist can have a more informal conversation, but there is a question about the ethics of using off-the-cuff comments from someone in the same way as information given in a formal interview. Reporters working in the highly competitive world of tabloid journalism may well use other methods to doorstep potential interviewees. Again, where a front-page exclusive and large sums of money are at stake, it's often tempting to go to greater extremes.

One particular issue when doorstepping potential interviewees is dealing with other journalists doing the same thing. This is more likely in high-profile stories where there may be a number of news outlets chasing the same material. Don't be put off if you see someone else knocking on a door and being turned away. The resident may change their mind, or your approach to them may simply be more successful. If they say they've already spoken to another journalist, if they've not agreed an exclusive deal, then you should also attempt to speak to them. Your interview may be better, and they may well give you different information. There is a danger of harassment if numerous reporters approach the same person, but one polite request before being turned away is unlikely to raise this issue, even if your potential interviewee has been approached several times.

Joining a media scrum outside a building poses its own problems. In the new media climate, these circumstances are more likely to involve people already in the public eye such as politicians or celebrities. For a print journalist, the challenge in a large press scrum will be working alone. They will need to station themselves close to the entrance of the property to ensure they are able to hear any exchanges with the resident. If a car enters or leaves the property they would ideally want to be able to see inside, to establish who's in the vehicle and/or see their facial expression. This isn't easy when a host of television cameras and press photographers are trying to do exactly the same thing. Another practical problem for those working alone is that they will need to leave the area to find food or visit the bathroom. News reporters often tell stories of how they missed an important moment outside a house or court building, because they popped around the corner to buy a sandwich. When working with a photographer or camera crew there can be less pressure, as they can be available when you're not, but the reporter is then under pressure to supply their colleagues with the very best information about the possible movements of the interviewee. Broadcasters will also need to ensure there is a suitable position for any outside broadcast vehicle to beam the pictures or sound back to the studio. More information on this can be found in Chapter 9.

Reporters and camera crews call these long doorstepping days 'stakeouts' for a good reason. They can be boring and stressful, but getting the only photograph of a politician hunched in the back of a car on the day they resign or catching a few mumbled words as a high-profile figure walks across the pavement can be highly lucrative and even make a journalist's career.

The death knock

A death knock is probably one of the most difficult jobs a journalist can do. Everyone is moved by the plight of someone who has just lost a relative in difficult circumstances, and knocking on their door unannounced can be a miserable experience. Up until the spread of social media, the death knock often started with a polite request for a photograph of the person who had died. Increasingly these images are now sourced online or are provided by well-prepared police press officers, who understand the media's need for images.

When a crime or serious accident is involved, there is also a growing trend for the police to secure and publish a statement from the family of the person involved very swiftly, and this will include a request for the media to leave them alone. It would be highly unethical and very unwise indeed to ignore such a plea, as the news outlet may then be excluded from further interviews or news conferences. Sometimes a news conference is organised to allow a victim's family to speak.

On the rare occasion when you are still asked to knock on the door of a victim's close relative, the best way to tackle things is with great courtesy and professionalism. Make it clear at the outset that you are from a media outlet and point out that many other people will be speaking to the press about the person's loved one. This should not on ANY account be framed as a threat, but simply some polite information that may encourage the person to consider putting forward their own story. Journalists from tabloid publications may also be able to offer money to interviewees, but there are both ethical and legal issues to consider, particularly if this person may be part of a court action or called as a witness in court.

More frequently, you may be required to speak to neighbours or friends about a dead person. This is generally a little less stressful, although people's reaction to a journalist on the doorstep can occasionally be aggressive. Sometimes people are surprisingly keen to speak. They may simply want to share their distress, express outrage or pay tribute to the person they have lost. You may be surprised to discover that some people find talking about their experiences therapeutic. As long as you don't take advantage of their need to talk and remember you're a journalist, not a counsellor, there is nothing wrong in allowing someone to talk through their distress with you.

There is little that can prepare you for the experience of doing a death knock. Some people find it easier than others, and the reward of getting paid for a story or securing a scoop can compensate for the embarrassment. In the end, you are simply doing your job, and by remaining courteous and professional at all times and leaving the premises immediately you are asked, you are doing as much as you can to reduce any distress. The same people who shout abuse on their doorstep may well read your publication themselves and will have given little thought up until then about how such interviews are secured.

Interviewing vulnerable people

There is a group of people, broadly described as 'vulnerable', who must be treated with special care when preparing for interviews. For most journalists this means children, disabled people, some older people and anyone suffering from a physical or mental illness or acute emotional distress.

You must ensure that the person you choose to interview is able to give informed consent. This means that they understand who you are, why you are speaking to them and can make an informed judgement about what will happen to the interview you record. So for example, someone with dementia may understand that you are a journalist and that you are giving an interview, but they may not be able to weigh up the implications of appearing in your publication and any personal repercussions this may have.

It's not always easy to make these decisions in practical working life, and what you do will depend as much on your own personal judgement as the rules and regulations. Children have the most protection. Some broadcasters have a strict rule that written parental permission is needed to interview anyone under eighteen. Others go further and insist permission is needed to show any identifiable child in video footage. Section 1.28 of the Ofcom code gives broader guidance:

> Due care must be taken over the physical and emotional welfare and the dignity of people under eighteen who take part or are otherwise involved in programmes. This is irrespective of any consent given by the participant or by a parent, guardian or other person over the age of eighteen in loco parentis.

Which means that even if a parent gives their consent, the journalist is still responsible for the child's wellbeing. The IPSO code is less strict. It only requires consent when the child is speaking about their or another child's welfare. Remember teenagers in particular will sometimes claim to be older than they are. If you're not sure, ask for some proof of age or consult a youngster's parents as a precaution.

If you are working with children over a longer period of time or they will be in your care without a parent or guardian, then you must implement your employer's child protection policies and follow their guidelines. If in any doubt, speak to a senior member of staff and don't cut corners. A child's safety is of paramount importance.

Not every disabled person is vulnerable, but some are. Reporting of physical and learning disability has changed dramatically over the past decade or so, but there is still a great deal of progress to be made. The key thing to remember is that your interviewee is a person and not a disability. There is no need to mention their disability unless it is relevant to your story.

Some of the language used to describe disabled people in everyday speech is not accurate or appropriate. People are not 'confined' to a wheelchair, they 'use' a wheelchair. Many disabled people are not 'suffering', they 'have' a condition and having a disability does not make you a 'valiant hero struggling to overcome the odds', unless that really is the point and context of your story. One of the easiest ways to get the language and tone of your report right is to consult the person you are featuring. Ask them if there are any terms they find offensive, and if you're struggling with language, get their guidance on how they would like to be described. There are a number of excellent organisations, which are also happy to provide help and advice. The charity Mediawise has some helpful online resources.

With the growing number of older people in our population, journalists can sometimes be faced with interviewing people with dementia or other memory disorders. This can raise some very difficult issues, as you may not be able to assess someone's ability to give their informed consent from a brief conversation. If you are speaking to someone who you suspect may be unable to give their consent, it is wise and of course ethical to try to contact a family member to ask their advice. A quick knock on a neighbour's door will often give you all the information you need. Anyone from the age of 50 to 110 can be described as an 'older' person, but many people will now be working into their seventies and are not in any way vulnerable. When working with older people try to be careful with your use of language, and if in doubt, again ask the person you are interviewing how they would like to be described. Not every older person is a 'plucky pensioner' or a 'tragic victim'.

Particular sensitivity is needed when reporting mental illness. Again it's wise to follow some broad guidance. For example, your interviewee is a person and not their condition. So they are 'a young woman who campaigns for better understanding of bipolar disorder' rather than 'bipolar campaigner'. Mental illness is an illness and many people recover; they are not always 'sufferers' of their illness. Think carefully what imagery you use to create graphics. By using visual clichés, such as a person weeping in a darkened room, you can be helping to perpetuate misconceptions about some conditions such as depression.

Special consideration should be given to researching and reporting of suicide. Of course, any decent journalist will be extremely sensitive about the coverage of such a story, but the reporting of suicide can unfortunately lead to copycat behaviour. So it's really important to consider this when writing copy. Experts advise against the use of the term 'committed suicide' and advise writing 'died by suicide' instead. Don't oversimplify or try to explain the suicide if you're not able to reflect the complexity and context of the event. Avoid going into detail about the method and circumstances of someone's death, particularly if they've used an unusual

---

Remember:

- Familiarise yourself with your employer's policy and code of practice before door-stepping.
- Always respect a direct request to leave someone alone.
- Be courteous and professional and don't hound or harass.
- Get advice and prepare thoroughly before interviewing vulnerable people.
- Be careful with the language you use and avoid clichés.
- Special care should be taken when reporting suicide.

method. Don't describe the location as a 'suicide hotspot' or mention a rise in suicides in a particular geographic area, as again this can encourage others to imitate the behaviour. If possible, try to reflect the devastation suicide has on family and friends.

If you're in any doubt, get professional advice. Suicide is an incredibly complex subject and the results of insensitive reporting can be dramatic. The Samaritans have some very excellent advice on their website and the BBC College of Journalism also has teaching resources that deal with some of these issues.

Planning an interview

Preparing a good interview is one of the trickiest and most frequent challenges a journalist will face. Of course, you need to research your material and decide the focus of your questions, but every truly great interviewer will also tell you that you should also be a great listener who is flexible and able to respond to the answers you get. The skill lies in the balance. There are four main stages to an interview: preparation, forming a relationship, getting the questions right and finally listening and responding. As this book is focussed on research skills, most of the advice will be on the earlier part of the process.

There will be many interviews, particularly for journalists working in daily news, where there will be no chance to prepare. These interviews are difficult, and even an experienced journalist will walk away sometimes realising they've missed something important. As I've already mentioned, there's much to be said for using the very basic journalistic method of jotting down the five Ws (why, what, where, who, when) and the additional H (how) before you start. Alternatively, such news interviews are rarely long, and you may well have an idea how you will use the material you gather, so you can choose to focus only on securing the quote or clip you might need for your final report. It's an uncomfortable truth for most news journalists, that the clichéd question 'How did you feel?' will often elicit the colour and emotion needed to make a good interview quote.

When you have more time to prepare, the temptation is to write down a whole list of questions. This can be a really poor strategy and can often make the interview worse rather than better. Firstly, it's hard to focus on someone when you're desperately reading through a list of questions and trying to pick the most relevant. If you simply cover the questions in order, there's a danger the interview won't flow naturally. Clutching a well-thumbed sheet of paper can also make you appear lacking in confidence and anxious. Of course you should have some questions ready, but they are not a shopping list to be adhered to at any cost. Here is some advice, which should help you to be more flexible:

Understand your subject

It's far easier to do a good interview if you have a really good understanding of the area you will be discussing. Aside from being better prepared, the very process of explaining the subject to yourself will help you to draw out the relevant information from your interviewee. For example, if you found it hard to understand a particular scientific concept during the research process, then your audience will too. Once you've grasped the subject, you can help your interviewee to cover the relevant material in an accessible way. A genuine understanding of your subject will also help you to come up with the best questions in a natural, flowing way. You will instinctively know that an interviewee has forgotten or glossed over an area that's important. If you are interviewing someone about their book, film or exhibition, make every effort you possibly can to see their work. Harry Crawford is a former BBC Radio News Presenter. 'Reliable, in-depth research is vital. There will always be some types of interview you can do "off the cuff", but if a guest or contributor sets you straight live on air . . . you'll sound like a fool.'

Write notes

Writing notes is not the same as writing questions. Start by drafting an outline of the relevant areas for your interview. Consider whether your interview will be just a few brief comments, or if you will have a long time to explore a variety of issues. One of the most common errors made by new journalists planning shorter interviews is not to establish a clear angle for the conversation. If you go to interview an angler about a recent spate of thefts of unattended property from a riverbank, it's not relevant (and a waste of time) to ask about what it's like being an angler and what fish he might catch in the location. Clearly the main area to be covered by the interview is the issue of the thefts.

Once you've established an angle or specific area for the interview, then narrow this down further into two or three areas for discussion. You could choose to ask your angler about the police operation to catch the thief, but practically he may not know much about this aspect of the story. Equally if you have done a research interview in advance, you may know the fisherman is keen to criticise the police operation, and so this might be an area to cover. Be practical about how much time you have to do the interview and how you plan to use the material you collect.

Decide on 'the point' *what direction am I going?*

Every interview, however long or short will have a point or purpose. Even in a long and complex analytical dissection of an issue, such as those on the most serious news programmes, the interviewer should be clear about the point of the discussion. As Today Programme presenter James Naughtie explained to the students of the BBC College of Journalism (2013): 'There's really only one point to every interview. There's a core of every interview and it's usually quite simple and you will do a better interview if you work out what it is before you start.'

You may choose to ask a whole series of basic questions first to 'soften up' your interviewee, or you may decide to catch them unawares by going for the most difficult question first. Some of these tactics can be decided in the run-up to the interview, when you've spent a little time chatting and got the measure of your interviewee. However without a clear focus for the interview, it's easy to go astray.

Remember the practicalities

There is little point wasting your time doing a twenty-minute interview, when you know you will only use a brief quote in a longer report. If you're short of time, don't be embarrassed about explaining this and asking a couple of clear questions. If you've prepared your interviewee well in the research interview, they will be expecting a fairly swift meeting. In contrast, if you're planning a longer feature or profile interview, then you will need to prepare far more material. There may be time to cover a good deal of content with your interviewee, but you should still have an idea what 'angle' or 'peg' you think is most interesting. It will give you a starting point and some ideas for additional questions if the conversation doesn't flow naturally. In this multimedia world, there is always the chance your material might be 'reversioned' or used in a different media format. Have this in mind as well.

Writing the questions

This is the point where you can plan some questions. For a short, factual interview, you may end up with just two or three key points. If you're planning a longer interview, don't put your questions in a rigid order, but group them together under each of the subject headings you want to cover. This will allow you to move more fluidly between ideas. Finally go back through your notes and highlight any really key questions that you know you must ask.

Once you have prepared two or three key questions, take a look at the language you use to express them. Keep the questions short and to the point, and you'll get better, clearer answers. Think about the questions your audience would like to ask if they had the chance and ask those. It's not wise to preface questions with a long rambling explanation unless it's absolutely necessary. A good interview is rarely about the interviewer, and it's more important to elicit the best answers from your interviewee than to show off how articulate you are.

Remember, the same question can be phrased in dozens of different ways, but each will bring a slightly different answer. The tone of a question can be important, because it's natural to reflect that in the answer. The question 'You were lying weren't you?' will get a very different response to the question 'Some of your critics have suggested you were not being entirely truthful. Do you think they have any justification for that?' It is also important not to patronise. If there's a danger an interview might become clichéd or overly sentimental, then take a look at the way you phrase your questions to ensure this doesn't happen.

Consider a structure

If your interview is long enough to merit this, work through the subject areas and consider how you might like to move from one to the other. If you have sensitive or difficult subject matter to cover, think about where in the conversation you might discuss it. You don't want to appear insensitive or prying, as the audience will lose sympathy. So it may be valuable to build a rapport with the interviewee not only to encourage them to speak more freely but also to make the reader or listener more comfortable.

Listen and respond

This is the skill that is perhaps the most simple to describe and the hardest to learn. A great interview may be revelatory, but it will sound like a conversation. When you're speaking to an interviewee, it's vital to look at them and listen to them. Watch their body language and listen to their tone of voice. If something appears emotional for them, you can then choose to avoid it or return to the subject and elicit a more detailed answer. Your audience is expecting you to ask questions, it's your job, and so you can dig much deeper than you might do in normal life. Follow the interviewee's line of thought and only move away from that when the subject has been naturally exhausted. That way you appear sympathetic and open. Where needed, you can refer to your notes and move the conversation on to another topic. This can be a very successful way to conduct a hard-hitting and challenging interview without sounding insensitive or rude.

Interview

Katherine Baldwin is a freelance journalist and former Reuters correspondent. She's been a foreign correspondent in Brazil and worked as a political reporter and general news correspondent in the UK. Here are her tips on interviewing.

How do you start building contacts and get people to talk to you?

If you're working in an industry or an area, you need to try to form relationships with people so that when you need to interview them, they're more willing to speak to you. The journalists who are the best at their jobs are those who are willing to spend the extra time to get to know people, take them for a coffee, chat to them, so they trust you. I would do my research on the person before I approached them for the interview, and I would try to come up with some good reasons why they would want to talk to me. Maybe they are very passionate about the cause you're writing about. Or perhaps the exposure you're going to give them might benefit them.

How do you research an interview?

I was always taught not to ask the obvious questions. You've got a very short time with people, especially if they're busy, important people. If you ask the questions anyone could find the answers to on the Internet, then for a start they're going to think you're foolish, and they won't respect you. They probably won't give you great answers, and you'll have wasted your time. I've always been super thorough with my research because I know people respect you more if you ask questions they haven't been asked before.

I would find out as much as I could. I would look at their LinkedIn profile, what's been written about them on Google or Facebook. I would read previous interviews that they've done, things that they've said in the past, look up all the basic facts. So then what you can do is ask the deep, tricky questions that no one else is asking – these are the ones they'll respect you for.

Do you take a list of questions, or just notes of broad research areas?

I would have some form of list of questions, in case I get stuck, but I think it's a real art to make sure you're listening to the answer. That's where recording your interview can be helpful because that takes the pressure off your note-taking and you can really listen, although I'd always take notes as well. I think it's important to have a good number of questions in the bank because the last thing you want to do is run out of things to say.

When you first start out, it's worthwhile recording or listening back to your interviews. Also listen to interviewers you admire and see if you can spot their methods or tactics. Like so many of the things in this book, good interviews come with practice and confidence. If you expect to get it wrong sometimes, then those mistakes won't feel quite as bad.

> **Remember:**
>
> - A good interview needs rapport with the interviewee, the right questions and careful listening.
> - If you don't have time to prepare, use the five Ws as a starting point.
> - Make sure you understand the subject before preparing questions.
> - Don't make a rigid list of questions to follow; write a selection and be prepared to abandon them.
> - Listening is the most important element of a good interview.

Managing your interviewee

One thing new journalists often forget is how nervous interviewees can be. What might be routine to you can be a major milestone for your terrified subject. Even media veterans like politicians can get nervous, and they have the added challenge of doing multiple interviews when they might also be tired or more concerned with something else in their 'inbox'.

It's wise to give an interviewee as much practical information as you possibly can. Take the time and trouble to let them know how much of their interview will be used, when and where. It will avoid confusion later on and prepare them for possible disappointment. If you might not use their comments at all, warn them in advance. Don't encourage them to post their likely appearance on every social media network, only to cut them out of your edit or final draft.

Many potential interviewees now receive media training. In fact, some journalists earn money by helping interviewees avoid other journalists' questions! The quality and content of media training varies from the dismal to the excellent. An interviewee who has been well trained will generally be a delight to interview and understand well how to tackle difficult questions without appearing rude or evasive. Those whose training has been less successful will appear stilted and cagey. It's often best to allow your audience to judge their responses for themselves.

Some interviewees will ask to see questions in advance. There is no hard and fast rule about this. It can be a disaster if your subject insists they will only answer those questions and then prepares a learned answer to recite. This looks particularly bad on broadcast media, and you might be better asking them to read a statement. If an interviewee is more flexible and simply wants an idea of the area of questioning, then that can be fine. You should explain to them that you won't be sticking to those questions, but they are indicative of some you might ask. If you're having an interesting and engaging conversation, they probably won't even notice you've moved to another subject.

A very few interviewees will ask for 'copy approval'. They will want to see your story in advance of publication or listen back to their interview. Most journalists refuse to show their copy to an interviewee before publication, and it's generally seen as poor practice. Many news organisations don't allow copy approval at all. Even if you do have some flexibility, I would advise strongly against playing back a video or audio interview to a guest. It's easy for them to start asking to repeat sections, which is time-consuming and rarely gets a better result. When organising interviews with some high-profile subjects or sometimes celebrities, offering copy approval may be the only way an interview can be secured. You should always discuss this with your editor, and ideally this should be made clear to the reader too. A brief sentence at the end explaining the interviewee asked for some sections of the interview to be changed or removed prior to publication should be enough.

Broadcasters have a particular problem when preparing interviewees for live or recorded programmes. Giving them help and information wherever possible can get a far better interview. Don't advise an interviewee you'll only take a couple of minutes when you know full well you'll be an hour and don't be late or run over your allotted time. All these basic errors are likely to make your interviewee less receptive and even angry.

There will, of course, be occasions when you're incredibly nervous too. It's not generally a good idea to own up to this (unless it's aimed at putting your interviewee at ease or giving them a false sense of security). New journalists can occasionally get great interviews because their subjects don't expect them to be prepared or underestimate their ability. Generally though it's better to hide nerves under the cover of quiet professionalism. I think most of us would prefer to be respected rather than pitied. Prepare well, work slowly and think clearly, and you may not come out with a groundbreaking interview, but you will probably get a successful and professional one.

Remember:

- Consider your interviewee's nerves.
- Give them as much information as you can.
- Don't raise an interviewee's expectations if you may cut their contribution.
- Some interviewees have media training. Don't let their tactics put you off.
- Avoid giving an interviewee copy approval or letting them review a recorded interview.

Planning a court case

Most new journalists learn the basics of court reporting as part of their training, which means they should be able to produce a clear, legal account of any court proceedings, but getting the right interviews and content to cover a big court case takes a lot of research and preparation.

It's rare now for any news organisation to send reporters to court regularly to follow proceedings and write up interesting or unusual cases. Some news agencies provide this service, and increasingly local police forces have started publicising criminal prosecutions. There is a debate about what this means for local justice and accountability, but more practically, this raises some challenges for a reporter who might only be sent to the final few days of a high-profile court case or may be expected to dip in and out of the hearing. Despite this reduction in court coverage, newspapers and websites do still carry a considerable amount of copy on court cases. You're much more likely to be asked to attend court if you're working for a local agency or newspaper, than you would be as a reporter in a broadcast newsroom.

Court reporting is a daunting experience for new journalists and most reporters can remember their first big professional court case. Nobody expects a new reporter to know everything, and it is far better to raise any worries or questions with your editor or a lawyer. The information below is intended only as a guide to the basic research work that can be done to help prepare for court reporting. It is very important indeed that you understand the legal restrictions in detail from a current legal textbook and keep up to date with changes in the law.

Before heading to the court, make a quick phone call to the 'listing office', where you can ask for details of the timetable for the case, the name/s of the magistrate or judge and the administrative team for the hearing. The Courts and Tribunals Judiciary media team may occasionally be able to provide information on very high-profile cases. Make sure you ask for the details of any facilities for the media and, in particular, any reporting restrictions which may have been put in place earlier in the case. Remember, it is your responsibility to find out about and comply with any reporting restrictions. Not knowing about them is no defence.

Spend some further time researching the background of the case. Check your own publication's earlier coverage and hunt out relevant images or video footage of the event and the subsequent police investigation and arrest. You might need to book an artist to produce sketches for you inside the courtroom. If you're working for a broadcaster or are expected to produce multimedia content, you will need to do some filming in advance of the hearing, as you will want images to illustrate your reports. Also think about whether you can create maps or graphics to help your audience understand what happened when the crime was committed. Some locations you might consider filming are:

- The location where the crime was allegedly committed.
- Footage that illustrates the movements of the accused before or after the crime was committed.
- Shots of materials involved in the crime (perhaps the items stolen or the getaway car).
- The police station where the investigation was centred.
- The home/workplace of the accused.
- The home of the victim/s.
- The exterior of the court.
- A possible reconstruction.
- Anywhere where others may have felt the impact of the offence.

During the court case you won't be able to use any footage that might influence the decision of the jury. In particular there may be restrictions on publishing images that were used during the original reporting of the story, especially shots of the accused. This is particularly important when 'identification' is an issue and a witness may be expected to pick out the alleged criminal from video or photographs. As a basic rule of thumb, during a court case you can only report what's presented to the jury. If you're not sure about which material can or cannot be used, it is VERY important to consult your editor or a lawyer.

On arrival, journalists wanting to shoot stills or produce video reports should establish where the 'precincts' of the court begin, as they will need to stand outside these. In older court complexes, this generally means you can stand on the pavement; but for more modern court complexes, this can be a real challenge, and you may need a long lens. In some very large court complexes, it may only be possible to secure footage of people leaving or arriving at court in their cars. The accused may well be arriving in a prison van at another entrance. If that shot is important you may need to find another vantage point. For very important legal cases it's a good idea to visit the court in advance to ensure you have the right technical equipment and possibly more than one camera point.

Shooting footage of people arriving or leaving court is actually illegal under Section 41 of the Criminal Justice act of 1925, but it's become common practice. The only participants who should not be filmed are jurors. Of course it's not always possible to know who the main players in a court case are until it's started. The best way to get around this is to get to court early and film everyone who arrives at court. Keep a careful note of what they look like and

Figure 7.1 Camera crews at Maidstone's court complex must stand behind a row of bollards!

what they're wearing, then when you get inside you can cross reference your footage with the various lawyers and witnesses. If you've accidentally filmed some of the jurors, it's best to delete those shots, to ensure you can't use them by accident. Keeping notes like this will also help you to identify the best interviewees at the end of a court case.

When you get inside the court, turn your phone to silent! Then identify yourself to the staff and ask for any relevant paperwork. This will help you with your report. This is another opportunity to ask about reporting restrictions. Sometimes, these can be posted on the door of the court. It's worthwhile introducing yourself to any other journalists covering the case. They are in exactly the same position as you and will have the same challenges and problems. A friendly colleague can often help with names and spellings. Like you, they will also have to leave the court to file a copy, and you can aid them by keeping a note of any important developments while they are out. Ideally, they can do the same for you. Remember, now you can tweet from court, and you may find the Twitter feeds from other journalists in court helpful. Also remember you MUST check any facts, as you are responsible for the content of your reports.

One way to speed up your court reporting is to prepare chunks of copy in advance. You are not able to include much background detail in your copy, but you will need a paragraph explaining the basic details of the case, such as the names of those involved and the time and location. So this can be written in advance. For example:

> The accused was allegedly involved in an incident in the George and Tomato pub in the town centre in May of this year. During the evening of the 12th, it's claimed, a number of people became involved in a brawl, which left three men injured. The accused is charged with violent disorder and affray. He denies all the charges against him.

You can see from this fictitious example that much of the factual information will remain the same throughout the reporting of the case and can be repeated in all your copy. You can then update the story by writing a new opening paragraph, with all the latest events from the courtroom. This method can be particularly useful if you're being asked to provide hourly copy to update a website.

It's also possible to prepare a series of stories for all the most likely verdicts. Sometimes with one or two charges, this can be relatively straightforward, but with more complex cases this can be a bit of a nightmare. Even if it's not possible to consider all the possible outcomes, you can write the bulk of your story in advance with background detail and information about the case and those involved. Some police officers and other officials will be prepared to give interviews in anticipation of various verdicts, and there is nothing to stop you contacting other potential interviewees to conduct interviews, as long as your actions do not prejudice the final verdict. This material can all be kept ready for reporting after the case finishes.

Figure 7.2 Reporter Chris Coneybeer on deck during the last days of *HMS Ark Royal* © Chris Coneybeer

Interview

Chris Coneybeer is a freelance journalist and trainer. He spent many years as a television correspondent for BBC South and has attended many major court cases. Here is his advice on researching a court case.

What preparation should a reporter do before heading into court to cover a big case?

You should know the names of the defendants and what the charges are, but you must check spellings and the details of the charges when you arrive. Charges are sometimes changed, dropped or new ones added. If it's a big case, it's likely it will be following an incident that's already been covered. You should familiarise yourself with these details, but remember that you can only report what is said in front of the jury while the trial is underway. It is important to plan and pre-shoot material. This could include scenes of the crime, pictures or court artist drawings of the accused and witnesses. But be careful to check if identification is an issue in which case you must not use pictures that could influence the jury. You can also pre-shoot material for use at the end of the case. This might include interviews, pieces to camera, reconstructions, maps or graphics. One other useful thing to do is to write your intro and the beginning of your report. You will have to adapt it according to what happens in court, but it will give you a great head start.

If you are going into a new court – what are the things to look out for?

Check the court list on display when you arrive to find out which court you are in. Make a note of the name of the judge. Go into the court, make friends with the usher, tell them who you are and ask where the press bench is. Make sure you have your press card with you. You won't be allowed to sit in the press bench without it and will have to go to the public gallery, a humiliation! Speak to the clerk of the court, check the name of the judge with them and especially check the charges. Speak to the barristers, get their names and check spellings. Make friends with your fellow reporters. You can help each other as the case progresses, especially if you're popping in and out.

Do you have any advice or tips on how to juggle the challenge of being in the courtroom to cover a developing case and needing to come out to file regular reports?

You cannot be in two places at the same time, even if newsrooms and producers think that's perfectly possible! Choose your moment to come out very carefully. If you're in the middle of hearing a vital piece of evidence, ignore the newsroom and stay with it. When they move on, come out and file. Make sure you have written your piece before leaving the court. While you are there, no one can bother you. Once outside, your phone won't stop and the newsroom will pester you relentlessly. When you go back in, ask your new reporter friends nicely if you've missed anything important. Do the same for them when they file.

What are the challenges faced by television reporters when covering court cases?

When the case is over, you need to do lots of things at the same time. You need to polish your script. Your structure should already be in place, and most of it should already be written. You need to chase people for interviews. You will sometimes want to challenge the guilty and ask them for a comment, maybe run down the street after them. Unless they're on their way to prison, of course! You need to record your own pieces to camera. And if it's live, stand in front of the camera and say something sensible. The biggest challenge for television reporters is finding pictures. This is utterly vital if you are going to get people to want to watch your report. Pre-shoot as much as possible and use your imagination.

After the case you'll be expected to catch some of the main players on the steps of the court for interviews. Increasingly now, police officers and lawyers will read prepared statements, but do ask if they'll do an interview as well. These interviews need to be quick and will be a test of thinking on your feet, but if you've kept good notes and followed the case carefully you should be able to ask relevant questions.

Remember:

- Research a court case before you head to the courtroom.
- Prepare as much as you can in advance.
- Check every practical detail when you arrive at court.
- Keep up to date with the law that relates to court reporting.

Things to do

Build your contacts

Find an interesting character who would make a good profile interview. Now, make a list of every person you can think of who they might be related to, work with or come into contact with. Using this list, identify two other people who you could also choose to profile. For example you might pick someone who tattoos city bankers or is the barber to Wimbledon tennis stars.

Practise your research

Using your list, contact and set up an interview with one of your profile choices. You can make this a text, audio, video or multimedia profile. Once again using the research you've already done, set up two or three additional interviews to add colour to your piece.

Research in action

Plan the three or four interviews you have arranged. Conduct a research interview with your main profile subject. Consider how that interview will differ from those that will be used to add colour and background material. In which order should you do the interviews? Finally, complete the profile piece.

Visit your local magistrates or crown court. Prepare for your visit in advance and introduce yourself to the court staff when you arrive. Spend a couple of hours watching the cases being heard. Familiarise yourself with the routine and language used and then start writing shorthand notes for some of the cases.

Issues to discuss

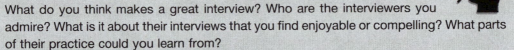

What do you think makes a great interview? Who are the interviewers you admire? What is it about their interviews that you find enjoyable or compelling? What parts of their practice could you learn from?

What responsibilities do journalists have when reporting on and interviewing disabled people? Is it the role of a journalist to report on the world as it is or work to bring about change?

Many newspapers have cut their dedicated court reporting teams to save money. How do you think this has affected their readers? What role do you think journalists should play in monitoring the criminal justice system?

Places to learn more

Books and journals

Adams, S. and Hicks, W. 2009. *Interviewing for Journalists*. 2nd Edition. London: Routledge.

Bakker, P., Broertjes, P., van Liempt, A., Prinzing, M. and Smit, G. 2013. 'This it not what we agreed.' Negotiating interview conditions in Germany and the Netherlands. *Journalism Practice*. 7 (4) 396–412.

Boudana, S. 2015. Impartiality is not fair: Toward an alternative approach to the evaluation of content bias in news stories [online]. *Journalism*. Available from: http://jou.sagepub.com/content/early/2015/03/02/1464884915571295.full [accessed 5 January 2016].

Lisheron, M. 2013. The Email Interview Debate [online]. *American Journalism Review*. Available from: http://ajr.org/2013/11/04/e-mail-interview-debate-2/ [accessed 29 May 2015].

Lundell, A. 2010. The before and after of a political interview on TV: Observations of off-camera interactions between journalists and politicians. *Journalism*. 11 (2) 167–84.

Quinn, F. 2015. *Law for Journalists*. 5th Edition. London: Pearson.

Sedorkin, G. 2011. *Interviewing: A Guide for Journalists and Writers*. 2nd Edition. London: Allen and Unwin.

Subramamian, R. 2014. Covering Mental Illness. *Journalism Practice*. 8 (6) 809–25.

Online resources

Guardian List of Great Interviews	www.theguardian.com/theguardian/2007/sep/10/greatinterviews
Mediawise Disability Advice	www.mediawise.org.uk/diversity/people-with-disabilities/
Samaritans Suicide Reporting Advice	www.samaritans.org/media-centre/media-guidelines-reporting-suicide/advice-journalists-suicide-reporting-dos-and-donts
Teeline Shorthand Online Course	www.teelineshorthand.org/index.html
Twenty Interviewing Tips for Journalists from Media Helping Hand	www.mediahelpingmedia.org/training-resources/journalism-basics/475–20-interviewing-tips-for-journalists

References

BBC College of Journalism. 2015. *Focusing an Interview* [video, online]. Available from: www.bbc.co.uk/academy/journalism/article/art20130702112133417

BBC Worldwide. 2007. *Jeremy Paxman's Infamous Michael Howard Interview – BBC* [video, online]. London: BBC. Available from: www.youtube.com/watch?v=Uwlsd8RAoqI [accessed 10 June 2015].

Coates, A. 2013. *Interview. Evan Davis, journalist*. How did they do it? [online]. London: Howdidtheydoit.net. Available from: http://howdidtheydoit.net/2014/03/ [accessed 10 July 2015].

Foord, E. 2015. *Interview: Jeremy Paxman* [online]. Cambridge: Varsity. Available from: www.varsity.co.uk/news/8538 [accessed 10 June 2015].

Naughtie, J. 2013. *Radio Interview Tips: Jenni Murray, James Naughtie, Libby Purves* [video, online]. London: BBC College of Journalism. Available from: www.bbc.co.uk/academy/journalism/article/art20130702112133435 [accessed 12 May 2015].

Sussman, G. 2001. *Tales of the Junket* [online]. London: The Guardian. Available from: www.theguardian.com/film/2001/oct/05/pressandpublishing.artsfeatures [accessed 12 June 2015].

Where not referenced, quotations are from interviews, emails or social media conversations with the author.

8 Print and digital text

Introduction

The term 'multimedia' is now used so frequently in the context of training new journalists, I'm writing this chapter with some trepidation. With newspaper sales continuing to fall and continued discussion of a print industry in crisis, it can feel as if journalists with a passion for words are at best marginalised and at worse redundant. It's worth remembering though that around seven million Britons still read a daily national newspaper (according to ABC figures published on the industry website Press Gazette in 2015), and there are indications that the decline in broadsheet readership may be slowing or even leveling-off. Many millions more read newspaper websites based in the UK, with the Mail Online remaining one of the most popular news sites in the world (Press Gazette, 2015). For many journalists, such as feature writer and columnist Adam Lee-Potter, the attraction of black and white print remains supreme: 'A decent newspaper . . . is life's cheapest luxury and as such, worth fighting for. What else costs pennies yet can entertain, educate and inform?' (Adam Lee-Potter, 2014)

Magazines too remain incredibly popular. Sales did fall in 2014 according to figures from ABC (in *Press Gazette*), but that doesn't take away from the fact that seventy five per cent of UK adults still read magazines, whether that's in print, digital copies or online (National Readership Survey, 2015).

Added to this are the first glimmers of a resurgence in long-form feature writing on the web. News websites do specialise in getting material posted online as swiftly as possible, aware that most people now turn to their phones or tablets as soon as they hear about a story on social media. However, in 2013 a piece of interactive, multimedia long-form journalism called Snow Fall, published by the *New York Times*, won a Pulitzer Prize. The BBC has followed suit with several longer online pieces including features about the Rwandan Genocide and mysterious Icelandic murders. These pieces of journalism do feature graphics and video, but there is still a significant amount of text.

So while the print and text landscape is undoubtedly a difficult one, readers do still want and value the written word, and there are opportunities for journalists who want to tell stories with text.

This chapter covers:

- Hard news
- Planning across multiple text formats
- Features
- Pitching
- Specialist journalism
- Trade publications
- A word of caution

Hard news

As we have seen, there is still work for new journalists who are keen to research and write daily and weekly news, but equally there are many keen to take up that challenge. This means newspapers and their websites are among the most competitive and high-pressured journalistic environments. For those who rise to the challenge, the job can be extremely rewarding. Beirut based freelancer Venetia Rainey, believes news reporting is still one of the best ways for a journalist's work to make an impact.

> It was a summer trip to Israel and a refugee camp in the West Bank that changed my mind [from fashion journalism to international reporting]. I blogged about the entire trip and got a lot of comments from friends who told me how interesting it was to hear a different perspective on it all (plus a few more hostile messages!). It was the first time I felt I had written something that might change people's minds or at least spark debate ... Within a year, I had booked a trip back out to Jerusalem and proceeded to make it my home for six months and pursued a career as a foreign correspondent.

The process of researching hard news stories begins with many of the skills described in the earlier chapters of this book, but for journalists working in the newspaper industry, the real pressure lies in constantly sourcing new and exclusive material. This has led to some of the most publicised and highly criticised practices revealed during the investigation of the tabloid phone hacking scandal. Although the climate has undoubtedly changed, for new journalists the challenge lies in researching great content without straying across ethical boundaries.

The independent regulatory body, IPSO is still relatively new, but in the light of recent events, it focuses particularly on the issue of harassment. Clause 4(ii) says journalists 'must not persist in questioning, telephoning, pursuing or photographing individuals once asked to desist; nor remain on their property when asked to leave and must not follow them. If requested, they must identify themselves and whom they represent.' IPSO also has a harassment service which aims to help people who are the focus of news stories. It includes a 24-hour emergency hotline. There is also a phone service for journalists to call, if they feel they are being pressurised to break the Editor's Code.

Despite these new safeguards, in May 2015 the Labour Party MP Chuka Amunna withdrew from the party's leadership contest, claiming that press intrusion on his family and friends was one of the factors which forced him to make the decision. At the time of writing, none of the journalists involved in reporting his story appear to have broken the IPSO code, although many would question the judgement of the reporter who allegedly doorstepped Mr Amunna's 102 year old grandmother.

The rest of this section focuses on some of the research skills used frequently by journalists working in daily news for print and text. Multimedia and broadcast journalists may also find these sections useful.

Working with news releases

Whether they like it or not, journalists are frequently asked to work with news (or press) releases. Journalists working in multimedia or broadcast newsrooms will naturally need to rework the content and record additional material to produce their stories, but print journalists must decide whether and how much they need to rewrite what they've been given. In larger, well-staffed news organisations reporters will be given the chance to check out the story and carry out additional research and interviews, but unfortunately in some newsrooms, it's becoming increasingly common to publish publicity material verbatim or do a few rewrites to make the content more appropriate for the publication's audience. If we assume that the vast majority of decent journalists, given the time and support, do not want to sit at computers retyping news releases, how should they go about turning the publicist's 'spin' into a decent news story?

The best way to approach a news release is to see the content as a puzzle. The publicist who wrote the copy put together the pieces with two purposes: first, to present their employer in the best possible light and second, to leave out or hide any negative information. So the journalist needs to untangle the elements of the puzzle to highlight the most relevant elements for their readers and also spot any missing information. The brief (fictitious) news release in Figure 8.1 is a classic example.

This news release for a fictional company in a fictional town appears to tell a good story, until you read the last paragraph. This suggests there will be job losses, which have been glossed over. The number of jobs shed is missing and should certainly be investigated. A wary reporter might also investigate the size of the new site to see whether the company might be downsizing and reducing its operations. There is also a question to be asked about an old industrial site close to the town centre, which may well be contaminated and could prove to be a long-term eyesore. It would be very unwise indeed to simply follow the angle offered by the news release.

If you're not sure where to start when researching the background to a news release, make a brief list of everyone you can think of who might be affected by the story and contact them to ask for their reaction to what's happening. In the case of XXZ Engineering, a quick call to the relevant trade union would reveal their concerns about possible job losses. Phoning the council would reveal whether it supports the planned move and a local resident or civic society might have a great deal to say on the possible derelict industrial site left close to the town centre.

If you are in the position of being forced to reprint news releases verbatim, without being able to do any checking or research, you should attempt wherever possible to explain the source and context of the story to the reader. For example, it's perfectly reasonable to include the phrase 'according to publicity material released by the company' in your copy.

Agency copy

Agency copy is another source of news, which can pose particular problems for journalists working in text. News agencies provide an invaluable network of news sources for larger broadcasters and newspapers, which may treat their material as an initial source, and for smaller

---

XXZ Engineering Ltd
Factory Road
Bigtown
BG5 PPE

NEWS RELEASE
For immediate release

BIGTOWN'S LARGEST EMPLOYER ANNOUNCES MAJOR MOVE

XXZ Engineering is proud to announce the company is to move to a purpose-built headquarters on the outskirts of Bigtown. Work will begin on the £5m office and factory building later this year, with the firm due to move early next year.

XXZ is Bigtown's largest employer with more than a thousand members of staff working on the factory floor and in various office and support services. The new headquarters will allow XXZ to purchase and install new cutting-edge equipment and widen its product range. It will also offer staff an attractive new working environment.

Planning permission for the move will be sought from Bigtown Borough Council over the next few weeks, but the site on New Road has been earmarked for a factory development and XXZ's plans comply with the requirements of Bigtown Council's Ten Year Development Plan.

XXZ has been at its current site on Factory Road for more than a century. On leaving it will clear the site and aid Bigtown Council in finding an alternative use for the land, which offers excellent opportunities close to the town centre.

During the move there will be redeployment of staff and managers anticipate some downsizing of the workforce. A full staff-support and redeployment service will be put in place.

FOR FURTHER INFORMATION CONTACT THE XXZ MARKETING TEAM ON :
marketing@xxz.com or Telephone: xxxxxxxxxx

Figure 8.1 A fictitious press release, with some concealed secrets

news organisations, they can be the only source of international news. Unlike a news release the journalist, like you, is looking for the most interesting and relevant angle, but unlike you, they are writing for a general news audience and don't have an understanding of your readers.

Many excellent newspapers and websites reproduce agency copy and add a clear credit to show where the material came from. If the story is relevant to your audience and well written, this is a perfectly reasonable thing to do. More often than not though, you may be required to check and rework the copy. In this instance many news organisations will remove the agency 'credit' as they can be sure the information is correct and can give their name to the copy. If you're presented with a piece of agency copy to rewrite, start by trying to verify the main facts. You can do this by calling your own stringers on the ground or corroborating the information against other reports from the scene. Once you're happy that the material is accurate, then you need to consider how it can be made relevant to your audience, both by changing the writing style and possibly reordering the factual information.

The BBC College of Journalism offers one very valuable and important piece of advice about using agency copy. A number of agencies are based in the US or use American English. It's very important not to simply cut and paste material, which is incorrect in the UK.

> Take care not to pick up US spelling from the agencies ('color', 'TV programme' etc). This policy also covers job titles (eg: US Defence Secretary Donald Rumsfeld – and not 'Defense'). However, US spelling will be retained when we are using the official name of a place, an organisation, building.
>
> (BBC Cojo, 2015)

If you're working in local or regional news, you may need to develop a local angle from the copy. You can do your own research into what impact this story might have on your local area. For example, agency copy may mention that a government scheme to fund local flood defences will include a project in your area, and all you need to do is to find out how much and where. You will then need to rewrite the copy, with the local angle at the top and the context given in the national copy further down.

Remember:

- Hard news reporting is one of the toughest journalistic disciplines.
- In a competitive environment it's important to maintain legal and ethical standards.
- Good journalists don't cut and paste news releases.
- Treat a news release like a puzzle to solve and identify the real news angle.
- Where possible, check agency copy and rework for your audience.

Planning across multiple text formats

If you're covering a news story for a local newspaper you are likely to be writing text for the print edition, website and several social media accounts. It can mean a lot to do, and you may need to produce a variety of 'reversioned' material in a very short period of time.

Planning ahead can make this easier. First of all, ensure you understand your editor's priorities. Some news organisations are 'web first' which means you'll be expected to update the website regularly. Others use their web content as a 'taster' to sell their printed editions. So you'll be expected to print a brief synopsis online and then spend far more time producing a more complex print story. It's also important to establish when and how you are expected to update social media platforms. Most news organisations expect you to start Tweeting and posting Facebook updates from the moment you arrive at a breaking story. Some may even expect you to 'live blog' the event before working on your main copy.

If you chat through these requirements before heading off and have a clear plan in advance, you're far more likely to balance all these elements successfully. If necessary, write yourself a schedule of deadlines and, if you need to keep on top of a variety of text outlets, set reminders in your smartphone.

Before you head out, do some brief research on the hashtags people are using on the ground to ensure you're using the most relevant and popular. This is particularly important if you're starting to cover a running story. There's no point in starting your own brilliant hashtag if everyone else is using another. You also want to know which hashtag your audience is using, because different hashtags are used to bring together different groups of people and different aspects of a story. Tools like Tweetreach, Hashtagify and Hashmash can help you to do this.

It may be possible to prepare some material in advance. This can be particularly useful when you're expected to produce regular Twitter updates. It's much easier to spend a few minutes coming up with some very short phrases for your copy before you head out of the newsroom. These can be saved in draft form for later use.

Remember:

- You may be expected to produce text across a variety of platforms.
- Preparation can help you to do this successfully.
- Research the social media coverage of your story before you start reporting.

Features

News writing is one of the first skills new journalists learn and once you have mastered the 'knack' and had plenty of practice, it becomes relatively straightforward. Feature writing can be much more of a challenge. First of all you need a great idea. Then you must sustain a longer more complex piece of writing in a style tailored to your target publication. It's tougher than many accomplished journalists make it appear.

A feature is pretty much any kind of journalism that's not 'hard news' or an editorial, review or comment piece. There are numerous ways to categorise the different kinds of feature. Here's a list of some common types, although it's not comprehensive and I'm sure some journalists would argue that it could be shorter or divided into further sub categories:

- News feature
- Interview/profile
- Human interest
- Trend
- Personal experience
- Historical
- Background
- Follow-up
- Analytical

Each of these types of feature can be written for a general publication such as a newspaper or for a more specialist audience. So, for example, you might write a sports historical piece about the development of croquet in the UK or a human-interest business piece about the billionaire behind a new website.

Generating ideas

Coming up with feature ideas is never easy. Many of the methods covered in Chapter 2 can be used to help you, but a great writer also needs to be able to think laterally, coming up with fresh ways of seeing familiar subjects and creative ways to approach content.

There are hundreds of books and websites which claim to improve your creativity, but one factor, which is common to all people who combine creativity with real productivity, is hard work. If you want to come up with great feature ideas, you need to come up with lots of fresh ideas, record them in a structured way, discard the bad ones and research the good ones thoroughly. Here are some methods, which can help to spark the creative process:

- *Develop a routine*
  Successful writers will often describe how they force themselves to write a certain number of words daily. The number of words will depend on their speed and style of writing, but this discipline ensures they are constantly generating and exploring ideas. Of course, some of the work will be excellent and other sections will be discarded, but writing daily offers the best possible opportunity to be creative. Some journalists set themselves the challenge to come up with two ideas a day. Not every idea will be great, but there will be a selection as a starting point.

- *Get out and talk to people*
  There's a reason why many writers choose to work in coffee shops or libraries. While much of writing is about people, it can be a solitary profession. Great ideas come from human contact, so get out and about, listen to conversations and speak to people. Make a particular point of speaking to people who aren't like you. Spending time with someone who is much older or younger than you can reveal a new perspective on a familiar topic.

- *Read obsessively*
  Even if you're not writing every day, you should be reading daily. What you read will depend on your journalistic area of interest, but it should at least be a daily newspaper or news website, magazines and websites in your own area of specialism and, ideally, some more specialist material such as trade publications, academic journals and blogs. If you are still struggling a little to find your own journalistic voice, then reading great writing can be inspirational. With very little effort, you'll build your vocabulary, learn elegant and creative sentence structure and find inspiration for your own work.

- *Relish the obscure*
  A good feature will surprise and delight the reader and a great way to do this is to come up with the unexpected. From people who make clothing for ferrets to professional dream translators, these people all exist and can be written about. Spend a couple of hours with Google and follow some random thoughts. Who knows where you will end up? Journalism is one of the few professions where browsing the Internet at random can work, so why not enjoy it?

- *Spider diagrams*
  These diagrams can help with lateral thinking and work particularly well if you've been asked to come up with a feature on a specific topic, but are looking for a new peg or angle. Start with the subject in the centre of a large sheet of paper and then begin writing

down everything you can think of connected with the subject. Link the ideas up with lines. Don't make any rules, but once you've filled the paper, filter out one or two good thoughts that might make the core of a feature. Write each at the centre of a new piece of paper and this time write locations and people down to help focus the original idea into a practical piece of work.

- *Use a checklist*
  If you find a spider diagram a bit too 'freeform' then you can start with a checklist. The man credited with developing the 'brainstorming' technique in 1939, Alex Osborne, produced a list of possibilities to help change an existing idea. His original list was: Substitute, Combine, Adapt, Magnify, Put to other use, Eliminate and Rearrange. Some of these ideas are not suitable for journalism, but others work well. If everyone is looking at one aspect of a story, why not magnify it and concentrate on one particular detail? You could rearrange a story and start from an unexpected angle, or see what happens when you eliminate a section of a story and focus in on something less obvious.

- *Break things down*
  If you have a pretty good idea of the broad subject area you're planning to cover (or have been commissioned to write something on a general topic) then doing some general research can start to generate new ideas and angles. Speaking to the organisers of an event may bring up a particular problem they are facing. Someone involved in an accident may have survived a similar incident several years earlier or have lost a relative in the same tragic circumstances.

- *Keep an 'ideas file'*
  Whether it's a brown envelope stuffed with bits of paper or some notes on your smartphone, you should be keeping things that interest or intrigue you. This 'ideas file' can be a valuable resource, especially when you're struggling to come up with something new for a looming deadline.

- *Do something else!*
  If you've had enough of staring at a blank computer screen, go outside and get some fresh air or do something repetitive such as ironing or vacuum cleaning. Let your brain continue working in the background, while you distract yourself. Just make sure you write down or record any ideas that come to mind.

Observation

A journalist working in print or text must become adept at recording their own experiences and those of others and transforming them into words. When you're starting out, collating facts and inserting interview clips can seem relatively straightforward, but writing those longer, more creative pieces can be a real challenge. One of the research skills you need to develop is observation. Journalism isn't creative writing, but a good journalist should still be able to use words to paint a picture of a place, experience or event.

It's relatively easy to describe a story from your own point of view, and this may be why many new journalists enjoy writing opinion or 'first person' perspective pieces. Some of the best writing though, comes from being able to draw the reader into the experiences of a third person, whether they're a sportswoman, hospital patient or celebrity.

When you're working at a story, make sure you spend a few minutes noting down some descriptive material about the weather, sounds you can hear, smells and memorable sights. A video journalist may be able to film an abandoned teddy bear, but you can write about it. Put yourself in the shoes of the people involved in your story or feature. You will already have asked them about their emotions and thoughts, but consider how you might describe their story in a way that will really help your reader to understand their experiences.

Journalists at work

Tania Willis is a freelance, multimedia journalist based in London. She's worked at the Press Association, London Live TV and Metro UK. Here she describes how a published feature was refined and developed from her original idea, with the help of contacts and her editor.

'I had observed a trend socially, amongst friends and the general public in the growing amount of men opting for non-invasive cosmetic surgery. So I spoke to a contact who does beauty and cosmetic PR to see if she might be working with any clients who could provide data or case studies to back up my idea. She came back to me with a story about a company which is introducing a new non-invasive fat freezing procedure. I needed to make sure the procedure was medically safe and approved, so I checked with the British Association of Aesthetic Plastic Surgeons.

Then I went ahead to pitch and discuss the idea with my editor at metro.co.uk, and she advised me she'd be more interested in a story about health fads. I went back to research fat freezing some more and saw that it had become popular with both male and female reality TV stars. My PR contact came back to me with a case study to interview about the operation. The woman had been inspired to have the treatment after seeing 'The Only Way is Essex' stars having it done. So I was able to interview her as well as the doctor administrating the treatment.

I developed the story in a multimedia sense by filming a behind-the-scenes video, as well as creating poll to see if readers would want to get the treatment done themselves. I also put together a fact box detailing which celebrities had undergone the procedure'.

Pitching

Freelance journalists spend a lot of time researching and pitching their stories to news organisations. Even journalists working for big media outlets are sometimes asked to pitch to colleagues in production meetings. One of the most difficult aspects of pitching is deciding how much research to do before you offer your story to an editor. If you do too little then you won't be able to sell your story successfully. If you do too much and the story is turned down, then you've wasted a lot of valuable time.

It's easy to find advice online about how to make a great pitch, but in some respects, having a good idea and researching it well, should be enough. No editor is going to turn down a brilliant idea with a great angle and well-planned content, even if the freelancer is so nervous they fall off their chair. If done well, pitching can form a valuable part of the research process. As journalist Kate Spicer told *Stylist Magazine* in 2011:

> Don't underestimate the importance of the pitch; if you can get your idea across clearly and succinctly in a pitch, the feature will write itself. If the pitch is a sloppy unfocussed mess you'll have trouble knowing what the story is about yourself, let alone the editor.

So it's wise to see the pitch as part of your planning and research process. If you're not sure how much to plan, then put yourself in the editor's shoes. How are they going to know that you really want to write for their publication (and that they're not your fifteenth pitch of the day)? How will they be sure you've got a good idea? How are they going to know you can write and structure the story for their audience? How are they going to be sure you can deliver the story you promise?

When you look at it from this point of view, it's easy to see what information you should include.

- Do some research on your target publication before pitching and make sure what you're proposing suits their audience and guidelines. Don't tell them how much research work you've done. Show them by tailoring your information to their audience.
- Tell them your idea clearly and simply and why you think it's so good. Is it just plain new? Do you have access to a unique interviewee? Is it funny or informative? Just one sentence should be enough to ensure they understand why you think your story is great.
- Show them you can write, by preparing your cover line. Chances are if you know how to write a catchy cover line, then you'll be able to write the rest of the story. Don't bother writing any more unless asked.
- Finally, if your piece involves getting access to particular key players or interviewees, reassure the editor by letting them know you've already got this in hand. Don't tell them hopefully that you'd quite like to interview Michelle Obama, when you have no hope of delivering. There's no need to do your interviews, but contact the interviewees to confirm they're free and willing to speak to you within the relevant timeframe.

Pitching can be done in person, but it's often done by email nowadays. So do make sure you have a professional email signature and everything you write is correctly spelled and punctuated. Don't forget to follow the social media accounts of relevant features editors and consider contacting them that way. If you can deliver a good pitch in a Tweet then you're probably worth their money.

Specialist journalism

If you have a passion for or expertise on a particular subject, then there may be a career for you reporting in that field. Of course, if your passion is root vegetables, there is probably a bit less competition than if you wanted to report on Formula One racing, but if you really are a petrolhead and can write well, then those opportunities are still there. There are dozens of different journalistic specialisms. This section provides a brief introduction and some advice on the research skills needed for some of the most popular journalistic specialities.

Political journalism

Political reporting is one of the foundation stones of daily news journalism. Whether you're a local newspaper reporter attending the occasional council meeting or a seasoned Westminster heavyweight, part of your job is helping the public to understand the mechanics of government and hold those in power to account. Many political reporters start out in local news journalism and build their first political contacts through their local councillors. If you work as a political journalist, it's important to have a good basic grounding in public administration, both on a local and national level. This section provides some research basics and advice from one of Westminster's best known correspondents.

- *Local government*

  Government in the UK is divided into local and national government. Local government funding is broadly made up of money from the Westminster Government (or Scottish Government in Scotland), Council Tax revenues (or rates in Northern Ireland) and revenues from non domestic (or Business) rates.

  Local government in England can have one, two or three tiers depending on where you live. Some areas are governed by 'unitary' authorities, which deal with all local government administration. Other areas have two councils, a district or borough council, working alongside a larger county council, with responsibilities divided between them. In some areas, there are also parish or town councils. The system is complex to allow for the diverse nature of the country. In Scotland and Northern Ireland, there is just one level of local government. Wales has a single tier of councils for 'principle areas' but also has a layer of community and town councils.

  In each form of local council, there will be elected council members (councillors) and the civil servants who carry out the daily job of running the authority (officers). The councillors are politicians, but the civil servants are public officials. If you're researching a story into a local council, the press office will be a good place to get practical information and contact officers. If you want to speak to a councillor however, it's often far quicker and easier to contact them directly. Most will have their contact details online.

- *Devolved government*

  The UK has three major devolved bodies: The Scottish Parliament and The Welsh and Northern Ireland Assemblies. The Scottish Government has the most power and is likely to be given further responsibilities. The Welsh Government has slightly fewer powers, but is still in charge of large areas of life in Wales including the NHS, transport and education. The Northern Ireland Government has fewer responsibilities, but it does oversee areas such as health, education and policing. Controversially, England does not have a devolved government.

- *UK government*

  Just like local councils, the Westminster parliament has elected members (MPs), but also includes the mostly appointed House of Lords. (There are a few peers remaining who have inherited their titles, and some religious leaders sit in the Lords.) Parliament examines and challenges the work of government, passes laws and allows the government to raise taxes. Parliament is known as the 'legislature'.

The government runs the country and is known as the 'executive'. It is supported by the Civil Service, which does the day to day running of the country. The political party which wins enough seats in the House of Commons either forms a government on its own or joins with another party/parties to form a coalition. The party's leader becomes the Prime Minister and appoints the cabinet and government ministers. A minister may be an MP or a member of the House of Lords. The work of the government is scrutinised by a system of select committees which are made up of MPs.

Hansard

This is the official report of what goes on in the UK parliament and is published daily. It's named after the one of the very first publishers to print reliable records of events in parliament. Today, members' words are recorded by Hansard reporters and are published verbatim, apart from editing to remove repetition or errors. Records from the mid nineties onwards are available online. Hansard is a vital resource for any parliamentary researcher.

Working at Westminster

The Westminster parliament has its own press gallery, which includes representatives of around 300 different news organisations. A specific number of press passes is issued to each news organisation, and they choose which correspondents should carry those passes. The reporters must also undergo security clearance. A smaller group of press gallery reporters are also Lobby Correspondents, given exclusive access to parts of the Palace of Westminster, in particular the Members' Lobby. The lobby is less powerful than it used to be, and some of its special privileges have now been extended to other reporters, but the role does still have considerable importance. MPs may speak to Lobby Correspondents under lobby terms, which mean the stories must not be attributed to them. Lobby journalists may also be invited by Downing Street staff to attend regular briefings; some are open to other journalists, but some offer entirely exclusive access. Up until the latter part of the twentieth century, these meetings were kept entirely secret, but now they may be attributed to 'The Prime Minister's Official Spokesman'. You will also hear political correspondents speak about 'Downing Street Sources' when reporting information given to them in these briefings. Correspondents may also attend a variety of lunches and other social occasions, which may be on or off the record.

The lobby system has come under criticism for allowing politicians and reporters to become too familiar. There is clearly a danger that some journalists may be wary of reporting stories, which could be controversial and risk their access to their political sources, but one could argue this is an issue with many areas of journalism. Some critics have accused the lobby of being lazy and relying on political briefings rather then checking and sourcing original stories. Attitudes to lobby journalists certainly changed following the revelations of the MP's Expenses Scandal. The story was not broken by lobby correspondents, and in 2009 *The Guardian*'s Westminster Correspondent David Henke accused the lobby of being too chummy: 'The club atmosphere is rife in Westminster. It ranges from parliamentary press gallery lunches (which are on the record) to private luncheon clubs set up by lobby journalists themselves.' Henke does concede though, that in the world of 24-hour rolling news, lobby journalists do face a much heavier workload than they used to. Just like journalists across our entire profession, they are sometimes not given the time or resources to do more in-depth research.

Journalists at work

Nigel Nelson is the Political Columnist of the *Sunday People* newspaper and is the longest-serving national newspaper political editor. He's a member of the parliamentary Press Gallery and a Lobby Correspondent. He says personal contacts are vital for his job.

'Politics is a contact sport. So most of my material comes from conversations with politicians, their special advisers, or Whitehall officials. As a political journalist I get a much better feel for a subject by talking it through with someone involved in its implementation rather than trying to research it online.

Even though there is now so much information available at the click of a mouse nothing beats face-to-face conversation, though before sitting down to an in-depth interview with a senior politician Google remains my primary research tool beforehand. And one can usually work out what information can be trusted and what can't.

As I am a columnist I also need this kind of personal interaction to try out my own attitudes to a particular issue. It prevents me making assumptions that later turn out to be false because there was something I did not take into account.

That does not mean there is no paperwork. Every morning I will scour the Hansard official report, particularly the written answers. Sometimes there is a set of figures published for the first time, which will form the basis for a story, or a question an MP asks of a minister will spark off an idea worth pursuing. Curiously political journalists read Hansard in different ways. Another journalist will spot something which makes a story which I completely miss, and vice versa'.

Financial journalism

One of the fastest-growing areas of journalism in the UK is the provision of specialist financial information, and that means there are jobs for new reporters. The term 'financial journalism' covers a wide range of specialist fields including economics, personal finance and business journalism. You could be reporting on anything from how to open a bank account for a child right up to a complex analysis of city derivatives trading. If you're considering a career in financial journalism or are working on your first story, here are some research basics, a few important terms and advice from a young financial reporter.

Companies House

Companies House is a valuable resource to journalists, and according to Editor-in-Chief of investigative website Exaro, Mark Watts, it's one that's often overlooked. 'Familiarise yourself with everything that can be found out from Companies House. I'm often amazed how few journalists really know.' Company accounts and annual reports can all be accessed for free and downloaded. The only drawback at the moment is that they are only available as .pdf documents and (as we have seen in Chapter 4) this can mean a lot of extra work for journalists hoping to analyse the data using spreadsheets and other database software. You can also find contact information for officers and some senior company executives and other details such as the dates for future accounts to be filed.

Reading annual reports

Your first company annual report can be pretty daunting. It's the document that is intended to summarise how a public company has performed in the past year. It's aimed at current and future investors and so, although it has to be factually correct, it is also written to show the company in the best possible light. Many big companies now post illustrated summaries of their annual report online and provide information for journalists. Try to resist the temptation to write your story from this material, as it won't give you the full story. You can always go back and use the analysis when you've read through the full report.

The first section of a financial report generally includes statements from senior managers such as the chairman, chief executive and chief financial officer. Thinking as a sceptical journalist, you should be wary of any overly positive language in this part of the report. Does this seem reasonable, given what you know about the company and its performance/share price in the past year? Are there any things missing that you would have expected to be there? Look at the language. Does it use repeated phrases or unusual terms? This might give away an attempt to promote a particular line or approach to the figures that follow.

Most reports will also include strategic material, looking at the market environment, the year's aims and objectives and sales and marketing information. Take a look at these and see if the tone and information are similar to that of the senior management reports. Does all the information tally? Are there hints of hidden problems or possible success stories to come?

Every company report must include an Independent Auditors' Report. Auditors review the company's accounts and its procedures to give an external assessment of how reliable they are. Their report will explain which parts of the company's accounts they reviewed and what they found. Even if you're not able to understand all the complex details, a long report is something to focus on. There won't be much to write about a company with a clean bill of accounting health. If the auditors raise a lot of potential issues or concerns, then this might be time to pick up the phone and speak to one of your expert contacts to see if they have any more information.

One area of business practice which has been very controversial in recent years is executive remuneration (how much the managers have been paid). It's well worth taking a look at these figures in the annual report. Even if you don't find a news story, you'll be able to remind yourself that journalism is rarely a well-paid profession!

Making sense of company accounts

Once you have a sense of the tone and context of the report, it's time to start reading the figures. Again with some practice, this isn't that difficult. As the *Financial Times* Business Editor, Sarah Gordon explained to a 'Women in Journalism' event in 2013, 'You don't need a degree in maths or economics to understand the technical stuff. Understanding company reports and balance sheets are the easiest skills to pick up. What's difficult is explaining why this matters to your readers.'

If you're going to be working long-term as a business or financial journalist, then it would be worthwhile buying some books and learning company accounting in some detail, but here is a very brief introduction.

The Balance Sheet shows what a company is worth. It includes the company's assets (things of value it owns like buildings, land, stock or even cash). It also shows the firm's liabilities (generally bills that need to be paid or money it owes), alongside the amount investors have invested in the firm. Some very simple maths will allow you to decide whether the company is solvent. There are various different ways of doing this, but basically you can calculate whether the company is likely to be able to keep on trading in the immediate future. The Profit and Loss Statement will give you similar information, but it covers a period of time rather than the figures on the Balance Sheet, which are recorded on a specific day.

Depreciation and amortisation refer to how much the company's assets have lost value over time. They are ways of allowing the company to spread the cost of investment over a period of time. Depreciation refers to tangible items like buildings or equipment, while amortisation refers to intangible assets such as intellectual property. Once you have factored depreciation and amortisation into the calculation you reach the company's Operating Profit.

The last stage in accounting before you can finally reach the company's so-called 'bottom line' is to factor in tax, interest and 'exceptional' and 'extraordinary' items. Even if you can't make head nor tail of the figures, it's important to take a look at the exceptional and extraordinary items, as they can be used to hide anomalies in the company's accounts. Finally, it's worth taking a look at the company's cash flow. This is the money that's coming in and out of the business. You should be asking whether this has changed dramatically in the past year or so and why.

Trading basics

This section is not intended to provide a comprehensive or detailed explanation of financial trading, but most news journalists will need a basic understanding of 'The City'. So here is a brief glossary:

- *Bonds*

  These are a form of debt. A company, city or government will sell bonds to raise money for a specific period of time. When the bond matures, they will return the money to the lender with an agreed sum of interest. There is a market for buying and selling bonds before they mature.

- *Commodities*

  These are physical substances, which can be bought and sold. A commodity is usually a product that is unprocessed such as oil, grain or metals.

- *Derivatives*

  These are not physical substances, but instead 'derive' their value from something else. They are often agreements between traders to buy or sell something in the future or in particular circumstances. Futures contracts, forward contracts, options and swaps are all forms of derivatives. They are incredibly complicated but do serve a purpose. They can help producers such as farmers and oil companies sell their products at a set price at regular intervals, to help them avoid lots of ups and downs in the market. They allow producers to plan for the future. However critics warn there are relatively few companies involved in the market, and this means there is serious risk for those investing in this system.

- *Dividend*

  This is a sum of money paid regularly by a company to its investors. It's basically a 'bonus' for holding the shares, paid from the company's profits.

- *Funds*

  These are pooled investments, which allow investors to put their money together and buy a variety of stocks, shares and bonds. Generally, they are a way to reduce the risk of investing in the stock market. Hedge Funds however, have been particularly controversial, because they are very risky indeed. Many trade in high-risk derivatives and also invest with borrowed money. This is known as leveraging.

- *Stocks and shares*

  These terms are used pretty much interchangeably although they do mean slightly different things. Stock refers to an overall investment in a company while shares are the specific measure of the investment. So for example an investor may own stock in Company D because she holds a thousand shares.

Interview

Myriam Balezou is a journalist for the online markets intelligence and analysis publication Deal Reporter. She works with a team providing specialist news and information for hundreds of traders, investors and bankers.

You work in a specialised area of financial journalism. How did you move into your current job?

I have a journalism training and also did a course in Forex and trading. I previously worked for a financial media firm for 2 years and then in B2B PR with a focus on technology. This niche background knowledge allowed me to work as reporter covering the 'booming' TMT (telecom, media and technology) M&A sector for a trade magazine. I then moved on to work for a financial newswire covering M&A activities and risk arbitrage across all sectors focusing on European listed companies.

How did you go about building the background knowledge you needed for your job?

During my time at the financial media firm, I was fortunate enough to get a lot of 'on the job training', consulting the editorial team on a daily basis and shadowing senior staff during client meetings. I also attended regular industry events as a delegate and listened to the latest developments in the industry on a regular basis, even if only passively. I realised much later how much I had learned and taken onboard.

What sort of research do you do daily in your role?

When a new deal breaks, I don't necessarily know the subject, the sector and its trends (it can be a deal about a chemical firm, oil and gas, transport and logistics, real estate, retailer etc.) Everything is thrown at you, and you need to understand the intricacies of the sector in a very short amount of time. I usually read a lot about the sector as a whole (latest news and development, upcoming legislation etc.). I listen to companies' conference calls. I read their annual reports in detail. I speak to sector bankers, analysts, lawyers and consultants on a daily basis to understand the mechanism of a particular situation and talk about current and future trends and the next expected deals. I also cover risk arbitrage, so I write a lot about merger reviews. For this, I constantly check the European Commission (or other European domestic competition authorities) and study previous cases and decisions that could be used as precedents for a particular company or sector.

There are many great opportunities in financial journalism, and yet new journalists are often nervous about applying for jobs. What advice would you give them?

Don't be afraid or intimidated and go for it, especially if you want to be challenged and learn new things on a daily basis. It is also a great way to combine your passion for writing and still be in the corporate world. Become an expert in a niche industry and you will be able to apply the same investigative reporting skills in every sector. You will get to engage with a great variety of people, from the local farmer in Texas to the high-flying banker in London. You will learn to adapt to your audience and become extremely knowledgeable with time. Working in financial journalism has been such a steep learning curve for me and an enriching experience.

Financial bodies

If you want to write about wider economic policy, you'll start to come across some of the major financial bodies involved in international economics. Here are some of those which are mentioned most frequently.

* *Bank of England*

   The Bank of England is the central bank of the United Kingdom. It was set up in 1694 and has a wide range of responsibilities. It issues bank notes, is the UK government bank and creates the overseas monetary policy for the country.

* *European Central Bank*

   The ECB is the central bank for all the countries that use the Euro. It's responsible for maintaining financial stability in these countries, implementing monetary policy and issuing currency and holds the foreign reserves of the Euro countries.

- *Financial Conduct Authority*

  The FCA is the regulating body for the financial industry. Its job is to ensure that companies operate ethically and with integrity. It regulates around fifty thousand businesses and is funded by the companies it oversees.

- *FTSE*

  The FTSE (pronounced 'footsie') is a series of measurements (or indices) that show how well products traded on the London Stock Exchange are doing. The most commonly quoted measure is the FTSE 100 which measures the success of the biggest 100 companies on the stock exchange. So when the FTSE is 'up' it means that a significant number of shares in these companies are rising in value.

- *International Monetary Fund*

  The IMF is an organisation formed by 188 countries. The organisation monitors economic and financial developments across the world. It provides statistics, economic advice and training and lends to countries.

- *London Stock Exchange*

  The London Stock Exchange is one of the oldest stock exchanges and is the third largest in the world, based in the City of London. A stock exchange is an organisation which offers services allowing traders to buy and sell stocks, shares and other financial products.

- *Wall Street*

  Wall Street is a street in New York, but in financial terms the name generally refers to all the US financial markets (in the same way 'The City' refers to all the financial institutions in the City of London). Wall Street houses the world's two largest stock exchanges: The New York Stock Exchange and the NASDAQ.

- *World Bank*

  The World Bank is a financial institution aimed at the reduction of poverty. It loans money to developing countries to spend on investment. It gets its money from a variety of sources including selling bonds and donations from donor member governments.

Working in financial journalism does require a good deal of specialist knowledge and can be daunting, but as Myriam Balezou points out, it's also well rewarded and offers a variety of interesting and varied jobs. A little effort early on could lead to a very lucrative career.

Sports journalism

Let's face it; it's hard to work as a sports journalist if you don't have a real passion for sport. Most sports reporters draw on a lifetime of expertise, learned from watching and playing their favourite sports. The UK has a wonderful tradition of sports journalism and the largest association of professional sports journalists in the world (The Sports Journalists' Association).

If you want to specialise in sports journalism, first and foremost you need to be a good journalist. You'll already know about sport, but that doesn't mean you won't have to develop many of the other research skills in this book. One area of particular importance to sports journalists is numeracy. You may have all the figures on your smartphone, but they're not much use if you don't understand them and can't explain them clearly. As award-winning sports journalist and academic Rob Steen wrote in 2014, 'An inability to comprehend why some numbers are more significant than others is a bigger obstacle to being a sports journalist than mediocre literacy.'

Sports commentary

Broadcast sports journalists face a particular research challenge when preparing for a live commentary. Not only do they need to have been through all the facts and figures, but they need to commit them to memory or at least have them easily to hand. Most commentators do learn the players' names by heart and they try to link them to something physically distinctive, so they are easy to identify in the excitement of a match or competition. They will also have a system of crib sheets. Each reporter will have their own format, and it's important to develop yours if it's a career path you're keen to follow. In 2015 BBC Sport's Steve Wilson explained how he prepared a football commentary for every eventuality: 'You watch tapes of them play. You go and watch them play, watch them train. Do all your stats and that stuff. . . . I spend a lot of time at home just researching silly things. Just in case they happen.'

Science journalism

Science journalists and writers are an eclectic bunch. Some come from a journalistic background, others are scientists who have developed their love of communication. Each route into the profession offers its own challenges. Journalists can struggle to grasp the complexities of scientific research, while scientists can find it hard to simplify their knowledge enough for an average person to understand. If you're planning a career in science journalism and would like to know more about the craft, there is an Association of British Science Writers, which offers some great advice on its website.

Good science writers bring a science story alive, with people and atmosphere. The best way to do this is to start with rigorous academic research, but then get out and meet the people involved. If the scientists have made a breakthrough, how many people might it affect? To what extent? And how long could it take to make any genuine impact? There is more detail about some of the practical research skills required to report academic research in Chapters 3 and 4.

One of the biggest professional criticisms made of science reporting is the tendency to overplay the importance of scientific research, particularly medical advancements. When you do your research, ensure you have a realistic and accurate understanding of the implications of the findings. Don't exaggerate when writing the intro, even if an over-excited editor is pressuring you. This is particularly important when researching health stories. It can be incredibly damaging and ethically questionable to present every research finding on cancer or Alzheimer's disease as being a 'major breakthrough'. You're harming your own credibility as a science writer and potentially hurting or misleading hundreds of people who have these conditions.

Science conferences

Conferences are great places to source science stories, with dozens of papers being presented and discussed. Organisers do often arrange press briefings which can help you to prioritise your time, but remember every other journalist will be using those briefings as a basis of their work, so if you want to come up with something original, do your own research work too. It's really important to prepare in advance and read as many papers as you can before you arrive. Even better, contact some of the scientists who will be at the event to arrange interviews in advance and get their advice on what's really new and exciting.

Entertainment and celebrity journalism

Entertainment and celebrity journalism are incredibly popular career routes for new journalists and the subjects are also popular with audiences, as the success of the tabloid newspapers, gossip magazines and celebrity websites such as Perezhilton.com and Popsugar.com proves. Some celebrity journalism amounts to little more than copying and captioning publicity photographs and reprinting information passed on by public relations companies. Broadcasters and broadsheets do have entertainment reporters, but they will be tasked with covering major events and researching and sourcing original material as much as is possible. Just as with all the other fields of journalism, research and contacts are vital in this field.

You also need a good understanding of the law and copyright issues. The phone hacking scandal and the development of privacy law in the UK have had a dramatic impact. While the Internet, magazines and tabloid newspapers are filled with unsubstantiated gossip, some celebrities do sue, and aside from the possible legal action, there is also the danger of losing access to valuable PR contacts. With celebrity news stories, it can be harder to defend any legal challenge to the story. In particular, it may be more difficult to prove the public interest defence. Some celebrity news court cases have resulted in incredibly complex rulings about which specific details of a story might or might not be in the public interest.

A good way to build your experience and contacts is to set up your own celebrity or entertainment blog. Try to find a niche and avoid copying other online content. You'll show far more skill if you track down your own stories and interviews. You may not get an exclusive interview with Madonna, but a beautifully filmed review of a local play or cleverly written profile of an up-and-coming band is far more likely to impress an editor. If you do start your own blog, be very careful where you get the images from and consider taking your own stills and video footage. There have been reports recently of a practice called 'copyright trolling' in the US, where lawyers deliberately scour the Internet for unauthorised images and make money by suing the blogger.

Trade publications

Trade (or B2B) publications are the ultimate specialist outlets. They are usually focused on a particular area of business, which can be anything from cheese making to international travel. (You may have seen some of the more arcane titles appearing in the missing word round of the BBC television show 'Have I Got News for You?')

Trade magazines and websites can offer excellent opportunities for new journalists. A publication that requires a deep understanding of an unusual niche subject may be prepared to train you, allowing you to build that knowledge on the job. One of the biggest advantages of starting your career in a specialist publication is the opportunity this gives you to move to

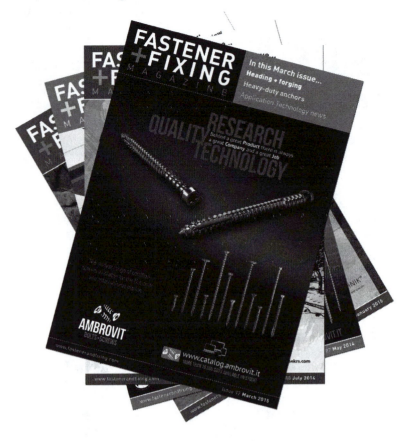

Figure 8.2 Trade magazines can help to hone your research skills and be a great career © *Fastener and Fixing Magazine*

a bigger organisation. For example, starting work in a little known trade magazine about catering could eventually lead to a job in a well-known food publication. The wages can be reasonable, and they can sometimes offer you the chance to develop longer and more complex pieces of writing for an interested audience. In short, they're a great way to hone your research skills; as journalist Chris Weale told the website 'Wannabehacks' in 2013. 'What I love about the trade press is the ability to properly research and explain issues … there is often an opportunity to write real analytical pieces … perhaps bringing in ten or more sources into an article.'

A word of caution

While specialising in one form of journalism can be enjoyable and rewarding, particularly if your specialism is also your personal passion, there are some risks and dangers. Spending many years dealing with one issue can distort your personal perspective and make it harder to spot a genuine story. There is also the danger that you may form friendships with your sources, and that can affect your journalistic judgement. It's wise to step back occasionally and check that you're doing your job as well as you can and that your judgement is still solid and independent.

Interview

Claire Edwards is Deputy Editor of *Fastener and Fixing Magazine* and *Fastener and Fixing Technology*. The publications provide news and information to designers, engineers and manufacturers of fasteners and fixings. Claire has been in her role for three years.

How hard was it to pick up all the specialist knowledge you needed when you first got your job?

It was extremely overwhelming when I first joined the publication. We're extremely specialist, and between them, my editorial colleagues have amassed over 50 years' experience. Luckily for me, I expressed an interest way back in the interviewing process to be educated. I requested one-to-one meetings with my Executive Editor, so I was able to 'pick his brains' as it were.

Having the naivety of being able to say 'I'm new – can you explain that please' is a luxury and perhaps your best research tool at the beginning – everyone is eager to teach you what they know, and 99.9 per cent of the time, revel in showing off their own knowledge. If you don't ask the questions when you've just joined, you'll regret it later on – when you're expected to already know the answer!

Do you think having such a specific field for your publication makes the research process easier or harder?

To be honest, I think due to our specific field, the research process is easier. I soon learnt the experts in the field (of which there are few and far between) and the most reliable sources. Once you build up relationships with these people and organisations, it is far easier to do your job. Our publication considers itself the *only* resource in our industry. This means we must trust and rely on everything we say and do.

It also means we have an extremely good name within the industry. If I was to pick up the phone to a managing director of a company and say: 'Look, I need your help with this project, I need to understand this process . . .', I know I would be quite welcome to visit the particular factory or warehouse wherever in the world they are.

Many new journalists tend to overlook trade publications when they're job hunting. What are the benefits of a job like yours?

The benefits of my job are that I'm now specialised in a very small industry. There are a handful of other publications that touch on topics that we cover, and I've been given the education that these publications could only dream of. I've seen first-hand manufacturing processes, which stands me at the front of the line if competing with journalists in this industry.

Also, in my experience trade publications run a very tight ship. We print a bi-monthly 150-page publication with only three editorial staff: two full time and one part time. Because of this, as a journalist you are expected to do more. You are given more responsibility and are expected to make a difference. You can also see the fruit of your labour. If I implement a specific idea, I see that directly making an impact. Sometimes in bigger publications, you don't see this. I've also been able to grow and gain confidence as a journalist. I have so much responsibility right now I would never have thought I left university just 4 years ago.

Things to do

Build your contacts

Attend a local council meeting. Prepare before you go by tracking down the agenda on the council website and looking for any particularly interesting items. At the meeting, introduce yourself to some of the councillors and add their details to your contacts book.

Practise your research

Choose three major employers in your region. Ideally, these should not be local authorities. Look at the relevant area of each organisation's website to see if they post news releases online. If they don't, ring the press office and ask if they have any recent news releases they can email to you.

Research in action

Using one of the research exercises above, develop your own news report. Think about what extra interviews you may need to do. You can use any medium you like to complete your report, but if you're producing a video report, you should watch some similar television reports first to get some inspiration.

Issues to discuss

Working reporters are now expected to file copy, update social media feeds, live blog and even take their own photographs. What do you think are the benefits and challenges of working across multiple formats at once?

Celebrity journalism is incredibly popular both as a profession and with audiences? What different kinds of celebrity journalism can you identify? Do they have different standards and ethics? Which celebrity publications are the most enjoyable to read and why?

Places to learn more

Books and journals

Adams, S. Gilbert, H. and Hicks, W. 2008. *Writing for Journalists*. 2nd Edition. London: Routledge.
Chadha, M. and Hsiang, I.C. 2012. News on New Devices. *Journalism Practice*. 6 (4) 431–49.
Levenson, E. 2015. *Creativity and Feature Writing: How to Get Hundreds of New Ideas Every Day*. London: Routledge.
Steen, R. 2014. Sports Journalism. *A Multimedia Primer*. London: Routledge.
Nicholson, M. and Sherwood, M. 2013. Web 2.0 Platforms and the Work of Newspaper Sport Journalists. *Journalism*. 14 (7) 942–59.
Rowe, D. 2011. Obituary for the Newspaper? Tracking the Tabloid. *Journalism*. 12 (4) 449–66.
Sugden, J. and Tomlinson, A. 2007. Stories from Planet Football and Sportsworld. Source relations and collusion in sports journalism. *Journalism Practice*. 1 (1) 44–61.

Online resources

Association of British Science Writers	www.absw.org.uk
Football Commentator Clive Tyldeslay's Website	https://footballcommentator.wordpress.com
Guardian Advice Pages on Science Writing	www.theguardian.com/science/science-writing-prize
Parliamentary Press Gallery Website	www.pressgallery.org.uk
Journalist Paul Conley's blog on Trade Journalism	http://paulconley.blogspot.co.uk

References

BBC School Report. 2015. *BBC Sport's Steve Wilson's tips on how to become a football commentator* [online, video]. London: BBC. Available from: www.bbc.co.uk/schoolreport/31510665 [accessed 2 July 2015].

Berridge, G. 2013. *Breaking into journalism? Don't forget the trade press* [online]. London: Wannabehacks. Available from: www.wannabehacks.co.uk/2013/03/20/breaking-into-journalism-dont-forget-the-trade-press/ [accessed 28 June 2015].

Hencke, D. 2009. *Westminster's Lobby is too Clubby* [online]. London: The Guardian. Available from: www.theguardian.com/media/organgrinder/2009/sep/07/david-hencke-westminster-lobby [accessed 30 June 2015].

Lee Potter, A. 2014. Truth and the Tabloids. In: Allan, S. and Fowler-Watt, K. (eds). 2014. *Journalism: New Challenges*. Bournemouth, UK: Bournemouth University.

National Readership Survey. 2015. *Magazines* [online]. Available from: www.nrs.co.uk/latest-results/facts-and-figures/magazines-factsfigs/ [accessed 30 June 2015].

Osborn, A. 2007. *Your Creative Power*. Fort Myers, FL: Myers Press.

Ponsford, D. and Turvill, W. 2015. *National press web ABCs for March 2015: Mail Online Dips to 14m after record February* [online]. London: Press Gazette. Available from: www.pressgazette.co.uk/national-newspaper-website-abcs-march-2015-mail-online-dips-14m-after-record-february [accessed 17 June 2015].

Ponsford, D. 2015. *UK mags lose circulation by average 6.5 per cent: Full ABC breakdown for second half of 2014* [online]. London: Press Gazette. Available from: www.pressgazette.co.uk/uk-mags-lose-circulation-average-65-cent-full-abc-breakdown-second-half-2014 [accessed 17 June 2015].

Steen, R. 2014. *Winning numbers will make your copy add up* [online]. London: Sports Journalists' Association. Available from: www.sportsjournalists.co.uk/courses-and-training/winning-numbers-will-make-your-copy-add-up/ [accessed 7 July 2015].

Stylist. 2011. *How to write a magazine feature* [online]. London: Stylist. Available from: www.stylist.co.uk/100/how-to-write-a-magazine-feature [accessed 29 June 2015].

Turvill, W. 2015. National newspaper circulations, May 2015: Mail on Sunday overtakes Sun on Sunday, Times remains only growing title [online]. London: Press Gazette. Available from: www.press gazette.co.uk/national-newspaper-circulations-may-2015-mail-sunday-overtakes-sun-sunday-times-remains-biggest-growing [accessed 17 June 2015].

Women in Journalism. 2013. *Business journalism: Could it be for you?* [online]. London: Women in Journalism. Available from: http://womeninjournalism.co.uk/business-journalism-could-it-be-for-you/ [accessed 29 June 2015].

Where not referenced, quotations are from interviews, emails or social media conversations with the author.

9 Broadcast and multimedia

Introduction

Most journalists today are expected to have a basic understanding of multimedia production. It may be as simple as adding a few smartphone photos to their social media site, but many employers now require all their staff to have good standards of video and audio production skills. It's no longer just broadcasters who can be seen lugging around bags of video and audio equipment. The rapid growth of online streaming means that reporters can even be expected to produce their own live programming.

Multimedia production offers a whole series of challenges beyond those of text and print journalism. Of course, a good multimedia researcher should understand how to check facts, develop a story and track down relevant interviewees, but they also need to ensure that audio and video material is well recorded in the most appropriate location, that interviewees give relevant information and are also able to speak in a clear and engaging manner. A successful researcher should also have a solid understanding of the technical requirements of their craft. It's no wonder that many new journalists find audio and especially video production complicated, confusing and hard. There are a lot of things to think about!

This chapter looks at the research skills needed to work in the world of radio, TV and multimedia production. It considers how these are changing over time and what these changes might mean for new journalists hoping to build their research skills.

This chapter covers:

- Finding a great multimedia interviewee
- Using archive material
- Planning a radio story or podcast
- Planning a video story
- Secret recording
- Researching for live broadcast or streaming
- Outside broadcasts
- Producing for multiple platforms
- Multimedia health and safety

Finding a great multimedia interviewee

One of the great pleasures of working in video and audio journalism is the chance to meet people face to face and give them the opportunity to speak for themselves. While broadcast and multimedia journalists still face the challenge of explaining and putting a story into context, they also need to find appropriate voices to illustrate their stories. The best interviewees add colour and personal testimony to a news story or feature. The voice-over of audio and video news stories tends to be shorter than the text of print pieces, and interview clips are generally used to introduce colour and reaction to the basic facts.

So what makes a good multimedia interviewee? The best audio or video performer is likely to have a combination of in-depth knowledge, confidence, articulacy and succinctness. Such a blend is rare, and it's understandable that some of the best contributors to television and radio programmes are in high demand.

The very best way to assess someone's suitability for a video or audio interview is to meet them in person, spend time with them and invest effort into briefing them, advising how they can best provide the interview you need for your particular production. Having time to do this is now rare and is generally the preserve of special reports for radio and television, news analysis programmes and long-form programme making and documentaries. When dealing with a sensitive or difficult subject, however, there can be no substitute for spending time with an interviewee, gaining their confidence and giving them a chance to prepare their story. You should chat with your contributor, allow them to talk through the story and clarify their opinions, both for themselves and you. You may well find that allowing someone to describe the same ideas or events a couple of times will help them to edit out any extraneous details, pick the best and most salient points and in effect rehearse the interview prior to recording. This process may be known as a 'research interview' and more advice on this preparation work can be found in Chapter 7.

For most daily news researchers, the only time they will meet their interviewees before a recording session will be on the phone. Again ideally, the more time you spend speaking to the interviewee prior to recording, the better the finished interview will be. Sadly in the pressures of a busy newsroom this isn't always possible, but there are some things to look out for.

Firstly beware of people who talk excessively. Although it's tempting to think they may make good performers on air, they may actually pose more problems than they solve. Many broadcast researchers will have booked 'a great talker' only to find the person who was overly talkative on the phone was also far too long-winded on air and failed to make their point clearly or provide a useful sound-bite. Equally, it's not ideal to cajole someone into doing an interview, when they are really not keen. Unwilling interviewees can be monosyllabic and grudging in their responses.

An ideal interviewee will be keen, know the subject matter well and have some idea how to keep their answers brief and tailored to your particular audience. One of the best ways to ensure this is to ask if they have done video or audio interviews before. If they have been on another news programme or contributed to a news report in the past, they are far more likely to be confident when doing it again. If your interviewee has never been recorded or broadcast before (and it's great to find new contributors), it's well worth spending a little time explaining exactly what you'd like them to do. It's also helpful to describe what they might expect when they arrive at the studio or you meet them on location. Useful information to give them might include:

- how long they will be expected to speak;
- how many questions they will be asked;

- how many people might be turning up at their home or office;
- what kind of recording equipment you will be using;
- whether you will be there or there will be a different team of journalists;
- how much time should they set aside in their day;
- what the name of the reporter or interviewer is;
- who will meet them at the studio (if they are coming in) and what they'll need to bring with them; and
- whether they will be able to get something to eat or drink.

This information might appear mundane or even obvious, but for a first-time contributor, it can be extremely helpful and will help calm the nerves that can often ruin an interview. A little kindness and understanding can go a long way and ensure that next time you ring a contact they are more likely to say 'yes' to you than to a rival television or radio station.

One of the most difficult challenges when choosing a good audio or video interviewee is deciding whether to favour a confident articulate interviewee over someone who is less entertaining but is a more knowledgeable contributor. In effect, do you go for the performer or informer? In an ideal world, you would have the time and resources to find someone who combines both skills, but when pushed for time, it can be easy to resort to a familiar face who you know will provide the interview and sound bites you need. You should always ask yourself though, whether you are getting the best information for your report and whether the person's authority might be undermined by regular appearances in the media or the fact that the audience might associate them with a variety of different news stories. Always be guided by your editor or producer. They will have their own preferences and a good knowledge of what your audience really wants. However, it is worthwhile trying where possible to provide a variety of voices, especially for media organisations which have particular remits for inclusivity and diversity.

Interview briefs

Researchers working for live television or radio programmes may be expected to write interview briefs. These are notes that the presenter will read to prepare them for the interview. It's another good reason why you should spend as much time as possible chatting to an interviewee and, if possible, do a research interview.

An interview brief should start with some practical information. This is the time to check the spelling of your guest's name, their correct address and any transport arrangements, where relevant. It's vital when concluding a preparatory telephone call to take note of two or three contact methods to make sure you can get in touch with your interviewee whenever you need to. Daily news interviews in particular are often changed or cancelled at the last moment, while longer interviews take a good deal of time to rearrange, so ensure you have a couple of telephone numbers for your interviewee, along with an email address. It's also worthwhile warning them that they might be contacted 'out of hours' just in case they have young children or elderly relatives at home or prefer to be rung on a particular number at a particular time.

The length of the brief will depend on the style of your live broadcast or report and the preferences of your reporter or presenter. Some will be grateful for considerable detail, particularly on an unfamiliar news story, while others might be happy with a few bullet points. Over-detailed briefs can irritate some presenters as they may feel it implies they're not well

GUEST BRIEFING:

NAME: Chris Smith (Female)

JOB TITLE: Chief Executive, Children's Transport Alliance (CTA)

TIME ON AIR: 16.25

WHY ARE WE SPEAKING TO HER?

She rang us and wanted to comment on the report. She's a leading campaigner to improve child safety on public transport. She's also the mum of a victim (see below).

WHAT SHE WILL SAY

- Children are major users of public transport – more needs to be done to protect them.
- Her son died needlessly.
- Nobody has paid attention to what she's been saying.
- The government must do more.
- She's calling for a meeting with the Prime Minister.

ABOUT CTA

www.xxxxxx.org.uk

The CTA is a campaign body and charity which was set up in 2008 by Mrs Smith, after her eight year old son was killed in an accident on a local bus. He was riding at the back when the bus stopped abruptly and he hit his head on the seat in front. Mr Smith is campaigning for better safety measures on all transport used for children and more awareness among bus and train manufacturers and transport companies.

BACKGROUND (Source: xxxx website)

An official report out today says more needs to be done to ensure the safety of kids on public transport. The number of children killed or injured in public transport accidents over the past year has doubled since 2010. The report is calling for more awareness among transport companies and better child safety measures on buses, trains and planes.

PRODUCTION NOTES

Chris is making her own way to the studio. Please can you book her a taxi into town when she's finished? Her contact numbers are Mobile: XXXXX XXXXX, Home: XXXXXXXXXXX Work: XXXXXXXXX She'll give you the address for the taxi when she arrives. Chris has never done a live TV interview before and is very nervous. She has asked to see the TV studio in advance and also meet presenter. I explained this may be hard, but if you can help would be good.

Figure 9.1 A good guest briefing includes brief points and more detailed background

prepared. If you're not sure, it's safest to start with a summary of the key points that can be read at a glance and then include more detail and background underneath. Treat the writing a bit like a news story; using the traditional print 'inverted pyramid'. (Take a look at Figure 9.1 for a fictitious example). As BBC Correspondent Jon Sopel explains on the BBC College of Journalism website (2013) 'The best brief is someone who'll say you've got this politician ... What is their viewpoint? What have they already said on the issue? Where are the areas of controversy? And out of that very quickly you can hopefully build in your head a reasonably structured interview.'

Case studies for video and audio

Great case studies bring any report or feature to life, but they're particularly important in audio or video reporting, where they can provide the most compelling interview material and images. In documentary making, these contributors may be called 'characters'. There is more information on the basics of finding case study contributors in Chapter 7.

Finding good case studies who are prepared to be recorded can be a real challenge for a broadcast researcher. It may be relatively straightforward to track down someone who has had a bad haircut for example, but finding a woman who will chat candidly about having an abortion or a man who wishes to talk about his experiences of childhood abuse can be far more difficult. Ideally, your case study should be of a similar age and background to the audience of your programme or website. So news aimed at a younger audience will often feature young people talking about the news and why it's relevant to them.

There is one school of thought that believes the predominance of broadcast journalism stories illustrated by case studies is not always a good thing. Some journalists argue that trying to illustrate the relevance of a story through the lens of one person's life can draw attention away from the complexity of some stories and detract from more in-depth discussion of the issues. Practically speaking, it is true that a case study does use up to twenty or thirty seconds of a short report and reduce the amount of time left for explanation and context. There are some television and radio audiences which have wide background knowledge, are extremely interested in news and already understand the relevance and importance of a news story. It may well be that they are more interested in an 'issue led' approach to storytelling, which includes fewer case studies and a more detailed analysis of the causes and implications. You'll certainly know if you're working on such a programme and will be expected to tailor your research appropriately.

Diversity

There has been consistent criticism of television news in particular for its tendency to include predominantly white, middle-aged, male voices. Clearly, this is undesirable when working for a public service broadcaster with a remit to represent the whole general public, but for private companies, offering such a narrow range of opinions can deter viewers and listeners and reduce the potential audience for advertisers. Finding interviewees from across the UK, with differing ethnic backgrounds and agendas can be hard in a country where white men still hold many of the most influential positions. Such an ambition should certainly not be used to skew or misrepresent a story, but a good researcher should always ask themselves if they are unwittingly overlooking unusual or iconoclastic points of view or whether there may be alternative options to a discussion panel of older men.

Remember:

- The best video or audio interviewee will have a combination of in-depth knowledge, confidence, articulacy and succinctness.
- It's always best to spend time listening to and briefing interviewees.
- Be guided by your editor; they will know what style of guest suits their programme.
- Great guest briefings combine a few quick facts with more detail if needed.
- Good case studies can bring a story alive, but they're not always appropriate.

Using archive material

It's hard to produce a report on a long-running story without using some archive material. Your audience needs the chance to review the facts so far and put the latest angle into context. Television and video news reports may also use so-called 'library' material to avoid spending time and money shooting fresh footage at regularly used locations. Covering stories about public buildings and general themes such as 'shopping' or 'motoring' would be typical opportunities to use library footage. This will often mean that researchers are asked to track down suitable audio material and video footage from the archives.

The methods for sourcing archive material will depend very much on your employer and/or budget. Large well-established news organisations will have their own archive of material spanning many years. It's generally free to use and well catalogued. The most recent material will probably be stored digitally, while older recordings might be on tape or possibly even on film. It's worth remembering that it can take quite a while to organise a 'format transfer' to make sure the material is usable in a modern newsroom. Any archive audio or video footage used to illustrate a current story should generally be clearly captioned on-screen or in the voice script. It's misleading to encourage the audience to think that the material was filmed on the day.

In smaller newsrooms or when working on special programmes, such recordings may have to be ordered from an archive company or news agency. This can be very expensive, and you should always check the cost of any material and clear it with your editor or supervisor before use. It is, of course, possible to download a great deal of archive footage from the Internet. Using this material without copyright clearance is illegal.

Electronic Press Kits

Many PR departments in companies, charities and other organisations are starting to record their own audio and video material for use on their websites and to offer professional news organisations. When packaged together, press releases, background information, photos and recorded material can be known as an 'Electronic Press Kit' or EPK. This material can be extremely useful, especially in these cash-strapped times. You should weigh up the relative issues and benefit before using such free footage. Some may be totally innocuous and will allow the journalist to illustrate a story quickly and easily; other material will have been carefully filmed to conceal particular aspects of a story or promote a positive image of the organisation. You should always ask yourself why it's being given to you and watch it through carefully. In a story where there's any controversy or debate, EPK recordings should not be used. They should only be used in such a report to illustrate an organisation's point of view, and it should be made very clear that they provided the material.

Remember:

- Archive material can take time to research and prepare.
- It can be very expensive indeed – always check with your editor.
- Library or archive footage should be clearly flagged up for the viewer or listener.
- Always consider carefully if you should use an EPK.

Planning a radio story or podcast

For those of us who work or have worked in radio or podcast production, it remains a uniquely intimate and engaging medium. Modern audio recorders are so small they can be used with little or no disruption in the field, and they can be far less intimidating and off-putting for interviewees than the large tape recorders of the past. This often allows a radio journalist or producer to secure interviews that might well not be available to their counterparts in video production. The medium also lends itself well to longer interviews, which can encourage interviewees to reveal more about themselves or talk in more detail about their experiences than might be possible in the fast-moving world of mainstream television news.

It may well be a cliché, but a vital skill for any audio researcher or producer is the ability to paint pictures with sound. This phrase is often used, but can mean anything from recording large quantities of natural sound to form an immersive 'soundscape', to choosing a brief telephone sound bite that will illustrate a story and engage the emotions of the listener.

With the growth of downloadable media and podcasting, we take our favourite radio programmes with us on buses and trains, into the workplace and increasingly overseas. This means audiences retain a close relationship with their favourite radio station which can provide a unique opportunity for interaction with journalists through email and social media. Phone-ins, networking sites and message boards all provide radio journalists with a real-time understanding of what their audience thinks, feels and wants. They are also a valuable source of case studies, expert comment and new ideas. A great radio researcher will have a very clear understanding of their audience. In local or regional radio, this means forming a strong bond with the broadcast area, while in national radio, listeners are spread across the country and increasingly across the world, drawn together into an interest-based community centred on the network or a particular programme.

Many live radio news programmes are now based on studio discussions and phone-ins. Researchers may be required to set up experts and case studies to get the conversation going and to also chase potential guests who have texted or emailed the show. In an environment like this, the ability to get on with people from all areas of life and be sensitive is vital, along with a great contacts book. When booking interviewees for recorded items, the location becomes much more important. Radio and podcast researchers should always consider the opportunities to collect natural sound to help illustrate their story.

In smaller radio newsrooms, there are no dedicated researchers, and reporters and producers are expected to do their own research. Where only short news bulletins are produced, this

Interview

Harry Crawford is a former reporter and presenter on BBC Radio Solent. He offers some straightforward advice on researching for radio news.

What are the skills a successful radio researcher and producer needs?

The ability to prioritise is very important. The chances are you'll always have more than one project on the go at any one time, so establishing which deadlines are the most important with your editor is crucial. Good communication skills are also essential. Keep people up to date with what you're doing, particularly if your research involves extended periods of time spent out of the office.

You produce stories for news bulletins and longer news magazine programmes; how do their requirements differ?

The two main differences are time and tone. Producing a piece for a news bulletin generally involves distilling a story down to a few lines and perhaps a brief audio clip for someone who may only be tuning in for five minutes at the top of the hour. The facts of the story will remain the same for your programme piece, but you'll have more chance to explore the various angles of the story and a slightly more conversational tone is sometimes expected.

Is there a danger that with many radio newsrooms being reduced in size, good research skills are being lost?

Possibly, although I have worked with some excellent journalists who got more research done in the 55 minutes between their news bulletins than some others did in a day. Your research skills generally improve the longer you're in the job, irrespective of how many people you're working with.

What advice would you give a new journalist hoping to start a career in radio journalism?

Don't be late. Ever. It sounds obvious, but if you're five minutes late for the 9 o'clock news, then you've missed it. Also be prepared to make less money than you might in other professions, but to have a much more interesting and varied working life.

---

might mean finding suitable interviewees to produce telephone clips to illustrate news stories. This may appear easy at first, but under tough time constraints, it can be very difficult and doing it successfully can take time and practice.

Planning a video story

Ask some experienced video journalists how they go about planning a video news story, and you'll get a whole variety of answers. The requirement for a traditional television news report to have a script, recorded sound and pictures throws up a whole series of production decisions to be made in concert, with each having an effect on the other. For example, a decision on the style and structure of a voice-over will be influenced by and have an influence on the way the relevant images are filmed. One of the most common questions asked by new television journalists is 'Do you edit the pictures first or write the script?', and the answer confusingly is often 'it depends'.

Whether the researcher is working for longer programmes or rolling news, there is one golden rule for television. The pictures are the most important thing, and coming up with interesting and relevant locations for filming is a vital skill.

Features and long-form programming

Some video news stories and longer documentary materials lend themselves very well to traditional film planning methods. These would generally be shoots that are based strongly on past events and involve the explanation of issues rather than breaking news stories. Planning documents such as 'shooting scripts' or 'storyboards' may be used to outline a structure, likely script and shots needed to tell a story effectively. Working on such documents is a complicated skill and more information can be found in many good books about video and documentary production. In addition, a whole variety of templates for such planning materials can be found easily online.

STORYBOARD TEMPLATE

Shot Number _____
Location in Rushes _____
_____
Audio _____

Shot Number _____
Location in Rushes _____
_____
Audio _____

Shot Number _____
Location in Rushes _____
_____
Audio _____

Shot Number _____
Location in Rushes _____
_____
Audio _____

Shot Number _____
Location in Rushes _____
_____
Audio _____

Shot Number _____
Location in Rushes _____
_____
Audio _____

Figure 9.2 A simple storyboard template for basic video production

For longer and more complicated film shoots it's common for researchers and producers to visit locations in advance to check they are suitable and plan the filming in detail. Such a visit is known as a 'recce' (shortened from the word 'reconnaissance', which is more familiar in a military context). A recce is extremely useful to establish whether the location is suitable for the crew, check out health and safety issues and the availability of power and other facilities.

If there isn't time for a recce in advance, a researcher on a factual film shoot should check out as much information as possible by telephone before the shoot. They should then tour the location on arrival, either alone or alongside the film crew. Questions a researcher should be asking might include:

- Who owns the site? Do we need to clear access with the police/local council/other public bodies?
- How good is access to the location? Will there be parking for our vehicles?
- Is there shelter, and what are the weather conditions?
- Is there a power supply, and do we have permission to use it?
- Is there a danger of noise pollution, perhaps from nearby roads or aircraft?
- Is the location safe for our interviewees? Do they have any disabilities?
- Will the crew need extra lighting or other specialist equipment?
- Can we return to the location if the shoot overruns?
- What is going to be interesting or attractive to film?
- Can I arrange for things to happen on site, to make the shoot more interesting?
- Have we done a risk assessment? (See Chapter 5).

Many production companies supply specialist checklists to help researchers complete all the information required before a shoot. Good early planning will often help to save time and money in post-production.

Figure 9.3 Documentary maker Mathew Charles working in Colombia © Mathew Charles

Interview

Mathew Charles is an award-winning documentary maker, who's also been a reporter for the BBC and CNN. He has been detained by the Belarusian KGB and embedded with the élite drug enforcement agencies of El Salvador. He explains the skills needed to research and plan a long and complex video shoot.

What skills do you think make a great documentary researcher?

You need to be able to delve well beyond the surface. You need time and a great deal of patience. A good documentary is also an investigation, so you need to know how to find information that sometimes might not be in the public domain. You need to be good with people too. Most documentary research comes from talking to people. You need to build up a rapport so you need the gift of the gab, but there are many times when you'll need empathy too.

You've worked in daily news and in long-form documentary making. What different challenges do you think they each offer a professional researcher?

News is about finding case studies. Documentary is about building characters. For the latter, you need to know a lot more about people you meet, not just where to find them. It comes down to time again and, obviously, being able to relate to people. For news, you don't have long to do your research; there's more pressure and tighter deadlines. But you don't need as much detail as you would for a documentary – that doesn't necessarily make it easier though. To get to the crux of a complicated political story quickly, for example, you need to have a lot of background knowledge you can rely on instantly.

What would you advise a new journalist hoping to get into documentary making as a profession?

Ideas. It's all about ideas. If you have a good idea, it will get commissioned. Also, it may sound obvious, but watch as many documentaries as you can. You need to know which subjects have been covered. You need to be able to critique them, and it helps to pick up ideas and techniques for future projects of your own too. You'll also need a thick skin and be able to take rejection. Lots of it!

What is the one thing you wish you'd known when you started out researching your first documentary?

How long it would take. I came from a news background and was often impatient. The edit process can take forever, or at least it seems that way sometimes, but of course it is important and well worth it in the end!

Daily and breaking broadcast news

Complex planning in advance is often not possible in daily or rolling broadcast news. Many smaller newsrooms have no planning team at all, while larger ones may be working a few days, or at most a week in advance. Where diary stories are being planned, then some of the processes remain the same as research in longer and more detailed productions.

With shorter packages, an experienced reporter will be able to jot the structure and script down in one sheet of paper or even work from a plan in their head. They will often plan pictures and words alongside each other. They may return for their video edit with a written script, but also have a clear plan for the pictures at the same time. Such 'on the hoof' planning becomes extremely important when researching and producing breaking news. Whether working alone or with a production team, a successful reporter will be expected to think quickly as a story develops and to track down key players, eyewitnesses and the right pictures on location to tell the story successfully. For a very big story, a reporter might well be providing live news reports and planning a more considered edited package for later news bulletins at the same time. It can be extremely hard work and require excellent research skills.

For important news stories, larger broadcast news organisations will often send a producer or researcher out on location with the reporter to help them research the story, set up interviews and organise the technical practicalities. It's a vital role and good on-location production skills are highly valued.

Stills and graphics

In most cases, dynamic moving images are the best way to tell a video story, but occasionally, a producer will need to research and design graphic images or use still photographs. Sometimes this might be simply because there are no pictures to illustrate a story. For example, you will often see maps used to illustrate breaking stories on rolling news channels, because there are no other images to use. Television journalists often use still photos of the victims of crime or of criminals themselves because the police or friends and family have supplied these. Sometimes, though, graphics are used because these are the very best way to convey a complex piece of information. Whatever your reason for producing a graphic, you must always be absolutely clear why you're using it and what you want to say.

There is a good deal about processing and visualising data in Chapter 4 which is also relevant to the production of graphics for television or video. The facts and figures must be carefully researched and verified, represented accurately and, where possible, put into context. There are some additional challenges though:

- *Time*
  Graphics produced for television and video can only be used for a limited amount of time; otherwise they slow down your film and can appear dull. So it's important to ensure the information conveyed is simple, clear and can be understood in just a few seconds. There's a real danger, when making things as simple as possible, that there may be a loss of context and nuance. You must make sure that you don't distort the information.

- *Text*
  Any text on video graphics must also be clear and brief enough to be read in a short time. In many cases it's necessary to make the language simple so that all your audience can understand it, and this can again pose the risk of oversimplification or distortion of the

story. You may notice that in some television news stories, text on-screen may only include a few selected phrases of the voice-over, to emphasise their importance. This helps to keep the screen uncluttered and makes the words easier to read. Wherever possible, ensure you include a few words to show the source of any facts and figures. This makes the graphic more accurate and can save valuable time in your voice-over.

Sometimes a graphic will need a title. Spend some time thinking about this. Make sure that, however short it is, it's accurate and it matches or reflects your voice-over script. Text and numbers need to be clear and bold. Don't be afraid of simple arrows which show movement up or down. They may appear obvious, but can really help to make sense of more complex facts and figures.

You need to check the size of your text on a number of different screen sizes. Remember not every viewer will have a 60-inch wall-mounted monster. And what about reversioning? Will your work be used on tablets or even smartphone screens? Then the text may need to be larger to be readable.

I can't emphasise enough the importance of checking the spelling on all on-screen text. Get a colleague to double-check for you and don't be rushed. A spelling mistake can completely detract from an otherwise excellent piece of journalism and result in numerous complaints.

- *Maps*
When you choose to create a map, think about your audience's current knowledge. A map illustrating an area close to home might have more detail than one showing a remote part of the globe. It's vital to ensure you spell place names correctly, and remember, there are some areas of the globe where boundaries and names are highly politically sensitive. If you don't have a policy in your newsroom, try checking with a local reporter. If a boundary is unclear or a place has two different names given by two different communities, then it may be necessary to explain this to avoid claims of bias.

- *Movement*
Include movement in your graphics where possible: not only for dramatic effect but also to help illustrate your point. Many modern video-editing programmes will allow you to create a moving image out of a still photograph by zooming in or panning across the picture. Using this simple technique can allow you to make a single photograph much more visually interesting. When producing a graphic to show numbers, such as a graph or pie chart, try to think of creative ways to move the image around and illustrate your point. However, don't introduce a lot of random movement for no clear reason, as this can detract from your story.

- *Creativity*
Remember a graphic doesn't have to be a simple illustration; think about using visual metaphors. For example an image of a bridge built in stages might be used to illustrate a process that must be completed in a particular order, as the bridge would collapse if a section is missing from the middle. A road sign might be used to show a number of alternative choices, leading to different results. Try to use real video footage if you can, perhaps blending in some of the shots from your video sequences. The complexity of your graphics will depend on the video-editing software you have available, your own or your editor's skill and the time available.

In the end though, as with all journalism, the most important factor when producing graphics is to convey an original, interesting relevant story to your audience. Without that, all your creative effort will be wasted.

Secret recording

When a broadcaster interviews a source there is a very clear point at which the interview starts and ends. Pretty much every interview begins with the ritual of switching on the camera or audio recorder, getting sound level and asking the interviewee to spell their name. The source knows exactly when they are being recorded and by seeing the recorder gives tacit permission for the material to be used. Occasionally though, it is necessary to record someone without their permission, and this raises a number of legal and ethical issues.

Secret recording includes using hidden cameras or microphones, cameras with long lenses at a distance, material recorded on a device before or after the interviewee is advised the device is switched on and secretly recording a telephone or online video call. Done without justification and proper planning, secret recording is an invasion of someone's privacy and potentially illegal, but as the Channel Four Producers' Handbook (2015) explains, it can be a powerful tool: 'Secretly filmed or recorded exposés have led to the revision of working practices, changes in the law, the closure of institutions and have even sent criminals to prison. Advances in technology have enabled a degree of infiltration previously unheard of.'

If you want to carry out secret recording, your first consideration must be the legal implications. If your subject takes you to court, the judge will have to balance your right to freedom of expression under Article 10 of the European Convention on Human Rights against your subject's right to privacy under Article 8. As lawyers Alison Castrey and Madeleine Heal write in the *Law Gazette* (2010) 'Their right to privacy may be outweighed by the public interest in being told the story.' So you must be absolutely sure that your story has a public interest justification, and there is no alternative way to acquire the footage you need.

There are a number of other potential offences which you commit when you film secretly. You may gain access to premises or an organisation fraudulently. In addition, there are two points at which you may breach Article 8 of the European Convention on Human Rights. Both the recording itself and the broadcast can involve an infringement of someone's privacy. It's not always an easy judgement and you may need to seek legal advice before you start.

Once you are happy that your plans can stand up to scrutiny in court, you must then ensure they meet the guidelines of any regulatory body. Broadcasters follow the Ofcom code. This gives further guidance on what might be considered to be 'public interest' and how that might be demonstrated. Most news organisations have a formal process for approving secret recording. It is very important indeed that you follow this; otherwise you might find you're in breach of your contract of employment or could lose an important commission.

Don't forget to carry out a full risk assessment before doing any secret recording. The equipment you use may pose its own risks, and then clearly, there may be a risk if the journalist's true identity or the nature of their actions is revealed to those they are investigating. There is information on risk assessment in Chapter 5.

Once you have made your recording, there is a separate decision to be made about broadcasting what you found. Again, this decision will be made with the advice of a senior member of staff and possibly a lawyer. You should then address the Ofcom requirement for fairness, and this usually means approaching the person or organisation you filmed in secret to gain their response. You don't need to show them the footage, but by contacting them in any way, you will immediately alert them to your work. At this point, some organisations will apply to a court for an injunction to stop the broadcast. This may be the first stage of their legal action against you and can be a complex process. As Castrey and Heal (2010) add: 'It is difficult to predict when the balancing exercise conducted by a court, between the media's right to freedom of expression and the individual's right to privacy, will fall in favour of an injunction.'

The most important thing to remember when considering doing any secret recording is to speak to your editor or another senior member of staff. Carrying on without their permission could result in your being sacked or even legal action.

Other people's recorded material

Occasionally, you may be given the opportunity to use material recorded by other people. For example, you might be given access to social media footage or material recorded on an answerphone or closed circuit television camera. Practically, you must first establish who owns the copyright to this material and get their permission. Then you will need to either secure the permission of those featured in the filming or conceal their identities.

If you wish to use the material without seeking the permission of those filmed or hiding their identities, then you will need to follow the same procedures as you would have done when recording the material in secret yourself.

Researching for live broadcast or streaming

Producing news material for live broadcast adds an additional layer of complication for the researcher. Depending on the type of programme involved, the journalist may well be required to track down and book live guests, organise transport, brief presenters or reporters and possibly plan the technical elements of an outside broadcast. In a rolling news environment this may well also be done in an extremely short timeframe. Organising a live guest for a radio or television news or magazine programme can take anything from months of planning to less than an hour between initial contact and broadcast. Entertainment shows or long-form interview programmes will require a lengthy production process, allowing time to negotiate with agents or staff working with high-profile politicians. Interviews with celebrities are often timetabled by their publicists to coincide with the release of films or new music tracks, and a 'bid' (or request) to interview them may need to be submitted many months in advance. In addition, an 'in depth' interview with an international leader may take many weeks of preparation and planning. In television, such shoots will often require more than one camera and a recce to check out the practical suitability of the location in advance.

In contrast, researchers booking guests for live rolling news programmes will need a contacts book full of guests ready and willing to speak with confidence at short notice on a whole variety of subjects. When a news story breaks, there will be an immediate rush to get commentators or eyewitnesses on the phone. Advice on tracking down such eyewitnesses can be found in Chapter 6.

Radio has a great advantage here, in that such phone interviews can be put straight through to the studio and on air, with little additional production work required. In a television newsroom, telephone interviews need material to fill the screen while they're broadcast. This might be live footage, relevant recorded material or a combination of still images and text known as a 'phone comp'. Such images will ideally include a photograph of the interviewee, which can be requested by email or MMS message. Choosing such images is often the job of the researcher. It is important, however, to make sure the reporter and interviewees and the technical team know about the availability of such images and also where in the interview they might be best played out.

In both radio and television newsrooms, the researcher may well be required to write an introduction or 'cue' for the presenter to read. This will guide the listener or viewer into the story and include details of the guest's name and why they are being asked to comment. The television researcher will need to check that the interviewee's name is spelt correctly on a caption, another formality that can be missed in radio, as long as the name is pronounced correctly. For speedy bookings on breaking stories, guest briefings are often bypassed. Much of the information given in such interviews is factual and will update the presenter and the viewers on events as they are happening. A good researcher will keep track of developments and use the information to brief upcoming guests and colleagues where relevant.

In many newsrooms, it can be the job of the producer to dial the interviewee from the radio studio or television control room and ensure they are ready to broadcast. Ideally it's best to ask the guest to use a landline for the interview to ensure the quality and reliability of the phone connection.

Remote interviews

Increasingly Internet video calling services and smartphones are being used to get live guests on air quickly. In radio these can provide better sound quality, while of course on television the viewer is able to see the contributor. In the case of a television interview, the researcher will need to brief the interviewee on setting up and lighting their webcam at home and make a note of their username. Arrangements will need to be made to feed the output into the television studio. In some newsrooms this is done directly in the studio gallery or control room, while others take in such feeds via a central control area. Once again, the researcher will need to check the spelling of the contributor's name, as this will appear in an on-screen caption.

Once a story has been running for a few minutes, the researcher will move their focus onto getting interviewees into the studio, or into a remote radio or television facility. This can be a difficult task, particularly at evenings and weekends, as the guest will not only need to be persuaded to contribute to the programme, but the researcher may also have to find a colleague to meet the guest at a remote studio or feed point. Once the guest is organised, satellite or ISDN (high quality telephone) links will need to be booked and guest briefings written for the presenter. For a researcher working in an unfamiliar newsroom, it's important to learn the procedures for booking ISDN links, satellites and remote studios.

When booking live guests, journalists can often overlook the importance of briefing the interviewee and putting them at ease, and yet this can have a dramatic influence on the quality of their contribution to the programmes concerned. If time allows, it's always worthwhile establishing whether the guest has appeared on radio or television before and offering them the chance to see the studio and meet the presenter.

Once again a well-maintained contacts book will be invaluable at such times, alongside a great telephone manner and the ability to think laterally and come up with innovative guest ideas. A talented researcher will not only be able to come up with ideas for interviewees to talk about breaking stories, but they will also do it faster than their rivals at other broadcast companies.

Outside broadcasts

When researching for live outside broadcasts (OBs), a basic understanding of the technology involved is vital. Whether you're working with a large production crew or as a self-op reporter, it's almost impossible to explain or fix a problem without some simple technical knowledge. If you're working alone and without a technical crew, you should receive full training on the equipment you are using, whether it's a traditional radio car or a satellite backpack. Make sure you're using the equipment safely and, wherever required, provide a full risk assessment.

Audio OB technology

Sending an audio feed from a location has always been cheaper and easier than sending pictures, and with the growing availability of Wi-Fi with superfast broadband along with 3G and 4G mobile communications, live radio broadcasting is becoming easier than ever. That shouldn't detract from the fact that providing high quality live radio transmissions of material such as music or theatre performance remains a highly complex and skilled job.

The oldest form of radio outside broadcast relies on traditional cabled technology. Integrated Services Digital Network (ISDN) lines are still regularly used to transmit high quality audio material down traditional telephone lines. Many broadcasters still use so-called 'radio cars' to transmit live audio back from location. These can have a satellite uplink, traditional VHF transmitter on a mast or Internet streaming. They provide a safe and reliable place for recording, editing and broadcasting and work well as a base station for a number of wireless radio microphones.

Some of the most recent developments in smartphone design allow the broadcaster to use apps along with Wi-Fi or mobile broadband to broadcast high quality audio material. The quality is limited only by the standard of the microphone used and the speed of the Internet connection. Such incredibly discrete technology has revolutionised the reporting of fast-breaking and unstable news stories such as civil disturbances and ground-based conflict, where larger broadcasting equipment would draw attention and possible danger to the user. Speaking into a mobile phone appears nothing out of the ordinary and can make the reporter almost invisible. BBC Radio Five Live's Nick Garnett has pioneered broadcasting live from a smartphone. He uses an app called LuciLive, and he told news:rewired (2012) he's been able to use it in the toughest conditions.

> I was sent to Doncaster to go and do a piece. It was a terrible day: it was windy, it was raining, and there was no way I could put a satellite up without it blowing off the roof of my car.

One of the major problems with all broadcasting on the Internet, both by cable or mobile network is the varying quality of the connection, which can change dramatically depending on the demands on the system and the service provider. A number of professional technical systems have been developed to overcome this, but they can lead to some delay in transmission, which can be problematic for live news broadcasting where interviews and conversation with a main studio may be required.

Video OB technology

There are a variety of technologies currently being used to send moving images from one place to another for live television outside broadcasting. Just as with audio, the oldest and most established is by dedicated fixed line telecommunications. Where such links are permanently set up for broadcasting they can be known as 'injection' or 'inject points'. They may be connected to a variety of different cabled telecommunications technologies and networks. Modern high-speed fibre optics allow high definition images to be sent live. Such fixed-line broadcasts rely greatly on pre-planning and finding suitable points well in advance.

Microwave links are well established for use in live television broadcasting. Utilising radio waves in the super high frequency bands, they are 'line of sight' connections, which mean the transmitter and receiver must be within direct sight of each other without large obstructions (buildings, mountains) in the way. The receiver is often set up on a major television transmitter mast and where the mast isn't directly in view from the transmission site, the signals can be relayed by bouncing them between points at the top of high buildings or geographical land-marks. The BT Towers in London and Birmingham are often used. In some cases, temporary relays can be set up if required. For very large or high-profile events, light aircraft can be used to bounce signals from the sky down to the receiver. These have a great advantage in that they provide an easy obstruction-free link to the ground, but they can prove extremely costly.

The most common technology for live outside broadcasting, well known to the general public, is via satellite. Uplinks for transmission can be housed in anything from a large truck offering full high definition and multi-camera video production facilities right down to satellite back-packs which can be carried by one person into the most remote and inhospitable locations. The smallest satellite uplinks weigh little more than fifteen or twenty kilos and can be checked in as airline baggage in rucksacks or solid carry-cases. Many foreign correspondents now carry a portable satellite dish which links to a network called Broadband Global Area Network (BGAN). BGAN can be accessed anywhere where there is a direct line of sight to the relevant satellite. There are different types of BGAN services, which offer different speeds and data allowances. Some allow only broadband and voice calls, while others can be used to stream video footage.

With the advent of faster mobile broadband, broadcasters are beginning to use domestic 3G and 4G mobile communication technologies to send pictures. This offers remarkably small and portable equipment and 'bonding' (or using several 3G or 4G lines at once) allows high quality HD or even 3D filming. The equipment is so small it can genuinely be carried or used in a rucksack and may also operate using Wi-Fi where there is not an adequate mobile phone signal. Of course the disadvantage of such a system is the availability of a reliable mobile communications signal and the reliance on the mobile network provider, but the low cost and portability of the equipment means it is already being used across the globe on everything from live sporting events, to news and even for low-cost Internet television channels. Such equipment can also be used to send pre-recorded material at high quality via File Transfer Protocol (uploading and downloading using the Internet).

In some very remote areas where a full satellite uplink may be too big to carry and there are no mobile communication signals, some broadcasters have used a number of bonded satellite phone signals to broadcast live television. This can prove an expensive option, but is more reliable than a 3G or 4G connection, particularly in broadcast situations where mobile communications may have been switched off by the emergency services or cut off by a natural disaster.

The OB planning process

One of the first tasks is to ensure the live broadcast equipment available is suitable for the job at hand. Some broadcasters will have their own OB vans and equipment, while others will hire in the kit they need. Before planning any live broadcasts, a researcher should ensure that the proposed location is safe and suitable for the equipment or vehicle being sent. Will it be possible to get a 'line of sight' connection if required; is there level and solid ground for a larger vehicle? Are there trees in the way of any equipment bolted on the roof or poor weather conditions that could put the equipment or crew in danger? Is there a possibility that a small satellite backpack might bring the reporter into danger or could even be stolen? It is often necessary to park an OB truck some distance from the place of broadcast, and this can cause problems because of running cables across rooms or through busy areas. Sometimes, they may need to be fed out through open windows or down staircases, which may require extra time to be spent on health and safety. The weather can also have an impact. All these factors should be taken into account, and the engineers and reporters involved should be given a clear briefing.

For larger more complicated broadcasts, the local authority and police force may have to be contacted along with private landowners to gain access to the best locations. Such a process can take months, but in the case of a big breaking news story, may have to be done in minutes. An experienced live television news crew will often take the decision to set up and start broadcasting on an important breaking event and then worry about moving or getting permission later on. Most broadcasters will have their own training and guidelines for planning such OBs, and it's important that even in the rush of daily news, they are not overlooked. As in many broadcast tasks, the best way to learn is from the staff who do the job on a daily basis.

Once all the practicalities and safety aspects have been settled, the next task is to ensure that the plans made in the office can be executed on location. In the case of television, it's important to know how many cameras will be at the site and how many 'paths' or individual lines there will be from the satellite truck back to the studio. If the producer wants to use more than one camera or send live and recorded pictures back simultaneously from the location, there will need to be more than one path, and the researcher will need to ensure they book adequate satellite links. Radio trucks too may have more than one path or feed. Sometimes radio and television broadcast facilities are combined on one truck. It's also important to know what kind of off-air communications there will be between the presenter and the studio; for example, will the 'talk-back' be via the satellite or another means of communication such as

Figure 9.4 Setting up a live OB © Nigel Phillips

a mobile phone line. Again, the ability of the presenter to hear events in the studio will affect the style and planning of the broadcast.

One issue, which is often overlooked by new researchers is the availability of light on location. While it can be daylight into late evening during a UK summer, light levels can fall very low by mid-afternoon on a cloudy day during the depths of winter. Again it's vital to check that an OB truck carries lights or the camera crew assigned to the team has lights with them.

Many broadcasters are keen to get live guests to an OB transmission point as this improves the variety and quality of their programmes. The researcher may well be expected to organise this. Although a relatively straightforward operation, it should be remembered that guests may have particular requirements for transport and introduce additional problems for location health and safety. Their mobility may be limited, and they should not be expected to endure adverse weather conditions in the same way that a professional broadcaster might be. In addition, some mobile broadcast locations are remote and difficult to locate. One great benefit of modern technology is the ability to provide a guest with a postcode or satnav coordinates to allow them to find the location easily. Remember also that they may need a parking space and security clearance in advance for some locations. The advice, as with booking all live interviewees, is to always include extra time for things to go wrong and to check and double-check all arrangements.

The final task for the OB planner is to ensure all the information they have gathered is recorded accurately and available to everyone else on the team. In a very large production, this might involve formal 'call sheets' which are sent to every member of the crew with their time and responsibilities on location. On smaller news OBs, usually a briefing will be emailed over to the reporter and producer on location, along with the technical crew, and a 'hand over' will be provided for the studio production team on the day.

Figure 9.5 Broadcast engineer Nigel Phillips rehearsing an outside broadcast © Nigel Phillips

Interview

Nigel Phillips is a freelance broadcast engineer based in the south of England. He has many years of experience working on OBs, from daily news stories to big international sporting events. He shares his advice on how to avoid those rookie journalist mistakes.

What sort of preparation should a good researcher or journalist do before arriving on the day for an OB?

Planning and preparation is vital, as you'll be working away from your usual environment. This might mean staying in a hotel overnight, and working an extended day as your story could develop. Be prepared to be outside in all weathers; this could mean having wet or cold weather clothing with you. Make sure you understand the objective of the OB. Have a good working appreciation of the technology used.

What questions should a journalist be asking you and your team to make sure the broadcast goes really well?

Make sure you ask what kit is being supplied for the OB, especially if it's not a crew you've worked with before. Obviously, you need to discuss the planned location of the OB, transmission times and whether there's any likelihood of working late or into the night. Think about whether you need any safety kit for the place where you're working. You'll need to discuss whether you'll need any camera kit to shoot video inserts and also whether those might need to be edited on location.

What are the most common mistakes which new journalists/producers make when working with OB teams?

First, lack of preparation and planning. This could be as simple as wearing the wrong clothing or assuming the story being covered will not develop and necessitate a very long day on location.

Second, it's easy to think the technical crew totally understands your contribution to the OB and your journalistic aims and objectives. Engineers may be travelling long distances to meet up with you in the middle of nowhere with little or no briefing from base, so patience and a welcoming coffee is always most appreciated!

Sometimes, producers have a lack of mechanical sympathy with the sometimes quite sophisticated equipment being used to achieve your live broadcast. It's common not to understand the basic principles of working in a remote location with problems such as two-way communications back to the gallery or studio presenter.

Technology is changing incredibly fast. It's now possible to stream live footage from a mobile phone on a 4G network. How do you think this will affect the work you and professional OB producers do in the future?

Equipment is getting much easier to use, so establishing a live link back to the studio is much simpler than it was a few years ago. It means that a journalist could be first on the scene and start sending back live reports via Skype, before a satellite uplink engineer is even aware of the story developing. With such a wide range of live transmission kit available, producers and journalists are now working with much more sophisticated live-link kits, which gives us more scope to be working flexibly in a rapidly changing news environment and not just utilising a sat truck.

Streaming

Video streaming from computers has been available for several years, but during 2014, two new video streaming apps, which used 4G or Wi-Fi connections became widely available for smartphones. Periscope and Meerkat were immediately popular and have opened up the opportunity for live broadcasting to virtually anyone. One of the main issues with the apps initially was the difficulty in finding good content. The only options for searching material were by location or person. However the opportunities offered by these apps were clear, and many journalists have already begun experimenting. As The Huffington Post's Jason Boucher explained in 2015,

> I can't wait for the first major news story to break using Periscope, but in the meantime I have to sift through live feeds of people walking, doing laundry, or driving, which is just not good content and boring to watch.

It's easy to see why easy-to-use live streaming could be an incredible breakthrough for multimedia journalism, but as with many other new technologies, there are legal implications. There's the possible invasion of privacy (how do you warn someone they are being filmed and broadcast to the world) and also the dangers of copyright infringement. Many organisations are already considering how to protect sporting events, live music and even movies from illegal live broadcast.

Producing for multiple platforms

While this chapter concentrates in the most part on the skills needed for either audio or video production, it's becoming very common for journalists to work across multiple platforms. For former BBC reporter and presenter Harry Crawford, it's one of the most significant challenges facing researchers today:

> One of the biggest challenges is making sure what you're doing works in more than one format. Radio doesn't exist in isolation anymore. Your story has to work just as well as an extended text piece for the website or as a 140 character Twitter message as it does as a piece of broadcasting. Cross-promotion is vital to building an audience.

In many media organisations, reporters and researchers produce written content alongside video or audio and material for social media networks. Researchers may need to consider the copyright implications of a radio programme being broadcast live in one country and then released as a podcast worldwide. In many broadcast newsrooms, the journalist might also be expected to plan web coverage, brief interviewees to ensure they understand their interview might be used on a variety of platforms and plan simple social media campaigns, soliciting contributions from listeners, viewers and readers.

Such multimedia working can throw up a whole variety of challenges and the larger and more complex the news organisation, the more complicated and difficult these problems can become. Some journalists would argue that a growing number of calls on a researcher's time can lead to cutting corners and reduce the quality of their work. For example, it can be argued that planning an audio feature is very different from planning a video shoot and that researching both pieces of work together may lead to the quality of both being compromised. Quite fairly, radio journalists working in multimedia newsrooms sometimes complain that their work is overshadowed by the priorities of their television colleagues, while newspaper reporters can often become frustrated when their newsrooms go 'web first', and they find their exclusives and breaking news stories published on the web before they appear in the newspaper edition. There may also be practical difficulties for journalists who are working for two or three different editors at once with different priorities and personalities.

Having said this, such multimedia researching is commonplace and works well in many news organisations. Many broadcasters and publishers would say that they have been able to cut costs and make working practices more efficient, which has kept them afloat and preserved jobs. The ability to communicate directly with audiences via social media has greatly enhanced producers' understanding of what their viewers, readers and listeners really want and think of their work. And for many journalists, working across different media has made their working lives more varied and interesting.

Remember:

- Booking live guests is about having great contacts and working at speed.
- OB technology is moving fast. You need to learn about the equipment available in your news organisation.
- Internet technology is cheap, but can cause problems such as inconsistent quality or delays on the line.
- Multimedia production is commonplace – some producers claim it is partly to blame for declining standards.

Multimedia health and safety

Multimedia production can be dangerous, particularly for journalists who are working on daily news or in hostile environments. According to the latest Health and Safety Executive (HSE) Statistics (2014), workers and contributors in arts and entertainment don't have as many accidents as those in the highest risk businesses, but the risk is certainly higher than those who work in regular administration roles. It is really important that you take seriously your safety and that of those around you. Aside from your legal responsibilities, no reasonable person would want to cause injury to themselves, a co-worker or contributor.

There is some basic advice on risk assessment for journalists in Chapter 5, but this does not cover the complexities of multimedia production. Most broadcasters and production companies, however large or small, will have their own rigorous health and safety procedures. Their employees will have received advice and training, and freelance staff must ensure they understand their employer's health and safety policies and are aware of the procedures for risk assessment.

Ultimately, your employer and the organisation in control of premises or facilities you use have overall responsibility for health and safety. In practice though, the HSE names 'the producer' (2002) as the person who is responsible for everyday health and safety. In many news shoots with small crews, the journalist will be the producer, and this means that responsibility can fall to you. Your employer must have put the correct procedures in place to support you and have given you the advice and training you need to ensure the health and safety of everyone involved in your production. It's really important that you respect any health and safety training that you receive, do proper risk assessments and raise any issues or concerns you have. Breaches of health and safety laws in the UK can be criminal offences. This pales into insignificance when you think that you might have to live with the guilt and shame of maiming or seriously hurting a colleague or contributor.

Remember

- Finding great interviewees takes time and skill.
- Spending time with a contributor and preparing them for an interview will always pay off.
- Archive material can be expensive and must be copyright cleared.
- Always use Electronic Press Kits with caution.
- Different research skills are needed for daily news and long-form programme production.
- A good live news researcher will have some basic technical knowledge.
- OBs require knowledge and planning.
- The health and safety of everyone involved in a production are paramount.

Things to do

Build your contacts

Listen to a radio news programme (ideally at least half an hour long). Note down each of the interviewees who appear in the reports or are live. Using the Internet, try to find contact details for each of the contributors. Are their direct contact details online or do their organisations have press offices? Which of them might be useful to you in future? Put the details in your contacts book.

Practise your research

Choose a story that interests you from one of today's newspapers. Now consider how you might turn that story into a video news report. Use your new research skills to track down a case study and interviewees. Also suggest two or three suitable locations within a reasonable travelling distance for filming on one day. You need not contact the contributors or get permission for the filming, but ensure you could do so if required.

Research in action

Following on from the research above, imagine you are a producer working on the story and you need to write a detailed brief for a reporter. Write a guest briefing for each interviewee. Use the Internet to dig out previous stories on the same subject or background information.

Issues to discuss

Social media is rapidly taking over from the telephone as a means of instant communication. How do you think broadcast journalists can best use social media? Can social networking contacts ever replace the telephone for broadcast researchers?

Current trends in multimedia news production favour the use of case studies. Discuss the benefits and disadvantages of using such case studies in audio or video news reports. Is there a danger that concentrating on personal testimony can detract from explaining more complex issues adequately?

The broadcast media in the UK are regulated in a different way to the print media. How does this affect the news coverage on radio and television, and what challenges or benefits might this bring for broadcast researchers.

Places to learn more

Books and journals

Adie, K. 2003. *The Kindness of Strangers: The Autobiography*. London: Headline.

Bock, M. A. 2015. Showing versus telling: Comparing online video from newspaper and television websites [online]. *Journalism*. Available from: http://jou.sagepub.com/content/early/2015/02/10/1464884914568076.full [accessed 5 January 2016].

Huffman, F. 2004. *Practical IP and Telecom for Broadcast Engineering and Operations: What You Need to Know to Survive, Long Term*. London: Focal Press.

McLeish, R. 2005. *Radio Production*. 5th Edition. London: Focal Press

Millerson, G. and Owens, J. 2012. *Television Production*. London: Focal Press.

Sedorkin, J. 2010. *Interviewing: A Guide for Journalists and Writers*. London: Allen and Unwin.

Snow, J. 2005. *Shooting History. A Personal Journey*. London: Harper Perennial.

Online resources

Broadcast   www.broadcastnow.co.uk/
BBC College of Production   www.bbc.co.uk/academy/collegeofproduction/

Media College	www.mediacollege.com/
Ofcom Code	http://stakeholders.ofcom.org.uk/binaries/
	broadcast/code-july-15/Ofcom_Broadcast_
	Code_July_2015.pdf
US National Radio Project	www.radioproject.org/
Videomaker Magazine	www.videomaker.com

References

Castrey, A. and Heal, M. 2010. *Secret filming and the case law that subsequently arises* [online]. London: Law Gazette. Available from: www.lawgazette.co.uk/law/secret-filming-and-the-case-law-that-subsequently-arises/54378.fullarticle [accessed 5 July 2015].

Channel Four. 2015. *Producers' Handbook. Secret Filming Guidelines* [online]. London: Channel Four. Available from: www.channel4.com/producers-handbook/c4-guidelines/secret-filming-guidelines [accessed 5 July 2015].

Health and Safety Executive. 2002. *Health and Safety in audio-visual production. Your legal duties* [online]. London: HSE. Available from: www.hse.gov.uk/pubns/indg360.pdf [accessed 5 July 2015].

Health and Safety Executive. 2014. *Health and Safety Statistics. Annual Report for Great Britain* [online]. London: HSE. Available from: www.hse.gov.uk/statistics/overall/hssh1314.pdf [accessed 6 July 2015].

Marshall, S. 2012. *5 examples of iPhone journalism from BBC 5 live's Nick Garnett* [online]. Available from: www.journalism.co.uk/news/five-examples-of-iphone-journalism-from-bbc-5-live-s-nick-garnett/s2/a551533/ Brighton: journalism.co.uk [accessed 13 July 2015].

Sopel, J. 2013. *Researching an interview: Jon Sopel and Libby Purves* [video, online]. London: BBC College of Journalism. Available from: www.bbc.co.uk/academy/journalism/skills/interviewing/article/art20130702112133437 [accessed 20 May 2015].

Where not referenced, quotations are from interviews, emails or social media conversations with the author.

10 Working overseas

Introduction

The challenge of researching a story, tracking down sources and gathering the best interviews becomes harder when you're working in a foreign country. Some nations may share our language, but have massively different cultures and traditions; others offer a linguistic challenge alongside the problems of acclimatising to a different culture. Governments all work differently, as do the legal systems and media organisations overseas. Added to all these obstacles, an unfamiliar country may have very different attitudes to openness, Freedom of Information and human rights.

These differences make it more complicated for any profession working overseas, but journalists face an additional problem. They may be asked to work in a country where journalism itself is seen very differently to the way they may be familiar with at home. In some countries journalists are viewed as those tasked with publicising the government's worldview and little else. They are not expected or, in some cases, permitted to question the government, its officials or other influential people. In many nations, journalists are viewed with suspicion or seen as a danger to public order and in some nations journalists are regularly imprisoned or even executed for doing their jobs.

This chapter is an introduction to some of the research challenges faced by journalists planning to travel and work abroad, with plenty of practical advice from those in the field.

This chapter covers:

- Getting started
- Freelance funding options
- Travel, transport and communication
- Sorting the paperwork
- Safety
- Personal Security
- What to take
- When you arrive
- Leaving in a hurry
- Travel journalism

Getting started

If you work for a larger media organisation, or have been commissioned to produce a piece of journalism then you will have already chosen your destination and you will have colleagues to help plan your trip. The cost of your assignment overseas will also most likely be funded. If you are travelling as a freelancer, either for a short visit or with the aim of settling overseas and working as a stringer, then getting started can be more difficult.

The research process starts pretty much as soon as you decide you want to work overseas. A good way to build experience is to organise a shorter trip abroad with the aim of returning with one or two stories to sell. It may be possible to personally fund a cheap flight and a few weeks in a youth hostel in the hope that you will return with material that editors will want to buy. Even if you can't get a commission before you go, blog about your experiences and contact editors as soon as you find something interesting to work on. You may come back with some commissions.

The other option for a freelance journalist is to take the plunge and move overseas permanently to develop a career as a freelance foreign correspondent. If you're trying to build a reputation, it's not a bad idea to choose an unpopular location to start work. There are obviously very many peaceful countries with warm environments and great living standards that already have plenty of journalists. By choosing an environment, which is less appealing or well known, you are far more likely to find buyers for your work. If you're not sure where to start looking, give some newspapers and broadcasters a ring to see where they are keen to recruit or send stringers.

Freelance funding options

If you can't find the funds yourself, there are a number of ways to raise money to cover stories overseas. It may be possible to borrow money through an ordinary consumer loan in advance of your trip with the aim of repaying the loan when you sell your story. Some reporters have had good experiences of crowdfunding, particularly where they have a compelling untold story to research and share. The best way to start with crowdfunding, is to look at a variety of websites to see which journalistic projects have succeeded best on each. Kickstarter may be the one of most famous sites, but Indiegogo and Rockethub are also general sites which include journalistic projects.

There are also some sites that specialise in journalism. Contributoria asks you to pitch individual projects. Uncoverage encourages funders to fund you personally and Beacon is a funding platform and publisher in one. Consider whether you can reward people for supporting your work, perhaps with a specially bound copy of your report or free access to download multimedia content. You can get inspiration for rewards by looking at other projects that have been successful in raising money. If you decide to borrow money or ask people to invest in your work with the promise of a return, make sure you don't raise debtors' hopes too high for a quick or generous return.

There are a number of organisations, which are prepared to fund innovative or unusual journalism projects. Some of those, which have offered grants over a number of years in the United Kingdom currently include:

- One World Media.
- European Journalism Centre – through its 'Journalism Grants' programme.
- Britdoc – through a number of funds with different criteria.
- The Manuel Rivera-Ortiz Foundation.

- The Firecracker Photographic Grant.
- International Women's Media Foundation (Howard G Buffett Fund).
- The Knight Foundation.

The Global Investigative Journalism Network also keeps an up-to-date list of organisations that offer grants for a variety of journalistic activities.

Writing a successful grant application

Although writing may be your profession, writing a grant application can be very different from journalistic writing. Make sure you research the grant provider and understand why they're giving away money. They will have aims and objectives and you will need to fulfil those. You should also read the application guidelines with care. If you know anyone, or can speak in person to someone who works at the funding organisation then do so. They will be far more likely to give you useful information and tips on what they are really seeking.

Have a clear idea of what you are trying to achieve with your piece of journalism and make sure you can boil it down into one succinct point. As investigative journalist Djordje Padejski wrote for the JSK Website in 2015,

> Keep your project description to one sentence no longer than 15 to 20 words. Think of it like the lead of your project. Even the most innovative projects can be defined briefly and described clearly. What exactly do you want to do or to develop?

Consider how your piece of journalism might bring about change, over and above being a great piece of reporting. For example, it may help to train new journalists, develop an innovative piece of software or raise awareness of an important issue. Be practical, explain exactly what you intend to do, what difficulties and challenges you might face and how you might overcome them. Where requested, include a realistic and detailed budget. The funders will want to see you are able to spend their money responsibly.

Another option to secure funding is to seek sponsorship or commercial support for your trip. Some media organisations have strict ethical rules on accepting money for foreign travel and accommodation. Their staff are not allowed to accept any funding and are not permitted to go on any funded press trips. Other organisations are happy for their journalists to report while attending PR events and trips and also find additional commercial funding for their work. In some publications any outside funding is made absolutely clear in the copy; in others nothing is said. This line between independent journalism and funded or paid-for content is becoming increasingly blurred in the online environment. If in doubt, check with your editor before seeking outside funding.

Remember:

- Going somewhere unpopular will make starting out overseas easier.
- Consider working in the UK and saving a fund to allow you to travel.
- There are some grants available, but competition is tough.
- You will need persistence and a great idea to secure funding.
- Sponsorship or commercial support may be an option.

Travel, transport and communication

Organising transport has become much cheaper and easier over the past twenty years, with the advent of online booking. It's relatively straightforward to organise transport to countries that are well connected politically and have a reasonably secure infrastructure. Many large media organisations subcontract travel arrangements to a specialist travel provider. This can sometimes be irritating, when you may not be able to organise exactly the travel options you would prefer, but a good commercial travel agent should be able to work with you. The advantage using a specialist company is that when your plans change or travel arrangements go wrong, then the agent will be able to change or make bookings for you.

If you're booking travel as a freelancer or for a small media organisation, most of the cheapest deals can be secured online, but it's well worth checking some of the travel advice websites for tips and also contacting specialist travel agents. Those that work with ethnic communities who travel regularly can have great deals.

Most people now know of the growing options for cheap accommodation overseas. Alongside many hotel booking websites, there are youth hostels, university halls of residence and websites that allow you to stay in someone's home. If these are not suitable or available, it's worthwhile contacting the local offices of companies with headquarters in your home country, academic research organisations or even language schools which can often put you in touch with reasonably-priced and reliable local accommodation. In countries with a warmer climate camping may also be a possibility, although it's important to consider keeping any filming or recording equipment secure.

Do remember though, if you have a hectic work schedule it can be really important to have comfortable, quiet accommodation. If you're travelling to a country where the food or water supply or even extreme heat may make you unwell on a short trip, it's worth paying a little extra for a comfortable room with some safe clean food. Important work trips are not always the best time to immerse yourself in the more challenging aspects of local culture.

Remote and inaccessible locations

Some countries are far more difficult to reach and it's not straightforward to book transport easily online. They do not have safe or reliable travel infrastructures, or can be cut off from the rest of the world for security or political reasons. Of course these problems are often the very reason why journalists wish to travel to these areas.

The first place to start when booking travel to these locations from the United Kingdom is the Foreign Office travel advice website. If there is UK government advice not to travel to a country or region, this will have important implications for your arrangements. Specialist insurance will be needed and you may not be able to rely on help from the Foreign Office if there are problems at your destination.

If an area is remote, but not subject to a Foreign Office warning, then there are a variety of places to find out about travel options and get useful advice. The destination's own government and tourism website may be a good starting point. In addition, the websites of some of the best-known travel guides can be good starting places, with up to date advice on the safest areas to visit and comfortable hotels. Again, it may be worthwhile getting advice from a specialist travel agent before booking transport, as they can offer valuable expertise. Before booking flights with lesser-known airlines you may also want to consult the European Union's airline blacklist and other safety records. If you're looking to book local public transport such as buses or track down a driver, Tripadvisor has a variety of forums where you can post enquiries and questions and can be a great place to find reliable local travel advice; such as hotels with reasonable standards and taxi drivers who can be trusted.

A number of organisations provide support for journalists planning to travel overseas. They are particularly valuable for freelancers. The charity One World Media runs regular public workshops and can offer funding and advice for young journalists working overseas. The Frontline Club in London is a meeting place for young and experienced foreign correspondents and also provides excellent workshops. It also runs a charity to support freelance journalists called Frontline Freelance. The Rory Peck Trust works to support freelancers abroad and the organisation Reporters Without Borders provides some useful publications. There are also a variety of companies and international journalism networks, such as the Global Investigative Journalism Network, which offer training, internships and other support programmes.

Remember:

- It takes time and effort to find cheap means of travel.
- Specialist travel agents can be a great option.
- Get good advice before travelling somewhere remote or inaccessible.
- Safety comes first when booking travel.
- Get as much training and advice as possible from other journalists before you go.

Sorting the paperwork

Once you've booked your transport, there will be a lot of paperwork to complete. You may be a seasoned traveller, but a working trip is very different from a holiday and particularly if you're working as a journalist.

Passports, visas and permits

You will need to check the passport, visa and other legal requirements for journalists working in your destination. Some journalists travel on tourist or student visas, but this needs to be a carefully considered decision. If you are caught working overseas without the correct visa and paperwork, you may be deported, banned from returning or face an even worse sanction such as prosecution and imprisonment. In 2013 three journalists for the TV network Al Jazeera were arrested and imprisoned in Egypt. There were many political issues surrounding their subsequent trial, but one of the charges was 'operating without a permit', which Al Jazeera fully admitted (2015). This was not the main reason for their prosecution, but the decision did not help their defence in court.

Some countries deliberately prevent foreign journalists from entering or have inadequate administration systems, and travelling as a tourist or student or even without paperwork may be the only option. Once again though, this must be a very carefully made decision and appropriate measures should be taken to reduce any possible risk not only to you, but also to anyone who works or comes into contact with you. In 2013 the BBC made a formal apology after allowing investigative reporter John Sweeny to travel to North Korea as part of a student tourist group. The corporation was accused of putting at risk the lives of the young people travelling in the group with the undercover reporter.

Remember if you do travel on a tourist or student visa you will need a good cover story and you won't be able to turn up at the airport with bags full of professional equipment.

Make copies of all your important documentation before you leave. Take a couple of paper copies with you and make sure you have access via the web to online copies. It may be worth leaving some paper copies with friends at home or giving them access to the online copies to print out.

UK government support

The Foreign Office provides a useful leaflet to explain the help and advice it can offer to Britons traveling overseas. It runs through how the government can help if you get into trouble and what action it expects from travellers to ensure they keep themselves safe. It is important to take a note of the British Embassy, Commission or Consulate contact details in the countries where you are travelling. If there is no British presence, you can contact the offices of another European Union country or, on some occasions, officials from Australia and New Zealand. The Foreign Office has an email service, Facebook page and Twitter feed which should also be monitored, particularly in more remote or unstable countries, but remember that help from embassy or consular officials is not a legal right. In difficult times you may well be on your own.

Some countries have foreign correspondent clubs in the capital cities. Some are membership only, but others offer accommodation and are excellent places to begin a period reporting overseas. If you'll be in the region for a while you may well be able to become a member. It's certainly worth making contact before travelling.

Insurance

Tourism travel insurance will not cover you if you are working abroad and will certainly not cover you for some of the additional risks you may be taking when working as a journalist overseas. It is important to approach a specialist insurer (several can be found with a simple online search; the Rory Peck Trust also provides a good list). The organisation Reporters Without Borders offers its own insurance policy; details can be accessed via its website. Expect this insurance to be expensive, especially if you will be travelling into a hostile environment. It is important to be honest about where you're going and what work you are planning to undertake, because if you try to keep some of your plans secret, there is a danger you will not be insured. Before skimping on insurance, consider what you might do if your policy proves to be inadequate or invalid. Do you have enough money to deal with an emergency or a plan for alternative help? It may be worth taking an American Express credit card with you, as the company provides access to its Global Assist Programme. It offers a hotline to call in an emergency and help with lost passports and luggage, money and legal support.

Health

You won't be able to work if you're unwell or injured. Your insurance policy should cover you for healthcare abroad and any additional risks you might be facing, but it's important to know where to access that care and whether you may need to take extra resources with you. You should do some research about each of the places you will be visiting. Hard though it may be to admit, in areas where local healthcare services are poor, you may want to identify a hospital, which provides higher standards of cleanliness and training. In general these are private facilities. American Embassies often provide details of healthcare providers on their websites. If you choose to attend public health facilities, you may need to take supplies with you, such as clean syringes and dressings.

Ensure you have any relevant inoculations before you travel. You may also need to take antimalarial medication. The best defence against malaria is not to getting bitten in the first place and good mosquito nets and insect repellents are also important. You should always take a basic first aid kit. If you're in a remote area also put together a pack of drugs and equipment you might need if injured or taken ill. It's wise to consider hygiene and take a selection of clean syringes and other medical equipment. Although you can't buy medication such as antibiotics off prescription in the United Kingdom, you may be able to buy them at your destination. In some countries, you are advised to carry antibiotics for possible intestinal infections. Find out your blood group before you go. If you have regular medication, then ensure you have enough supplies and keep a small slip of paper in your purse or wallet giving your blood group and giving doctors information about the type and dose of medication you need.

Remember:

- Make sure you get the right visa – a tourist visa may not be appropriate.
- Foreign journalists need permits in some countries.
- Don't rely on British diplomatic officials to come to your aid.
- Ensure your travel insurance is relevant and adequate.
- You may need inoculations or to take medication with you.
- Consider taking a good quality medical kit.

Safety

Journalists travel regularly to places that most people would not consider 'safe'. Even in the United Kingdom, you may be heading to the heart of a storm, while everyone else is staying inside or leaving the area.

The best way to ensure you have considered all the various risks involved in your journey and done your best to plan for them is to complete a risk assessment and this is particularly important when travelling overseas. Journalists working for larger media organisations will be familiar with completing these as a regular part of their job. For freelancers, this may seem less necessary, but a good risk assessment can serve as a really useful checklist to ensure you've planned comprehensively and done as much work as possible to keep yourself safe. The basics of completing a risk assessment are discussed in Chapter 3 and the charity, The Rory Peck Trust, offers some particularly good resources to help freelance journalists complete a risk assessment for an overseas trip.

Before you consider a trip as a freelance journalist, ensure that publications you might approach on your return will consider taking your work and will pay enough to merit the risk. Many reputable news organisations are becoming concerned about the risks some freelance journalists are prepared to take to secure stories and don't want to be accused of encouraging them. For example the French news agency, Agence France Presse, will no longer

Figure 10.1 Risk assessments should consider the impact of unfamiliar climate and landscape
© Mathew Charles

take freelance work produced in areas too dangerous for its own staff. In his blog AFP's Global News Director, Michele Leridon, wrote (2014):

> If someone travels to Syria and offers us images or information when they return, we will not use it. Freelancers have paid a high price in the Syrian conflict. High enough. We will not encourage people to take that kind of risk.

Your work might be bought by a smaller, more radical, news website, but will that pay for your trip?

Personal security

Depending on the nature of your assignment, start researching your personal security before you leave and get as much up-to-date information as you can when you arrive. Join relevant social media networks, such as the Facebook Group 'Vulture Club' which brings together several thousand foreign correspondents. This is the work that could keep you alive and it's worth considerable time and effort. If it's at all possible, try to find another journalist who is familiar with the area where you plan to work and ask them to check your safety plans. They will be able to identify any problems or issues very easily.

Training

If possible, get some relevant personal security training before you leave home. There are a variety of companies which offer 'hostile environment' training to journalists. These can be expensive, but extremely worthwhile. If you're not sure which companies are reputable and offer good value for money, contact one of the charities or professional organisations at the end of this chapter for advice. Some media organisations won't employ you if don't have hostile environment training and the courses often offer excellent first aid training.

Keeping in touch

When working in remote or unstable areas it is very important to make a plan for keeping in contact with someone at home. Ensure that if you disappear, your employer, relatives and friends have various ways to contact you or advise local authorities where you've been travelling.

There are different forms of so-called 'communication plan' and they will vary depending on your assignment, but the basic idea is to put together a network of people who can be contacted and can contact each other if anything happens to you. This will probably start with a person who is nominated as your next of kin in the United Kingdom, alongside any employer, commissioning editor or professional organisation. In the country where you are working you should also identify someone who can act on your behalf if anything goes wrong. This could be a friend or colleague or if you're travelling to an unfamiliar area the local office of a major broadcaster may well be happy to provide this service. You should also make a note of the relevant contacts at the local embassy, commission or consulate.

You should agree to make contact with your key contact at pre-agreed regular intervals. This could be a phone call, text or social media post. Agree with those contacts what they should do if you don't make contact. Clearly in areas of higher risk, action may be taken more swiftly, but equally these may be areas where communications are more difficult.

In the most difficult environments, do not identify yourself as a journalist unless you have to. Give practical information about your whereabouts to the fewest people possible, trust even fewer. It's important too to be vigilant and if there is a danger of being kidnapped, take defensive measures. In 2006 the BBC Correspondent Caroline Hawley told The Independent about her experiences working in Baghdad:

> We weren't to spend any more than 20 minutes in one place. Our security guys would keep a watch and if they didn't like an area, we left. We were filming in one area of town once and the same car was spotted driving past us three times so we had to cut things short and leave.

One of the most effective precautions when working in an unstable or hostile environment is simply never to assume you are safe.

'Proof of life' document

This document is only necessary when traveling to an area where there is a risk of kidnapping or other form of detention. It contains confidential information that would allow your colleagues and family at home to confirm that you are still alive. This generally includes a brief list of questions and answers that would only be known to you and someone close to you, the more obscure the better. It's not a perfect solution, but may provide your loved ones with some reassurance in a difficult situation and also ensure efforts to free you are continued. Templates for a communication plan and proof of life document can both be found on the Rory Peck Trust website.

What to take

Personal protective equipment

One area where you will certainly need advice is personal safety equipment. If you're going to a stable, relatively safe country you may be planning to work alone and want to take some practical precautions. For example you might want to buy a money belt. In hostile environments you will probably want to take a safety vest or helmet with you, or arrange to buy one when you arrive. There's no point buying the first kit you see online, as it may not be appropriate for the weapons and ammunition being used in the area where you are working. There are soft vests and those with plates, which provide some protection against rifle rounds. Any kit will also need to be fitted correctly and comfortable enough for you to work in and carry around with you. The charity Frontline Freelance offers some excellent advice on safety equipment and links to reputable suppliers. The charity can also loan equipment in some cases.

Professional equipment

The more multimedia production kit you take with you, the more opportunities you will have to sell content. If you're going to a relatively safe country you can take a laptop with video camera, audio recorder, tablet and of course smartphone. Remember to check where and how you will be able to access the Internet and take a look at the cost and implications of buying local SIM cards. Also remember that access to the Internet may not be as fast or reliable as you have in your home country. You may be unable to upload images or video. Whatever kit you take, make sure you have enough chargers for your kit. Take back-up batteries, adapters

Figure 10.2 Taking an OB kit overseas requires a carnet and plenty of luggage allowance
© Nigel Phillips

to help you charge from a car socket and if practical a solar charger. You don't want to miss a story because your phone is flat.

If you are travelling to an area with no Internet access, you may buy or hire BGAN technology, which allows satellite access to the Internet. (There is more on this in Chapter 9.) The decision to take this equipment has to be weighed against the risk of drawing attention to yourself or even being identified as a journalist.

Carnets

If you are travelling outside the European Union with a technical kit, which is clearly going to be used for professional media production you will need an ATA Carnet. This allows you to take the kit through customs without having to go through complex import and export procedures. In some countries it can help guard against having the kit 'confiscated'. A carnet is valid for a year. It's made up of a cover and vouchers and you'll need to make sure you ask for enough vouchers to cover your journey (depending on how many countries you intend to visit).

There is a useful government website explaining in detail how and when a carnet can be used (see Online Resources for this chapter). Bear in mind that you will need to apply for your carnet in advance from the London Chamber of Commerce and Industry. This can be done online or by post. You will have to pay a fee for the carnet and also lodge a sum of money as a bond, which can be retrieved on your return. This is a percentage of the value of your kit and is usually around 40 per cent. A carnet saves a great deal of time and bother, but is clearly not appropriate if you're travelling undercover.

Technology in hostile environments

If you're travelling to a hostile environment, then you will need to spend far more time planning how to take professional equipment into the country. Start with considering a back-up plan if your kit is confiscated at the airport (this happens even in relatively stable countries). You may be lucky and get to keep your smartphone, or you may need to buy new equipment when you arrive.

If you're planning to access the Internet, it's important to consider how secure your communications might be. Get advice from colleagues on the best SIM card to use and use an encrypted network such as TOR to access the web. In some areas it may not be possible to use any kit other than a smartphone, especially if you are working undercover. Finally it's important to consider whether it's safe to save any journalistic material on your computer or phone. You should certainly lock any files and encrypt your work, but even better try to get it uploaded onto some cloud storage as quickly as you can. Emailing it to a secret email account is a simple option. Even if you're relatively sure of your own security, consider the possibility of drawing attention to your colleagues and contacts. If necessary ask their advice as soon as you arrive on the best way to communicate securely.

Money

One other important aspect of your trip to consider is money. You will need far more than you expect and it's important to plan several ways to access funds, in case your cash gets lost or is stolen. If you are travelling to a remote area you will need to carry cash, but this puts you at considerable risk. Think about how you plan to transport that money. Break the cash up and keep it in different places. Are there locations where you might be able to store small caches of money? If you are working with colleagues ensure you have a plan if one of you loses their cash and make sure you have enough for all of you. Ensure some of your cash is in dollars as dollar notes are desirable in most countries.

Remember you may not have access to an ATM or your bank account, so nominate someone at home to send you money in an emergency. This can be done using transfer companies and the money can be accessed via a local agent (usually a shop) or in some countries the funds can be accessed on your mobile phone in a 'mobile wallet'. If you're planning to take a prepaid card or credit card, consider how you will access those funds and also how you can keep the card safe.

When working in some countries you will need money to pay local officials, checkpoints and for your own security. Don't underestimate how much this will cost and make sure you have access to the funds if you need them.

Personal life

If you are going overseas for while, try to spend some time with migrants from your destination country here in the United Kingdom. Take the opportunity to chat with them about the problems they faced when migrating. Ask about their food and traditions. Visit an ethnic shop to taste some specialities. If you are vegetarian or vegan, ask people whether your dietary needs can be met or even understood in your destination country. This research at home could be a great opportunity to write your first feature about your chosen country. As BBC journalist and former freelance James Longman told a workshop at the Frontline Club in 2012, his expertise and research gave him a massive head start.

> If you've got the network set-up you can then go to a place and . . . from Syria's point of view . . . there wasn't anyone with contact network that I had. I'd been writing about Syria for about a year previously. I had a way in.

Do as much online research as you can before you go, speaking to others who have worked in your destination. Look on Internet bulletin boards and chat rooms. Think about the things that you find most important at home and if necessary take them with you. I have come across seasoned travellers who take pillows, jars of pickle and even toilet rolls with them. In particular, consider whether poor hygiene is something that you might find hard to cope with and take washes, wipes and cleansers with you if you need them.

Remember:

- Safety is an absolute priority.
- When travelling abroad a risk assessment is vital.
- In more challenging areas set up a communication plan and prepare a proof of life document.
- Get proper advice and training on personal safety.
- Plan your medical care and take supplies if needed.
- Make a plan in case your money is lost or stolen.
- Don't forget to take those important personal items.

When you arrive

There will be some practical arrangements to make when you arrive. You'll need to set up a base and find somewhere secure to lock up any specialist equipment. If necessary organise local mobile phones or SIM cards and make sure you find somewhere with good Internet access.

Don't underestimate the problems caused by 'culture shock', particularly in countries which are very different to your own. You may have had great fun living rough on holiday, but working in extreme temperatures without adequate food or rest can be a dramatically different experience. If you have a very short time to complete your assignment, jet lag can also be a significant problem. Unless you are very short of time, allow yourself some space to rest and adjust.

As part of your risk assessment you should have identified a number of valuable contacts who might be able to help you when you arrive at your destination. You should have been in touch with them before you left and can now arrange some meetings. Contact as many local journalists as you can, as they will be valuable sources of information. It's likely the first people you will meet in most countries are people from your home country working overseas like you: businesspeople, those working for NGOs, charities and other groups. You will probably also come into contact with politicians and government officials. They will probably speak English and provide a particular view of a country and its people. Far harder is finding new and authentic voices.

Abigail Fielding-Smith is the former Beirut Correspondent for the *Financial Times*:

> I would say the biggest challenge for any foreign correspondent is getting beyond them. To some extent that's just about spending time in a place and if possible learning the language, but it's also about talking to everyone you encounter everywhere you go. Not interviewing them, but chatting and listening and being alert to what they're saying and asking follow-up questions and overcoming the social embarrassment of asking them if they'd mind introducing you to other people, if they are talking about someone who sounds interesting. You're never off duty, basically, and it's quite a weird way to interact with your environment, seeing everyone as a potential source.

When making contacts overseas, don't forget the power of online social networking. And don't forget the social network that's most popular for journalists in your home country might not be the most used in your destination. Consider setting-up social networking accounts both in English and the language of your host country. Even if you don't speak the relevant language fluently you can usually rustle up a few words with an online translation service, it can help people to track you down and understand what you do and who you are. Aside from anything, it's a nice gesture.

Interview

Venetia Rainey is a freelance journalist based in Beirut. She works in text, radio and film for some of the world's best known news outlets.

Clearly language can be a barrier for journalists working overseas, but what other challenges are there when researching stories?

Knowing the country well enough to root out the original, getting insightful stories is a big challenge. A lot of people think you can just parachute in and out of countries and just write the exciting stories, but proper journalism comes from a sustained and deep knowledge of not just the country, but the region it's in. To develop contacts, understand the nuances, and avoid going after stories that are clichéd; you need to have spent at least a few months somewhere. As a journalist, you can't just get to know somewhere by reading the news about it, that gives you zero insight into which stories AREN'T being told. You have to be on the ground figuring things out yourself.

Access can be a challenge, but in my experience that's more of an issue in Western countries. Getting hold of government ministers, militia chiefs and refugees is nowhere near as hard it might sound out here in the Middle East; all it takes is the right contacts and a lot of calling around. The lack of proper statistics and verifiable data – that's also a huge challenge for journalists in this region (the Middle East).

How do you start building a network and sources when you arrive in a new country?

Be sociable, get on Facebook, and contact the NGOs. The easiest place to meet useful people is at parties and bars, so going out and 'networking', no matter how horrible it sounds, is totally essential. Local journalists, in particular, are a mine of information; they're great people to touch base with when you land somewhere new. Other foreign correspondents can be super useful as well, and there will always be a network of them to tap into once you've won their trust/earned your stripes. Facebook is a great resource for both this, and for finding local events/parties/conferences that you can attend to meet people and network. Local and international NGOs are the go-to source for free field trips and finding stories outside the capital where everyone else is. A word of warning: it's a small world out here, so be careful about the first impression you make – if you stick around you will definitely be meeting or working with these people again.

Many journalists use local 'fixers'. What difficulties are there in finding someone you trust to work with and also making sure they are kept safe in difficult environments?

I've never used fixers, mostly because as a freelancer, I've never been able to afford them. My 'fixers' are contacts I've made for a story, NGOs who are taking me to visit projects, or friends I've made along the way – they're normally the ones keeping me safe! I do use translators, however, and as a rule of thumb, I only use people who have been referred to me by others. I then use my instincts as to whether they are trustworthy or not. Although obviously the stakes are not as high as for someone working in a war zone, a translator has the power to twist or totally omit what interviewees are telling you, so trust is important.

Translators and fixers

If you don't speak the relevant language, you will need to secure the services of translators and/or fixers. Large news organisations employ people specifically for this job, while local journalists, students or other English speakers will often supplement their incomes working with international journalists. There are a number of ways to track down a fixer or translator, but it's wise to get a recommendation, particularly in a country where there are security issues.

There has been heated debate about the role local fixers play in the work of foreign journalists. Some argue they are doing the work of journalists, without the payment or credit and are being badly exploited. Fixers themselves have begun writing about their experiences and raising concerns about the way the foreign press operates overseas; particularly those journalists who are not willing to spend time and effort living in an area and getting to know the people. If your fixer does much of the research and interview work for you, then you should certainly consider giving them a by-line or journalism credit. If they aspire to work as a journalist or want to build contacts with overseas news organisations then you should help and advise them wherever you can.

Both translators and fixers can be expensive. If they put their lives at risk while working with you, then you also have a moral obligation to consider their safety. Making sure your local team can move away from a particular area or start a new life can be very costly indeed and is generally not an option available to freelancers. If you can't pay, you may well still find people willing to help you. Make sure you understand why they are offering their help (do they have a vested political interest?). If they are hoping to develop their own careers ensure you give them any help you can in return. You will not aid your research work or build the respect and local contacts you need by exploiting people.

When you start work in some countries, prepare to see things and speak to people you find disagreeable or even offensive. You may disagree strongly with the way people behave or treat each other and working in some countries can be particularly challenging for women, but showing some understanding will help you to secure your contacts' trust. You may be writing a passionate campaigning piece about the treatment of a particular minority group, but you won't be able to understand the views or opinions of those you interview if you attempt to lecture or bully them. Read as widely as you can before you travel, be open minded and where you can, ask questions. Courtesy, good manners and respect will get you an awful lot further than you might imagine.

Leaving in a hurry

If you'll be working in a country where there is a danger you may have to get out quickly; it's wise to plan this on your arrival. You may want to buy travel tickets in advance to avoid drawing attention to yourself as you leave. In areas where there is no transport you'll need access to a vehicle and possibly someone to drive you to a border. Some journalists pack what they call a 'grab bag' with personal items and travel essentials (such as a passport and dollars) so they can leave the country in an emergency.

If you leave quickly, don't leave anything behind that might incriminate or endanger people who have helped you. You might also want to consider options for getting your journalistic work back by a different route. Consider travelling with decoy items and asking someone trustworthy to transport the material. If possible, upload anything you can via a secure internet connection and even consider sending material back regularly rather than keeping it all with you. Again get advice from people working on the ground and have a clear plan, to avoid being taken by surprise.

Travel journalism

Many new journalists aspire for a career in travel journalism. The specialism offers the chance to travel and experience different cultures without many of the challenges and dangers faced by foreign correspondents. Given this popularity, travel writing is a very competitive area and great research skills can put you ahead of the field. Here's Lyn Hughes, the Editor of *Wanderlust Magazine*, speaking to *Press Gazette* (2003)

> People wanting to be travel journalists must have good research skills, accuracy and thoroughness, as well as an understanding of what motivates the reader – people plan and book their dream trips as a result of what they have read in our magazine.

The best way to build a career as a travel writer is to read widely and write as much as you can. Look for a 'niche' and write a blog. Think about which audience you want to reach, as travellers come in all ages and with a wide variety of incomes. Learn about your industry by following some of the trade publications such as Travel Trade Gazette and Travel Weekly and keep in touch with other travel writers using networking sites. You will need to show an editor that you have a real passion for travel and an interest in the places you visit, over and above the possible 'glamour' of the job. Travel journalism isn't just about visiting luxury hotels abroad; writing about your local area or travels in the United Kingdom is a great way to practise your skills.

When you are travelling it's really important to keep notes; otherwise you risk returning home having had an enjoyable trip, but with nothing to write about. Your work is supposed to be journalism so keep an eye out for an angle or 'peg' and write your story around that focus. This will also make your first on spec articles easier to pitch. Great writing skills will help the reader to imagine your experiences and share the journey with you. Even better, if you can produce good multimedia content, that will make you more employable.

If you're looking for ideas to get you started and advice on pitching your ideas to travel editors, take a look at the features section in Chapter 8.

Figure 10.3 Travel journalist Lottie Gross takes some local transport in Kenya © Lottie Gross

Interview

Lottie Gross is an Assistant Editor at roughguides.com and a freelance travel writer. Her work has appeared in *National Geographic Traveller*, *The Guardian* and of course *Rough Guides*.

Travel journalism is one of the most competitive fields to get into. How did you go about developing your career?

I decided travel journalism was the route I wanted to follow half way through my journalism degree. After this, I tailored many of my assignments and internships/work placements to suit travel publishing (for example, I interned with *National Geographic Traveller* and spent two months in Kenya filming for my final project). This put me in good stead with experience in the industry and got me good references from important names and contacts. It was these contacts that got me my first paid professional commission and helped kick start my career in travel journalism. Despite much discouragement from older travel writers, I was persistent and resilient, two qualities any journalist needs.

What research do you do on a country before you go there?

I work for a guidebook publisher, so it's important for me to read what we've already published on the destination. I also read what our main competitors have published, as well as what the national papers have written. Finally, I check the news. Some destinations may not have been covered very recently (for example, many African destinations have been left behind in travel publishing due to wars in parts of the continent) so it's essential to know what's important to the country's people at the time. Social context is everything. All of this research allows me to decide how I want to cover the destination differently to what's already been published in the wider media.

Travelling for work is very different from going on holiday. How do you plan and prepare for a work trip?

It's important to understand what I want to get from the trip before I go. This way I'll know what I need to take notes on, where I need to put my focus and which questions I want to ask when I get there. While I may not know what stories I'll find when I arrive, having an idea of the kinds of angles I could explore is extremely useful for working on the ground. In terms of equipment, I always carry plenty of pens, a few notebooks and lots of business cards; a recorder or Tascam is extremely useful for interviewing and, of course, a camera for getting visuals.

How important is personal safety? What measures do you take to keep safe when working overseas?

Personal safety is always the number one concern when I'm working abroad: if I don't come home in one piece, then nor does my story. When travelling in developing countries,

I try not to wear anything that looks too expensive, and I always ensure I know exactly where I am at all times. Being lost can often lead to danger, so using a map or GPS on your phone (if safe to do so) is a good way to keep your wits about you.

Things to do

Build your contacts

If you are planning to work overseas, begin a contacts book for your chosen country. Start by creating a list of useful UK contacts in the country, such as local diplomatic staff, university language departments, foreign language schools and journalists. Send emails of introduction and ask if you might be able to meet them on your arrival.

Practise your research

Using the Internet and any other research methods you like, identify where migrants from your chosen country may have settled in the United Kingdom. Consider the following questions: Are they clustered in groups in some towns and cities, or spread across the country? What might have prompted their decision to settle in these places? How do their lives differ from the families and friends they left in their country of origin?

Research in action

Visit a family or business run by migrants from your chosen country. Produce a text or multimedia profile of an individual, family or the relevant company. Try to paint a picture of their experiences here in the United Kingdom and their memories of their country of origin.

Issues to discuss

Some large news organisations have stopped using material from freelancers in some conflict areas. They are concerned that freelancers are putting themselves in danger to secure dramatic stories. What risks would you be prepared to take to get a great story?

Which reporter do you think is better able to explain foreign affairs to an audience in the United Kingdom? A foreign correspondent sent from Britain to live and report from a country, or a local journalist who has grown up in the country? What relevant skills and knowledge does each journalist have and what challenges do they face?

Places to learn more

Books and journals

Adie, K. 2003. *The Autobiography. The Kindness of Strangers*. The Reprint Edition. London: Headline.

Bell, M. 2012. *In Harm's Way: Bosnia: A War Reporter's Story*. London: Icon.

Berrington, E. and Jemphrey, A. 2003. Pressures on the Press: Reflections on Reporting Tragedy. *Journalism*. 4 (2) 225–48.

Bourdon, J. 2015. Strange Strangers: The Jerusalem Correspondents in the Network of Nations. [online]. *Journalism*. London: Sage. Available from: http://jou.sagepub.com/content/early/2015/04/20/1464884915579333.abstract [accessed 5 July 2015].

Hamilton, J. M. and Jenner, E. 2004. Redefining foreign correspondence. *Journalism*. 5 (3) 301–21.

McNair, B. 2011. Journalists at war. *Journalism Practice*. 5 (4) 492–4.

Murrell, C. 2014. *Foreign Correspondents and International Newsgathering: The Role of Fixers*. London. Routledge.

Simpson, J. 2008. *News from No Man's Land. Reporting the world*. London: Pan.

Online resources

BBC Safety Guide	http://downloads.bbc.co.uk/mundo/pdf/safety-journalism_safety_guide_second_edition-v1.pdf
Beacon	www.beaconreader.com
Brits abroad – Government Leaflet	www.gov.uk/government/uploads/system/uploads/attachment_data/file/317474/FCO_Brits_Abroad_2014.pdf
Carnets – Government advice	www.gov.uk/ata-and-cpd-carnets-export-procedures
Contributoria	www.contributoria.com
Freelance Travel Writer Website	www.freelancetravelwriter.com
Frontline Club	www.frontlineclub.com
Frontline Freelance	www.frontlinefreelance.org
Global Investigative Journalism Network	http://gijn.org
Newsgathering Safety and the Welfare of Freelancers (Frontline Club Report)	www.frontlineclub.com/wp-content/uploads/2013/06/Safety-Report_WEB.pdf
One World Media	http://oneworldmedia.org.uk
Reporters without Borders	http://en.rsf.org
Rory Peck Trust	https://rorypecktrust.org/resources/safety-and-security
Travel Writers Life Website	www.thetravelwriterslife.com
Uncoverage	www.uncoverage.com/journalists/louis-dowse
Written Road	www.writtenroad.com

References

Al Jazeera. 2015. *FAQs. Al Jazeera's journalists on trial in Egypt* [online]. London: Aljazeera English. Available from: www.aljazeera.com/news/2015/03/faqs-al-jazeeras-journalists-trial-egypt-150317113 935704.html#reckless [accessed 7 May 2015].

Leridon, M. 2014. *Covering the 'Islamic State'* [online]. London: AFP. Available from: http://blogs. afp.com/correspondent/?post%2Fcovering-the-islamic-state-afp#.VX61W0uTlsv [accessed 15 June 2015].

Longman, J. 2012. *On the media – Becoming a freelance foreign correspondent* [online, video]. London: Frontline Club. Available from: www.youtube.com/watch?v=38lmI6YybmQ [accessed 7 July 2015].

O'Neil, B. 2012. *Debating the 'Journalism of Attachment'* [online]. London: brendanoneill.co.uk. Available from: http://brendanoneill.co.uk/post/18794475962/debating-the-journalism-of-attachment [accessed 12 July 2015].

Padejski, D. 2015. *15 tips on how to prepare a grant proposal for a journalism project* [online]. Stanford, CA: JSK. Available from: http://knight.stanford.edu/news-notes/2015/15-tips-on-how-to-prepare-a-grant-proposal-for-a-journalism-project/ [accessed 2 July 2015].

Press Gazette. 2003. *Tips of the trade: Travel journalism* [online]. London: Press Gazette. Available from: www.pressgazette.co.uk/node/28116 [accessed 7 July 2015].

Sengupta, K. 2006. *How to stay alive in a war zone* [online]. The Independent. Available from: www.independent.co.uk/news/media/how-to-stay-alive-in-a-war-zone-466980.html [accessed 15 June 2015].

Where not referenced, quotations are from interviews, emails or social media conversations with the author.

11 The future

Introduction

This is by far the hardest chapter to write in this book. What next for journalism? Which research skills will we use in twenty years' time? Technology develops so quickly, it's impossible to imagine. We have only a hazy view of the future, focused through the imaginations of a few brilliant and innovative people. Certainly journalists will need to adapt and find new ways to research their stories and share them with people. We will have to work hard to justify our role in an age of universal information and we may need to judge our work by different criteria.

So what factors will remain at the core of our profession? As storytellers, journalists will always need fascination for and understanding of other human beings. It is our humanity that allows us to create the narratives and stories that others want to share. As academic Jeff Jarvis writes: (2014) 'We have new tools to exploit. These tools require new skills and create new value. But at its core we serve citizens and communities.' At the moment, new journalists still need to develop the skills to deal with people face to face, but with the growth of social media we also need to engage in online conversations and form relationships with people through the hard obstacle of a plastic screen.

If our thoughts and ideas are to remain distinct from the torrent of information from social media, then we need to retain our ability to filter information; establish what's new and important; find a natural beginning, middle and end to a story; and place that material into context. Our journalism may come in the form of words, data, images or sound or a mixture of all of those, and so we will also need the knowledge and creativity to decide which media to use to tell which story.

This chapter covers:

- Production innovation
- Communication developments
- Wearable technology
- Drones – the opportunities and ethics
- Sensor journalism
- New ways to research and tell stories
- Journalism bots and who knows what!
- Funding
- The future of the researcher

Production innovation

Coding the future

While a few journalists have taken up coding to help them source material, the vast majority of reporters don't write their own programmes. This is partly a generational thing; there are many hundreds of journalists working today who trained before computers were brought into newsrooms, and many more who were never given the opportunity to learn to code at school or college.

Many young journalists still see their careers developing in a more traditional way through the print or broadcast media, and journalism schools often don't or can't teach coding. For those journalists who are fluent coders, the opportunities are growing, and this is leading to some reporters teaching themselves the skill. But many employers say they still don't need coding skills, and if they do, they are happy to recruit specialists from a technology background. In fact, it remains the case that many of the most successful journalism coders come from tech companies and learn journalism as a second specialism, rather than the other way around.

Journalists who want to conduct in-depth Internet and data research can clearly benefit from learning to write their own programmes. It means they can produce their own scrapers and develop tools for analysing and visualising information. Those who have a particular interest in sourcing material from the Internet will also clearly benefit from learning .html. These skills require an investment of time and effort though, as they need to be practised and the programmer needs to keep abreast of new developments. A journalist coder also needs to learn the right languages. Python and Ruby are ideal for back-end work such as scraping databases. For those more interested in working on websites, then HTML, CSS and JavaScript would be vital, but then mobile programming for apps uses Objective-C or Swift or Java. It's not an easy decision, and you may need advice before you even start.

So should new journalists learn to code? The answer is probably only if you enjoy it and can see the benefits, and if you think that's a direction your work may take you in the future. For freelancers in particular, the opportunities to develop your own web content and even make money from apps can offer a valuable income stream.

The future of apps

The growth of mobile apps and the spectacular financial reward for those who develop popular programmes provide a strong indicator of where journalists may be able to make money from their work in future. However, the development of apps both for research and publication of journalism is still relatively new and the focus remains on some of the more practical aspects of production such as video recording and editing and the dissemination of news.

Chapter 3 covers some of the best new apps for journalism research and they are growing in number every day. Most are not specifically aimed at journalists, and here perhaps could be an area of growth: journalists developing research apps for other journalists.

The next social network

The development of social media research will undoubtedly follow one thing – the audience. No sensible journalist looks for stories in a totally empty room, and in a similar way, no reporter will be looking for ideas and sources on networks that few people use. It will continue to be important for journalists to understand not only how to use social media but also who else uses the networks and why.

As we've heard, until recently Facebook was by far the biggest social media network in the western market, but the mobile image network Instagram has rapidly caught up in some countries. China's two large networks QZone and Weibo remain extremely popular with millions of members, followed in size by Google+, which has had a big impact in the United States. Snapchat is one of the fastest growing networks, but its members are mostly teenagers and young people. Twitter isn't huge, but is very influential, while LinkedIn reaches people at work. Not only is it important to understand who uses these networks, but it's also valuable to understand how they use them. Many Facebook users see their time on the site as a 'leisure activity', while people accessing LinkedIn are expecting to connect in a professional capacity. There remains a significant proportion of the older population who do not use social media at all.

So which social networks will we be using in the future? There seem to be two distinct trends. With the spread of fast mobile broadband, everything is becoming mobile, and that means people are far more able to use networks that share images and video. This may be one reason for the rapid growth of Instagram in the UK. Many commentators are focussing on live streaming through new apps such as Meerkat and Periscope as the next big fashion, but at the moment, much of their content is still publicised and shared through current social media networks such as Twitter; so it's not clear yet whether these services will generate their own networks. Nor do we have much idea about what will be popular, although it's likely that journalists will soon be able to access live material streamed by members of the public from news events. How much they will do this and what implications it will have for both copyright and privacy laws are up for discussion.

The second trend for social media is interestingly to become more niche and private. As freelance journalist Eleanor Ross (2015) wrote: 'Networks are becoming more specific and are moving away from the concept of public sharing and caring.' So while broadcasting your life on networks such as Twitter remains extremely popular, as already mentioned, there is already a growing use of more private networks such as Snapchat and WhatsApp among young people.

Communication developments

The spread of 4G, wireless Internet and mobile communication technology will continue to be among the biggest drivers of journalism innovation in future years. The past has shown that as technology has moved forwards, journalists have been quick to experiment and make use of the facilities on offer. As we saw in Chapter 9, there has been a rapid growth in the technology available for live broadcasting and Internet streaming.

So what next? The race is already underway to build a reliable 5G mobile communication network. Although there are no formal plans in the UK, Ofcom has started to work with communications companies. Everyone involved knows that 5G will need to be much faster than 4G (some scientists are suggesting it could be a hundred times faster). Even more important is a massive increase in capacity. If we are to see a big expansion in the 'Internet of Things', then there will need to be enough capacity for millions of everyday consumer items to communicate with each other. In theory, there would be nothing to stop your favourite food blog uploading health data from your smartphone and ordering groceries with the right nutrients, which could be delivered directly to your home. The website could even tell your fridge to display a menu for your week ahead, consulting your calendar to see when you would be out of the house and offering recipes to cook along with your favourite chef online.

Figure 11.1
4G technology has shrunk the size of outside broadcast kit – what will 5G bring?
© Nigel Phillips

Mobile devices continue to have faster chips, bigger storage and better kit on board. All the manufacturers are working to improve the quality of their cameras and screens. Mashable's Pete Pachale (2014) believes better sound recording could soon be on its way with a new chip from Qualcomm able to record directional sound.

With the new chip, the phone will be able to process sound in a way that captures it in specific directions. If you, say, just want to record audio from the person you're filming, you'll be able to tell your camera you just want his or her voice. So it looks like the quality of UGC material will soon be getting even better.

Wearable technology

If some of the new smartphone developments seem a little tame, that's because many of the most innovative minds have moved their attention elsewhere. In 2013 tech savvy journalists put on Google Glass and felt they had glimpsed the future. The futuristic glasses were groundbreaking wearable technology, relatively cheap and easy to use. As many began to use the glasses for journalistic projects they immediately began to see the journalistic opportunities for wearable technology.

The material gathered was unique in offering an immediacy and unrivalled sense of first person witness. Interactive broadcast journalist Tim Poole took a hacked version of the glasses to Istanbul, Cairo and Sao Paulo and streamed live from street protests; sharing a unique viewpoint with those who watched his experiences. In a 2013 interview he explained how the technology had changed his experience of reporting.

> It's the opposite of distraction. It's totally out of my frame of mind . . . I can totally forget about the camera and focus on the surroundings, just keeping in mind that if I'm doing something live I'm talking to people.

Journalism students at the University of Southern California became among the first in the world to use Glass for research and production. They set up their own blog of the project to record their findings. In 2014 filmmaker Aneesh Chaganty told them how the technology had influenced his work: 'With Glass, after a few minutes, people forget they are being videotaped and start being themselves. For journalists, this is a huge opportunity to get people comfortable and open up.' In some ways Glass is already old news. Google withdrew the product from the market early in 2015, but it's thought the company intends to replace the product with a new version, but the growth in wearable technology continues.

In September 2014 the Apple Watch was launched. It immediately posed a big challenge to news organisations producing content for the product and trying to keep the attention of a reader using a tiny screen. Little has been written so far about the opportunities it gives working journalists. Essentially it offers many of the facilities of a smartphone but in a much more discrete way. Sending and receiving messages and checking information can be done faster and almost invisibly. A contributor can be recorded, just by lifting your wrist close to their mouth. It can also be used to frame a shot on an iPhone remotely, so you can shoot images with the phone, without being anywhere near it.

Using such discrete wearable technology to record and broadcast live is controversial. It raises a number of ethical questions about the right to privacy and how contributors can be made aware that they are being recorded and broadcast. Interestingly though, wearable technology does offer an excellent opportunity for researchers wanting to record and review interviews for research purposes, where far fewer ethical questions arise.

Drones – opportunities and ethics

Drones (small remote controlled aircraft) are already being widely used in journalism, but so far have mostly been seen as production tools. It's no surprise that given the chance to shoot dramatic aerial shots for just a few thousand pounds, reporters and producers would have jumped at the chance. The opportunities offered by drones for research are beginning to be explored, and the potential is clearly great. Technically, they can do anything from recce a site for a film, locate an interviewee, squeeze into areas too small for a human, shoot research footage or even record material where it's unsafe for a researcher to go. The BBC's Future of News Report (2015) highlights the ability of drones to collect data in high-risk areas: 'Drones can . . . be used to count the number of people at large events or equipped with sensors to measure levels of pollutants.'

The current debate, though, is which of these activities are legal and ethical. In 2011 the data journalist Matthew Schroyer set up the Professional Society of Drone Journalists in an attempt to address some of these questions and to set up some form of ethical framework for practitioners to follow.

The law in most countries is also gradually catching up with these issues. In the UK, all drones used for commercial purposes (and that of course includes professional journalism) require a licence from the Civil Aviation Authority. In order to get this licence you'll need to show that you have basic competence to fly the drone (usually by completing a training course) and get proper insurance. If you fly the aircraft in quiet places within line of site, you will not need to do anything further, but if you want to film anywhere near people or other busy areas, you will need specific permission from the CAA. So such projects need considerable research input.

The Information Commissioner's Office (ICO) provides guidance on privacy laws and using drones on its website. Images recorded by drones could be subject to Data Protection Law. In addition, there are concerns that even seemingly innocent filming projects could result in the invasion of people's privacy, for example during test filming on the way to a location. The ICO advises:

Get to know the capability of your camera . . . to understand how it works. What is the quality of the image? How powerful is the zoom? Can you control when it starts and stops recording? Drone cameras are capable of taking unusual and creative pictures from original vantage points.

It also warns that using drones could break laws on harassment, and this should be considered when planning a project.

Interview

Ben Kreimer is a journalism technologist and BuzzFeed Fellow based in San Francisco. He's been using drone technology for three years and is now exploring new ways of using the aircraft for storytelling.

What drew you to work with drones?

In January of 2012, while I was a journalism student at the University of Nebraska-Lincoln, I began working with Matt Waite in the Drone Journalism Lab, (he started it in November 2011). The concept of drone journalism appealed to me because I love making and working on machines that perform some function. With drones in the context of journalism, I'm working on machines, drones that can gather content to tell a story in novel ways that are not possible otherwise. And when it comes to techniques and applications for drones, I'm constantly coming up with new ideas for how to use them in the context of journalism and beyond. The field is very new, so there are no right and wrong ways to do drone journalism. The work is entirely an exercise in creative problem solving, and I love it.

And finally, drones can capture images and video of the world from previously unseen perspectives. When I go out and work on projects in the field, I'm observing the world through the lens of a gravity defying and highly manoeuvrable flying camera, seeing and recording the world like it's never been seen before. That's absolutely thrilling for me.

Television journalists have been quick to use drones because of the aerial images they can secure. But in what other ways can journalists use the technology?

Using drones to capture aerial video and images is like using a computer for word processing. Both drones and computers are capable of doing much more dynamic tasks! With drones, there will always be a need to use them for capturing such aerial views, but the technology is also capable of much more. For example, recently I've been using drones in the process of turning real-world landscapes and structures into immersive, interactive three-dimensional (3D) environments for publishing and sharing online. These 3D environments enable media consumers to experience a space in ways that are impossible to convey in two-dimensional video and images. A 3D environment can virtually transport you to the place where the story is. And the 3D environments, which also support written annotations, give a media consumer the ability to explore an environment as they wish, rather than being restricted to the perspectives captured in images or video. Unlike watching a video clip or looking at photographs, both of which provide little opportunity for audience interaction, a 3D environment encourages and requires audience/media consumer engagement. Drones capture the photographs, which later become the 3D environments. Without drones it would be extremely difficult, if not impossible, to create such 3D environments.

I'm in the early stages of using drones as sensor platform, both for flying with a sensor while it gathers data and for deploying them in the field. One example is an air pollution sensor. On a drone, it could be used to make air pollution observations throughout a predetermined space, like around a landfill or other environmental hazard.

There are clear ethical issues when using drones, particularly when it comes to privacy. How do you address those in your work?

Your question makes it sound like ethical issues are very common when working with drones, but I don't think they are. I have yet to run into ethical issues with my work because everything I've done so far has been away from the general public. Most of my work has been in Kenya, Tanzania, India, and Turkey, and my video and photography projects have taken place in either rural areas or on private property. On an interesting note, when doing the 3D models, people don't appear in the final product.

It would certainly be possible to do unethical journalism with a drone, but working with a drone doesn't automatically lead to ethical issues. Most projects won't carry more ethical considerations just because a drone gets involved. Note that I'm not talking about the paparazzi here. I'm usually more worried about frightening people, so I fly from a point where I'm easily visible. But I also wouldn't use a drone to invade on someone's privacy, just like I wouldn't use my telescope or a telephoto lens to look into people's houses. If you wanted to spy, you would be better off with a telephoto lens anyway because a drone is noisy.

I think the drone ethics question receives too much attention, but that will fade. The first portable camera, the Kodak Brownie, created a very similar privacy scare, but that faded away, and now cameras are everywhere. Drones will be the same. I'm more concerned about the safety concerns around drone journalism. Inexperienced operators are a big concern to me. Drones are complicated machines. Even the ubiquitous DJI Phantom has quirks and limitations that have to be understood, or else crashes will happen.

Are you concerned that the widespread use of drones for journalism may alienate the public from journalists, who could see us more as spies than reporters?

Not at all. If anything I think non-journalists are more likely to spy on the public using drones. As long as drone journalists don't stray from pre-existing journalism ethics codes, like from the SPJ or more specifically the NPPA code of ethics for visual journalists, then there won't be many issues. But I am concerned that journalists could be seen as reckless if drone crashes start happening due to inexperienced operators.

Sensor journalism

It seems a natural progression that when journalists started to analyse large quantities of other people's data, some began considering ways to collect that data themselves. This has led to a number of new areas of analytical journalism, including the exciting new field of 'sensor journalism'.

Sensor journalists are working with engineers and other tech experts to access sensors that are already deployed or create and design their own sensor network. Sensors can measure virtually anything from traffic speed at a road junction to a person's body temperature. Sensing can monitor movement, noise, pressure, changes of light and chemical substances. Obtaining data from publicly owned sensors has grown more popular with the growth of open data and the ability to make Freedom of Information requests. Work is already being funded by the Knight Foundation in the United States (2014) to create a simple tool that journalists should be able to use to extract data directly from sensors and feed it directly into a computer for analysis.

Some early sensor projects give a glimpse of what could be achieved in the future. A 3 month investigation by the *Sun Sentinel* newspaper in Florida (2012) looked at the driving habits of police officers and discovered a shocking record of speeding both on and off duty. The journalists used data obtained from the sensors, which log drivers at various points as they pass through the toll road system. They noted the times the officers drove past two sensors and then calculated how fast they would have been travelling between the individual points.

In 2013 the *Washington Post* obtained data from a network of audio sensors designed to pick up the sound of gunshots across the city. The information showed there were far more incidents where firearms were used than the crime statistics suggested and also revealed insights about the way weather and time of day affected the number of shootings.

By far the fastest growing area of sensor journalism is in environmental reporting. This may have been prompted by the sheer scope of opportunity to collect data about human interaction with the natural world or equally a lack of faith in the data being collected and analysed by public bodies. The Earth Journalism Network of environmental journalists has been a keen supporter of the development of sensor journalism, providing training, assistance and information for reporters and campaigners. This is an area of journalistic research that has seen campaigners, educators and journalists working side by side.

Interview

Journalist and technology expert Matthew Schroyer is one of the pioneers of sensor journalism. Based in Oklahoma in the United States, he's been developing an open-source air quality sensor called the 'DustDuino'. With help from the Earth Journalism Network, journalists have been trained at Google's San Francisco office to deploy DustDuinos for research in the US, Mongolia, Brazil, and Indonesia.

What appeals to you about this relatively new method of research?

I've always been fascinated by both science journalism, and technology, so perhaps it was only inevitable to combine those interests. That being said, it occurred to me that sensor journalism might become an important and lasting practice, given wider trends occurring in the publishing world.

Revenue in the digital age is tied to page hits and impressions, and one business model that seems to be succeeding is aggregation, where news websites mine citizen reports, interpret the information, and verify accuracy and authenticity. Another promising business model depends on the scarcity of subject matter experts or people who can apply an uncommon depth of knowledge or rare skillset to a specific issue. Subject matter experts can produce long-form journalism, uniquely qualified analysis, interactive experiences, data journalism, and even sensor and drone journalism.

In essence, sensors allow journalism to evolve up the information food chain, and can provide the public with invaluable information. That is what appeals to me most about this new method of research.

What new skills do journalists need to develop to help them interpret this complex scientific data?

To interpret the data produced by the sensor, it helps to know how the sensor works and what it actually is measuring. Programming skills may be needed to analyse the information that is collected by the sensor and to produce compelling visualisations that accurately express your findings to the public. Statistical skills may be necessary in order to find correlation, test hypotheses, and determine whether data is actually significant. And if you need to develop a sensor for a novel application, you might need knowledge of circuitry and electricity. Fortunately, it's easier than ever to gain these skills. 'Maker' culture, maker spaces, and open-source tools and systems like Arduino and Raspberry Pi are demystifying programming and teaching a whole generation about circuitry, computers, and sensors. Also, open courses and the Internet are providing a great, non-traditional path to learn about science, mathematics, engineering and technology.

However, if I had to select one broad skill set that proved to be the most advantageous, it would be general scientific literacy. This doesn't mean memorising facts or equations, but rather, it means being able to find an article from a scientific journal, understand what it's trying to communicate, and extrapolate how that knowledge can be applied to your own endeavors. Indeed each sensor journalism initiative is its own kind of scientific mission with unique challenges and solutions, but to have any kind of legitimacy, the tools, methods, and analysis must be grounded in peer-reviewed scientific literature. I was fortunate to have studied engineering for a time during my undergraduate education, so I had a good foundation in chemistry, physics, and programming when I started developing technology in this field. Access to a good library of science journals and even science researchers, though, made all the difference in moving forward.

Why did you decide to build your own airborne pollution sensor rather than try to obtain data from other sources?

Primarily, in my fieldwork, I found many cases where air quality data simply wasn't available. For my Master's thesis, I visited an industrial part of Chicago that was grappling with crime but also with pollution. People were concerned about children studying and playing at a school that was near an old, dirty coal power plant. Health issues were widely reported in this community, but it wasn't until the people rallied together to collect soil samples that any action was taken. Those soil samples tested very high for lead, prompting state officials to deploy an air monitor at some cost. Regulatory actions followed. The key here is the community had to gather the data before any larger attention was given to this issue.

In another case, a tyre disposal operation not far from my home had caught fire, and the surrounding area was evacuated. Some reports I obtained indicated that this evacuation was prompted not only by the overwhelming odour and pervasive detritus from burning rubber, but also by air quality data obtained by sources on the ground. I worked for months to obtain that data through various Freedom of Information requests and even at one point received assistance from the state's attorney general, but in the end, the environmental agency either did not record the air quality data or had destroyed it. There was no way to accurately determine what the public had been breathing. That was very troubling to me and probably more so to people living in the situation.

Those are the events that inspired the development of my own environmental sensors, but there also were plenty of personal reasons. This seemed like an opportunity to contribute something original and useful, to meet and get to know communities, maker spaces, researchers, and journalists, all while gaining skills and experience in a number of increasingly important fields.

As more data from sensors is made accessible to journalists, what ethical issues do you think this raises?

The Tow Center for Digital Journalism at Columbia University published a comprehensive report on sensor journalism, and held the first sensor journalism conference, where ethical concerns were one of many issues that were raised. Both in the report and in the conference, journalists, researchers, and engineers cautioned about how sensor data could be used to identify citizens and track various aspects of their daily lives. Such information could be used by powerful interests, extremist groups, or individual actors for retaliation, vigilantism, stalking, harassment, or blackmail.

There is tension here between gathering crucial data that can help pinpoint problems, and preserving the anonymity and privacy of the public. It's important not to become complacent and assume that because this data seems innocent enough, that it may never be harmful in the future. We cannot know how this data may be aggregated and used to identify individuals in the future, or what harm that ultimately could cause. As more commercial sensors are brought into the household, and more journalism institutions seek public buy-in for wider-scale sensing projects, a key part of a comprehensive sensor journalism initiative may be to educate the public about the risks and rewards of these devices and the data ecosystems they represent.

Matthew rightly mentions some of the potentially serious issues, which are raised by the practice of sensor journalism. The opportunity to collect our own data at source, bypassing public bodies and those with vested interests could be incredibly empowering, bringing a new vibrancy and value to the work of journalists. With these opportunities, however, comes a whole new area of responsibility for researchers. They must ensure the data is collected rigorously and analysed professionally and fairly, and there is also the issue of privacy. As the 'Internet of things' grows we all face the prospect of having dozens of sensors in our homes connected to an open network. There is potential to collect information on anything from how often we wash our hands to whether we walk our dogs often enough. As journalists in the UK are well aware following the phone hacking scandal, some of our colleagues have squandered much of the trust given to journalists to access private data responsibly and use it for the public good. There is bound to be intensive scrutiny about how we choose to use it in future.

New ways to research and tell stories

This section looks briefly at an eclectic collection of some of the new ideas and technology that could change the work of journalists in the next few years.

Instant transcription

One of the most time-consuming and often dreary aspects of print journalism is taking notes and transcribing interviews. Most journalists have a story about the challenges and rewards of learning shorthand. With the gradual improvement of voice-recognition and transcription software, it may soon be possible to instantly turn recorded interviews into usable text. Some voice-recognition software companies have already spotted the opportunities their products offer journalists, but the best software still works by learning the speech patterns of one person. So the only really successful way to transcribe interviews is for a journalist to 're-read' them out loud to a computer. Anyone who uses the voice command or dictation facilities on their smartphone, however, knows the technology is improving fast and that it's only a matter of time before journalists will be able to interview a source and have an instant transcription ready to edit.

Digital subbing

Having your work subbed is part of the job of a journalist. We're all used to sharing our writing with other journalists who help to improve (or of course sometimes wreck) our copy. What if this role could be carried out automatically? There are a couple of apps which are just beginning to offer this opportunity. Grammarly is an enhanced version of a spellchecker, which is able to spot a whole variety of grammatical errors and misused words. Hemmingway claims to go a step further and help you to write more clearly. At the moment this software comes nowhere close to replicating the human touch, but that doesn't mean it won't be improved in future.

Linked data

We all know that pages on the World Wide Web are linked together into a network using hyperlinks. Now a new network is being created which allows data to be linked together in a similar way. By standardising the way data is made available online, it can be accessed and shared by multiple users, making it incredibly valuable to journalists. This linked data network, which is still in its earliest stages, has its own equivalent to URLs known as URIs and a standard way of categorising the data (data model) called RDF. Linked data means that sports web pages can be automatically updated with all the latest statistics from a central database. The BBC is already using a linked data network to update its sports pages and has published information about how that data is organised (2012).

Emoji journalism

Along with the proliferation of smartphones across much of Europe and the United States, has come the spread of emojis; the tiny images that were originally added to text to show emotion. Emojis are already spreading far beyond this use, with all sorts of artistic material being translated into the little pictures. In 2014, the website Vox took the first steps in emoji journalism by telling the stories of the year in emoji. The stories attracted some attention, but more for their novelty than their practical success. They each required a text translation.

The local Philadelphia news website Billy Penn has also pioneered the use of emojis for sharing news. Digital journalist and CEO Jim Brady told the Colombia Journalism Review 2014 'We've covered a debate using emojis, and are doing a weekly Spotify playlist based on the Philly news of the week. Both went over well with the audience.'

Music

The copyright issues raised by using music has made it harder to include in journalism, but the EU ruling that embedding material is not a breach of copyright (see Chapter 3), has brought new opportunities. Music bloggers have been embedding music and playlists into their content for a long time, but now playlists and other music content are beginning to be embedded or created for other online journalistic content. As with all journalism, it's really important to consider how your particular audience will want to access and use the material. Digital expert Paul Bradshaw recommends considering a variety of video curation and playlist methods on his blog (2013).

> It's worth thinking about the easiest way for people to consume that multimedia. Do you want them to have to play each video separately, on a blog post, or do you want them to be able to play them all together, with one click?

Aural creations

Some journalists and tech experts are taking the use of sound one step further. They are pioneering the use of sound to convey meaning in data. This area of investigation has been part of academic research since the latter part of the twentieth century, but experiments in using sound to share journalistic content are very new. The informal team at CSV Soundsystem have begun using music to tell digital stories. They have created music from financial data and even the usage of buses, called Ridership Rachenitsa (2013). There's no denying this approach to researching and sharing data is very niche, but that doesn't mean that a creative and clever journalist can't find a way to use this in a wider environment in future.

Journalism bots and who knows what!

In the early part of the twenty-first century, some reputable news organisations began publishing stories online that had not been researched, written or even checked by a human being. The first 'journalism bots' wrote these stories. They began as basic sports stats reports, but in 2014 Associated Press began publishing more than a thousand automated financial stories a month. These too were very specific forms of stories: short write-ups of companies' quarterly earnings, which could broadly follow a regular format. Managing editor Lou Ferrara explained the system on the AP blog (2014).

> When the earnings reports are issued. Automated Insights has algorithms that ping that data and then in seconds output a story. The structure for the earnings reports stories was crafted by AP . . . All conform to AP Style, the standard of journalistic style.

Also in 2014, the creatively named Quakebot wrote a story for the *LA Times* about an earthquake in the city. The algorithm, which created the copy, was written by journalist and programmer Ken Schwencke and gained some news coverage, but it was actually modelled on a similar bot which produces basic reports about murders in the *LA Times*' area. At the *LA Times*, human beings soon expand the automated stories with detail, colour and interview clips added. The bots are used for speed, to get copy online as swiftly as possible.

Bots still struggle with more complex stories. The *Washington Times* asked a writing bot called 'Content Forever' to write an article about online journalism. The bot's creator was artist and programmer Darius Kazemi. Its rather meandering and somewhat artistic article can be read on the *Washington Times* blog (2014). Only its first two sentences make any reference to the required subject.

It's clear that, when it comes to more complex structured journalistic work, bots are still a long, long way from being competent. They clearly struggle with prioritising, structuring and presenting the content. However, perhaps a bot could be programmed to perform the role of researcher, providing a human journalist with a pool of research material to construct a story. In some respects, the search engine Wolfram Alpha already performs some of this task, attempting to provide an intelligent answer to a question, rather than a list of ranked relevant information. It not only selects information but also tries to 'understand' a question and give the researcher the most relevant answer with context and background information.

Funding

Although the problem of funding journalism over the next few decades is far from solved, journalists have begun finding innovative new ways to pay for their work. Pitching is already a familiar process for journalists, and it may be that, in coming years, the challenge of raising money will become increasingly integrated into the research process.

Some journalism is already being funded by grants for specific projects or philanthropic donation. In the UK, the Bureau of Investigative journalism is funded by small donations from its supporters and also donors who believe in its mission and grant funding.

Crowdfunding has proved successful for some projects. The website Matter was initially launched with money from a crowdfunding campaign and crowdfunding has worked well for longer investigations, which can generate public interest. In 2014 the podcast Serial became the fastest ever downloaded podcast on iTunes and went on to win a Peabody journalism award. The factual podcast was a spin-off from a radio programme called 'This American Life'. It was a real-life murder investigation. The listeners were able to hear the work of the researchers unfold in real time and became fascinated by characters involved. The first series of the podcast was funded by a sponsor, along with the US radio station WBEZ (which produces 'This American Life'). A public appeal for donations during one of the episodes raised enough money to produce a second series, along with support from sponsors.

In 2013, journalists from the American National Public Radio show Planet Money wove their fundraising campaign into their storytelling. They decided to make and sell t-shirts. Anyone who pledged money for the t-shirt on the Kickstarter campaign would not only get a finished t-shirt, but would also fund an investigation to see how the shirt was made from growing the cotton right until the shipping of the finished product. More than twenty thousand people pledged more than five hundred thousand dollars to fund the project, and the result was a complex piece of multimedia journalism.

Websites such as Matter and Exaro have pioneered and trialled new ways of charging readers for content, with different levels of success. They continue, along with other new news organisations, to explore a combination of income streams such as the sale of 'added value' content, organisation of associated events such as conferences and training and syndication.

The need to sell journalism has always raised issues of ethics and conflict of interest and these modern forms of funding are no different. Creative and resourceful journalists will continue to find the money to tell stories that matter to them. There are questions to be asked, however, about the ways in which some of these funding models develop. In particular, how they may favour particular forms of journalism (such as financial reporting, which has access to rich revenue streams) and what impact this will have on the role of researchers.

The future of the researcher

One factor that has become clear when writing this book is the remarkable amount of knowledge and skill that new journalists need to acquire. They may not have to memorise large quantities of specialist information, as journalists of the past often did, but their understanding of both their audiences and technology is unrivalled.

A new journalist needs to know how to find information in a massively complex digital world, filter out the most relevant facts and present these in context, illustrated with real-life description and colour. In his 2014 report for the Reuters Institute, Philipp Rottwilm sounds a note of caution about the dangers of expecting too much from journalists.

> This new form of social journalism is increasing both the amount and pace of information input, as well as the output of journalistic work, arguably leading to cognitive overload, with journalists less able to filter and analyse their sources and detect and remove biases.

While few of us can see trends or technology more than a few months in advance, there is little doubt that one skill that all researchers will need in the future is flexibility. As US research expert Leigh Montgomery explains.

> Journalism research will require being facile with data of all kinds, in many forms. The best piece of information might not be in an article in text form. It might be in a video, or a social media post, or in a book published years ago. It can be written by people with a mobile device transmitting it from on scene in a response to a humantarian disaster or a typhoon or from Tahrir Square in Egypt. Reading and experiencing and being able to identify the best possible information outside of your experience or beat will be a critical skill, but . . . being able to quickly evaluate information – and misinformation – is a critical skill. Also working directly in a collaborative capacity.

We have already discussed how new production opportunities and funding methods may have an impact on the journalistic research process. Many journalists are also now questioning the traditional models of balance and impartiality, arguing there is a need for journalism to break free from these constraints to campaign on important issues. This model of journalism, sometimes called 'journalism of attachment', is clearly less controversial in some areas of our profession, such as the traditional print press, which has a proud tradition of campaigning for change. Even in the regulated world of broadcast journalism we have seen how notions of balance are being challenged, especially in the reporting of highly controversial areas such as climate change.

In whatever area of journalism you choose to build your career, your goal is no longer just to inform your audience, because they can find plenty of information on the Internet. The goal of the journalist must now be to guide, explain, enrich and engage. We need a strong sense of our own mission and the passion to explain and share that with the public, whether it's as simple as entertaining them with the ten best online cat videos or spending months researching an in-depth investigation into public wrongdoing.

At the heart of our professional lives remains our individual philosophy and personal ethical framework. We each follow this career path for a different reason and our aims and aspirations will vary. What is important is to think often about our reasons for becoming a journalist and what we hope our communications with the outside world will achieve. This personal compass will point a direction through our careers and allow us to develop the most relevant research skills.

'Only by recognising the primacy of principle can journalism change ethically and come out the other side still fulfilling the same democratic purpose for a new century a new technology and a new kind of information-wired citizen' Kovach and Rosentiel (2011).

Things to do

Build your contacts

Set up a profile on a new social media network (one that has been established in the past year). New networks don't have huge numbers of users, but try to make contact with as many people as you can who share your personal or professional interests. Did this social network offer any advantages over those you currently use? Have you made any new or unexpected contacts?

Practise your research

Put together an emoji translation, audio or video playlist to accompany a news story you have written recently. Does this content add value to your story? Or distract from the core journalism?

Research in action

Now post your emoji or playlist content online, either on your own blog or an accessible news site and share via social media. Monitor the reaction you get to your content. Does it encourage new interaction with your story? Might you attract new contacts and sources with such innovative journalism?

Issues to discuss

Do journalists need to stay on top of every digital innovation? Are some of the newest forms of journalism exciting new ways to tell stories? Or are they just a gimmicky waste of time?

What ethical and practical challenges do journalists face when they are charged with raising money to fund their own journalistic projects? Is there a difference between a freelance journalist accepting a commission from an editor and a journalist raising money for an investigation by crowdfunding?

Places to learn more

Books and journals

Agirre, A., Aiestaran, A., Ramirez de la Piscina, T. and Zabalondo, B. 2015. The Future of Journalism – Who to Believe? Different Perceptions among European Professional and Internet Users [online]. *Journalism Practice*.

Franklin, B. 2013. *The Future of Journalism*. Kindle Edition. London: Routledge.

Innovation Journalism Journal [online]. Available from: http://journal.innovationjournalism.org

Holton, A., Lawson, S. and Love, C. 2014. *Unmanned Aerial Vehicles* [online]. Journalism Practice.

Stephens, M. 2014. *Beyond Journalism: The Future of News*. New York, NY: Colombia Journalism Review Books.

Online resources

BBC Future of News Report	http://newsimg.bbc.co.uk/1/shared/bsp/hi/pdfs/29_01_15future_of_news.pdf
Civil Aviation Authority (UK) Advice on Drones	www.caa.co.uk/default.aspx?CATID=1995
Eat, Sleep, Publish – Jason Preston's Blog	http://eatsleeppublish.com
Glass Journalism Blog	http://glassjournalism.tumblr.com
Grammarly	www.grammarly.com
Hemmingway	www.hemingwayapp.com
Innovation Journalism Blog	http://blog.innovationjournalism.org
Jeff Jarvis' Blog	http://buzzmachine.com
The Mediashift Digital Journalism Blog	http://mediashift.org
Paul Bradshaw's Online Journalism Blog	http://onlinejournalismblog.com
Professional Society of Drone Journalists	www.dronejournalism.org
'Sensors and Journalism' – Tow Centre Report	http://towcenter.org/research/sensors-and-journalism/
Timcast (Tim Poole's Blog)	www.timcast.com
Thomas Levine's Blog	www.thomaslevine.com

References

BBC. 2012. *Sport ontologies* [online]. London: BBC. Available from: www.bbc.co.uk/ontologies/sport [accessed 2 July 2015].

BBC. 2015. *The future of news* [online]. London: BBC. Available from: http://newsimg.bbc.co.uk/1/shared/bsp/hi/pdfs/29_01_15future_of_news.pdf [accessed 30 June 2015].

Bradshaw, P. 2013. *Journalism *is* curation: Tips on curation tools and techniques* [online]. Birmingham, AL: Online Journalism Blog. Available from: http://onlinejournalismblog.com/2013/09/30/curation-tools-tips-advice-journalism/ [accessed 30 June 2015].

Clark, A. 2014. *What can Jim Brady's new site do for Philadelphia journalism?* [online]. New York, NY: CJR. Available from: www.cjr.org/local_news/what_can_jim_bradys_new_site_billy_penn_do_for_philly_journalism.php [accessed 25 June 2015].

Colford, P. 2014. *A leap forward in quarterly earnings stories* [online]. New York, NY: AP Blog. Available from: http://blog.ap.org/2014/06/30/a-leap-forward-in-quarterly-earnings-stories/ [accessed 25 June 2015].

Devine, T. 2013. *Ridership Rachenitsa* [online, video]. Available from: www.youtube.com/watch?v=tcnoBL0tvpc [accessed 30 June 2015].

Dewey, C. 2014. *This is what happens when a bot writes an article about journalism* [online]. Washington, DC: Washington Post. Available from: www.washingtonpost.com/news/the-intersect/wp/2014/12/16/this-is-what-happens-when-a-bot-writes-an-article-about-journalism/ [accessed 1 July 2015].

Fallis, D., Keating, D. and Petho, A. 2013. *ShotSpotter detection system documents 39,000 shooting incidents in the District* [online]. District of Columbia: Washington Post. Available from: www.washingtonpost.com/investigations/shotspotter-detection-system-documents-39000-shooting-incidents-in-the-district/2013/11/02/055f8e9c-2ab1–11e3–8ade-a1f23cda135e_story.html [accessed 25 June 2015].

Gascong, C. 2013. *Tim Pool and the use of Google Glass in journalism* [online, video]. YouTube. Available from: www.youtube.com/watch?v=kqz7KzH-CnY [accessed 25 June 2015].

Information Commissioner's Office. 2015. *Drones* [online]. London: ICO. Available from: https://ico.org.uk/for-the-public/drones/ [accessed 30 June 2015].

Jarvis, J. 2014. *Geeks bearing gifts. Imagining new futures for journalism* [online]. New York, NY: CNUY Journalism Press. Available from: http://press.journalism.cuny.edu/book/geeks-bearing-gifts/ [accessed 30 June 2015].

Kestin, S. and Maines, J. 2012. *Cops among Florida's worst speeders, Sun Sentinel investigation finds* [online]. Fort Lauderdale, FL: Sun Sentinel. Available from: www.sun-sentinel.com/news/speeding-cops/fl-speeding-cops-20120211-story.html#page=1 [accessed 2 July 2015].

Knight Foundation. 2014. *Creating a tool that will help data journalists and civic hackers collect data without a programmer's assistance or proprietary software* [online]. Miami, FL: Knight Foundation. Available from: www.knightfoundation.org/grants/201450255/ [accessed 2 July 2015].

Kovach, B. and Rosentiel, T. 2007. *The Elements of Journalism.* 2nd Edition. New York, NY: Three Rivers Press.

Kreimer, B. and Waite, M. 2014. The feasibility of using Small Unmanned Aerial Vehicles.3. for mapping news events [online]. In: Diakopoulos, N., Essa, I. and Hansen, M. (eds.) *2014 Computation + Journalism Symposium.* 24–25 October 2014. New York, NY: Colombia University. Available from: http://compute-cuj.org/cj-2014/cj2014_session5_paper1.pdf [accessed 26 June 2015].

Pachal, P. 2014. *5 smartphone innovations coming in 2015* [online]. London: Mashable. Available from: http://mashable.com/2014/12/12/qualcomm-smartphones-2015/ [accessed 5 July 2015].

Rangarajan, S. 2014. *The good and bad of glass* [online]. Los Angeles, CA: Glass Journalism. Available from: www.glassjournalism.io/2014/10/06/the-good-and-bad-of-glass/ [accessed 25 June 2015].

Ross, E. 2015. *Bye-bye Facebook: The future of social media for small businesses* [online]. London: The Guardian. Available from: www.theguardian.com/small-business-network/2014/oct/24/future-of-social-media-for-small-business [accessed 25 June 2015].

Rottwilm, P. 2014. *The future of journalistic work: Its changing nature and implications* [online]. Oxford: Reuters Institute for the Study of Journalism. Available from: https://reutersinstitute.politics.ox.ac.uk/sites/default/files/The%20Future%20of%20Journalistic%20Work%20-%20Its%20Changing%20Nature%20and%20Implications_0.pdf [accessed on 1 June 2015].

Vox. 2014. *The Year in Emoji* [online]. Washington, DC: Vox. Available from: www.vox.com/a/emoji-year-in-review-2014/politics-emoji-story-one [accessed 25 June 2015].

Where not referenced, quotations are from interviews, emails or social media conversations with the author.

Index